The
Fundamentalist
Mind

The Fundamentalist Mind

HOW POLARIZED THINKING
IMPERILS US ALL

Stephen Larsen

QUEST

BOOKS

Theosophical Publishing House
Wheaton, Illinois • Chennai, India

The Theosophical Publishing House
P.O. Box 270
Wheaton, IL 60189-0270

www.questbooks.net

Cover image: © Images.com/Corbis
Illustration credits:
    Pages 24, 25, 26: R. Larsen, 1970
    Pages 27, 37: Stone Mountain Counseling, P.C.
    Page 30: Stone Mountain Counseling, P.C.; USE2, J&J Physiolabs
    Page 66: Stone Mountain Counseling, P.C.; LENS Report Generator, Ochslabs.com

Cover design, book design, and typesetting by Beth Hansen-Winter

Library of Congress Cataloging-in-Publication Data
Larsen, Stephen.
  The fundamentalist mind: how polarized thinking imperils us all / Stephen Larsen.
p.   cm.
Includes bibliographical references and index.
ISBN-13: 978-0-8356-0850-3
ISBN-10: 0-8356-0850-6
1. Religious fundamentalism—Psychology.   I. Title.
BL238.L37 2007
200.1'9—dc22   2007030822

5   4   3   2   1   *   07   08   09   10   11   12

Printed in the United States of America

DEDICATION

This book is dedicated to the many victims of fundamentalist thinking around the world: "God bless us, every one."

CONTENTS

ILLUSTRATIONS

FOREWORD

Phil Cousineau

On the evening of September 10, 2001 I had a book reading in Berkeley, California, for the launch of my book, *Once and Future Myths.* After reading a few passages I asked for questions. First came an enthusiastic query about my old friend, mythologist Joseph Campbell, followed by an academic question about the relationship between art and myth. The last question of the evening, from a bearded and brooding student, took me by surprise.

"What is the *shadow* side of mythology?" he inquired.

Startled, I said the first thing that came to mind: "Fundamentalism." Then I took a deep breath and plunged in.

"My understanding of the relationship between the two," I said, "is that myth is to religion as math is to physics; they are special languages to describe what lies beyond ordinary words. Mythology is made up of timeless metaphors, symbolic stories; it is a kind of picture language of the soul that is not meant to be taken literally or historically. If we breathe new life into our myths in each generation, like artists such as Ovid, Shakespeare, Martha Graham, and countless others have done over the centuries, then myths have the power to electrify us.

"But," I added, "if we *don't* reanimate them they can degenerate into dogma. Let's not forget what James Joyce said: 'You can't teach an old dogma new tricks.' If you try and reason with a mean old dog, it turns violent."

Picking up my old leather satchel, I thanked the crowd and concluded by saying, "Myths are neither true nor false. They're either living or dead. They can inspire or conspire. That's why we have to beware of all the unquestioned myths that people live by."

Five minutes later I was on a shuttle to San Francisco International Airport, where I boarded a red-eye flight to New York. If all went smoothly, I would arrive around 9 a.m. and catch a taxi for the World Trade Center, where I was scheduled for an 11 a.m. reading at Rizzoli's Bookstore on the ground floor.

After a fitful night flight, I awoke a few minutes before nine, September 11, to the sound of screeching tires as we hit the tarmac at JFK. Seconds later, a scream came from a woman sitting behind me. I craned my neck in time to see her unbuckle her seatbelt and stand bolt upright with a cell phone to her ear. She swayed back and forth as we taxied down the runway, shouting: "They've hit the Towers, they've hit the Towers!"

An ashen-faced flight attendant staggered down the aisle and tried to calm her, but the woman could not stop sobbing. All around me passengers were gasping, some whispering the chilling word, *"Terrorists."*

When the doors of the plane were released I hustled past the cockpit, where the pilots were avidly listening to the radio, and down to baggage claim. There I watched the television monitors in horror as the first tower burned.

Outside the terminal, the world had come to a standstill. Nobody wandered far because there was nowhere to go. Hundreds of us waited for instructions from the airport or security, but none came, nothing but a swirl of rumors. I overheard a businessman say that the White House had been destroyed. A taxi driver bellowed that poison gas had been released in Chicago. A trembling pilot told a police officer she'd heard there were seven more "suicide planes" circling over New York.

Hearing these things, I backed slowly away from the terminal. Near the parking garage, at a few minutes before 10 a.m., I stood with a lawyer fresh from Kansas City who was frantic to get to his new job at Cantor Fitzgerald in the Twin Towers. Together, we stared out at the Manhattan skyline as the glaring red and gold fire-wheel of the doomed second plane hit the second tower. A restless crowd gathered around, muttering *"fanatics . . . terrorists . . . fundamentalists."*

After a sleepless night in a hotel I found near Shea Stadium, an executive from one of the book chains managed to send a town car to bring me into Manhattan. We had a mournful lunch on the terrace of a restaurant a few blocks from Ground Zero. An unnerving dust from the fallen towers landed on us as we shared our anger and our dread about our country's early response to the attacks. Eventually, he told me that the night before, in the middle of the blackout, he'd read out loud—by candlelight—to his family from *Once and Future Myths*. And now he wanted to talk about what the *mythic* implications of the attacks might be.

For the second time in twenty-four hours, my blood ran cold. The notion of speculating about the terrorist attacks seemed almost sacrilegious. But I had to admit I'd been struck by the unwittingly mythic references in the media, including those to paradise, heroes, villain, monsters, and the old battle between good and evil.

The image that haunted me most was one that had occurred to me while listening to the drumbeat of the war machine vowing to slay the "monster" that had attacked us. It was the image of the Hydra, the seven-headed sea creature. According to the ancient Greeks, the Hydra had the nasty habit of growing a new head each time one of the heroes tried to slay it by chopping one off. It was Chiron, the wise centaur, who revealed to Hercules that it took more than brute force to vanquish a monster that could disappear at will (under water) and grow eerily stronger every time you tried to kill it.

Chiron's advice was strangely prescient in light of the myriad-headed monster we now faced. "You must learn to *temper* your sword," he said. "Unless you learn to control your anger, your desire for revenge will destroy you." This cryptic remark refers to the annealing process of passing a blade through fire, which allows it to cauterize and close a wound. But the puissant image also reveals the depth of psychological insight that pervades so many of the myths. In this case it suggests that we must learn to control our animal nature, as the half-human, half-horse centaur knew better than most creatures. The tempered sword also suggests that it behooves us (so to speak) to know the true nature of our enemy, as well as any responsibility we might bear in the conflict.

After lunch, my new friend, the executive, confided that he would understand if I wanted to cancel the book tour and return home to my worried family. However, he said, if I wished to carry on with the tour I might be able to turn my book signings into something resembling town hall discussions about the recent suicide bomber attacks. I readily agreed, and he wrote out a generous travel-expense check on the spot.

Walking back to my hotel, though, my heart sunk when I saw etched into the strange ash fall on the windshields of cars, trucks, and emergency vehicles words that read like old WANTED: DEAD OR ALIVE posters: *"Revenge,"* *"The End of the World is Nigh,"* and *"Death to our Enemies."*

Fortunately, Dame Fortune smiled upon me. My first stop on the resuscitated book tour was a reading in Woodstock, New York that Stephen and Robin Larsen had helped to arrange. I arrived at the teeming book store in a fugue state, somewhere between reverie and exhaustion. The Larsens offered to help by joining me on stage. What followed was two hours of respectful speculation about the combustible relationship between myth and fundamentalism. All three of us had spent years writing and talking about how the rhapsodic aspects of myth lies at the core of religious ritual and ceremony and has inspired so much of our poetry, literature, art, sculpture, dance, and cinema. But that night we were compelled by the exigencies of recent events and the audience's insistence to explore mythology's darker side.

Myths *matter*, we agreed, because they are *overpowering* stories that give us a sense of identity, a place in the universe, a moral orientation, and a sense of meaning and purpose. But unchallenged myths lull us into thinking monolithically. The telltale sign of fundamentalism is rigidity, we said, which derives from literalism and intolerance. The minute any of us believe *literally* in our myths and become intolerant of any other worldview we will face immediate and fierce resistance.

"People are funny that way," I added, "they tend to bristle at the suggestion that you have the truth and they don't."

As the evening wore on, I found my perception of fundamentalism stretched by Stephen's expertise, ranging widely from mythology and psychology to biofeedback. His was a mind on fire. He patiently explained that it was ludicrous to suggest that human beings should have evolved past myth and religion. "We're neurologically wired for both," he explained, and then went on to give a fascinating description of the physiology of fear and "the pathology of a literal view of the world" that can lead to despair and suicide bombers turning themselves into human missiles.

His closing remarks especially helped me during the rest of my tour. He said that it was imperative to understand the implications of being intoxicated by one's own unswerving certitude. What's more, every one of us tends to revert to fundamentalist thinking in moments of uncertainty, crisis, anxiety, and especially trauma. Fundamentalist thinking raises its ugly head every time we find it impossible to comprehend someone else's point of view, or whenever we condescend to others as being less informed—or chosen—than we are.

*   *   *

As I was reading through this inspired new book of Stephen's, *The Fundamentalist Mind,* I realized that he has been brooding on these ideas ever since the events of 9/11 had changed our world. I use the word *brood* advisedly, in the best sense of giving ideas time, heat, light, and life. To do this work, he's read voluminously and counseled legions affected by the traumatic events in New York, Washington, and Pennsylvania. The result of his Herculean labors—the tempering of his sword—is to give us in this work what I believe to be one of the most important books of our time.

Stephen humbly begins by admitting that he was totally unprepared for how "profound was the alienation and dissociation of the entire modern world [and] how the world itself seemed to have lost its soul." Thus braced, he goes on to explore the phenomenon *holistically*, in terms of mind, body, and soul.

He explains first the "exquisite correspondences between the brain and myth," then the "physiology of the fear-driven," and finally the dire impact on the spirit due to the "disorientation and loss of meaning in a fragmented society." But his real breakthrough is the humanist perspective allowing him to see that fundamentalists "cannot think or behave in any other way." In a manner that seems incomprehensible, they may not even *want* to do so because their way of thinking provides them with "a total account of what's true" and relieves them of the burden of having to make decisions on their own. The repercussions of a rigid worldview are vast when those with religious and political absolute certainty are in collusion. But Stephen's is more than just one more description of cultural pathology. He suggests that there will be no personal or collective peace until we all recognize the potentially dark side of our own mythology.

One of the grace notes I've gleaned from *The Fundamentalist Mind* is a clearer glimpse of perhaps the most quintessential fundamentalist myth of all, the belief in a Chosen People. This is the tragically widespread belief that one particular group—whether religious, political, scientific, or cultural—is the only one graced with the truth. Campbell most keenly expressed this invariably tragic belief that one's group is special and exclusively blessed by saying, "You worship God in your way, and I'll worship Him in *His*."

Moreover, Larsen cautions, we are *all* susceptible to fundamentalist thinking at one time or another; hence what he calls "five-minute fundamentalism." The dark side of our own personal mythology emerges whenever we feel superior and act sanctimoniously. We see such behavior in the scientist who condescends to religious people, the artist who dismisses athletes, the jock who disdains intellectuals, the psychologist who refutes the different schools of philosophy, and the politician who despises all but his or her own party.

Thus we get a harrowing glimpse of what Emerson must have meant when he wrote, "Man is a god in ruins." There may very well be something divine in our core, but history shows time and time again how we have turned our paradise into ruins and, not unlike Samson, have pulled the temple down around us. This, in a nutshell, is what Larsen means by "perilous rapture," the dangerous side of spiritual experience that too often leads to sense of entitlement. In his memorable phrase, "glimpses of enlightenment do not excuse claims of privileged knowledge."

The antidote, Stephen believes, and as he explores in his final chapters, is for us to be eternally vigilant about our own deepest-held beliefs. Citing the Swedish philosopher Immanuel Swedenborg, he writes, "No one should be instantly persuaded about the truth—that is, the truth should not be instantly so confirmed that there is no doubt left. . . . [That would be] second-hand truth." Swedenborg thought, points out Stephen, that "habitual good thinking inclines us toward the state called 'heaven,' and habitual bad thinking toward 'hell'—which, like heaven, *is not a place but a state of mind or spirit*. Swedenborg's idea of evil thus precludes it being projected out onto others. If you really want to take on the problem of evil, address it in your own psyche."

* * *

Shortly after I completed my twenty-one-city book tour, I returned home to the Bay Area and immediately arranged a lunch with my old friend, the great historian of religion, Huston Smith. The first thing he wanted to know was what I'd experienced on 9/11. What I needed to know from him was whether or not his faith had been shaken by the recent relentless attacks on religion, and whether he now regretted naming his most recent book *Why Religion Matters.*

"No, none whatsoever," he said firmly. "Religion doesn't matter *less,* but clear thinking about it matters more than ever. The heart of the conflict cannot be blamed on religion. It was an *abomination* of religion, which has always been rooted in the belief of love of our fellow human beings and the transcendent aspects of life."

Rather than the inevitable consequence of religion, he went on to say, the suicide bombers' decision to turn themselves into human missiles is *radical* fundamentalism, the hijacking of myth and religion by political ideology. *Fundamental,* he reminded me, is essentially a good word that should simply remind us of our *foundation,* the essential truths of our spiritual life. But fundamental*ism* is a bad word because, he quipped, "all *isms* end up in schisms."

Ironically, he sighed, terrorists ultimately defeat their purpose of defending their religion by downplaying the universal message of traditional religion, which is compassion. The other tragedy, he concluded, is that fundamentalism takes the profound need to believe that the truth we perceive is rooted in the unchanging nature of the universe, which is an "indispensable necessity," and turns it into doctrine, which is another name for fundamentalism.

Though Dr. Smith resolutely shies away from dispensing any form of advice, he then came as close to doing so as I've ever heard him. He asked that we remind ourselves that "we are in good hands" and suggested that, "in gratitude for that fact, it would be good if we bore one another's burdens." His recommendation was that we ask our opponents what we might do *for* them rather than *to* them.

After I left Dr. Smith's home that day, my mind wandered back to Ground Zero. On my third and last night in Manhattan after the attacks, I had spoken for a few minutes with a New York City fireman who was standing next to the barricades, covered in soot, coughing from the fetid air, emotionally distraught. When he met my gaze, I gently asked him how he found the strength to keep going back into "The Pile" and the courage to search for survivors.

"It's not heroic," he said, wearily, "if that's what you're thinking. He took off his boots for a few minutes before going on. "It's necessary. This is what I do. Everybody has to do *something* while the world is burning."

This brilliant and timely book is Stephen Larsen's own necessary work while the world continues to burn, and it just may help us find the strength and courage to do our part, or at least the compassion to understand what sets off the conflagrations.

Phil Cousineau
San Francisco
September 2007

ACKNOWLEDGMENTS

My book arose from the ashes of 9/11. As a New Yorker, I felt the scorching breath of the misunderstood god come all too close, blighting the lives of many people and an entire city that I love. The only way I could deal with the monstrosity of that event was to try, as a psychological thinker, to understand the extreme conditions of mind that allow such things to happen. The intervening six years from researching to writing this book have shown that the fundamentalist mind abroad in the world is not chastened in the aftermath of the human tragedies it produces; to the contrary, it is willing to enact even greater violence in the attempt to show, somehow, ever and again, that "our god is greater than their god." It is this mentality we have to slough, as a species, like an outworn snakeskin.

My first instructor, who spent most of his life trying to flee from the fundamentalist mind inflicted on him, was my father, the Reverend Harold B. Larsen. My barrister father-in-law, Col. Robinson P. Searson, though reared in the conservative South and scarred by PTSD, emerged from the foxholes of World War II as still one of the most thoughtful and loving agnostics I ever met. His daughter, Robin, my best friend and lover for forty-three years, always helps me see the other side of each issue and the inextricable connectedness of the web of living things.

Joseph Campbell saw all of this coming—a whole culture-mind that seems determined to confuse metaphor with something concrete and mythic with historical forms. This book partially represents my decades of reflection on his seminal ideas. Dr. Edward C. Whitmont, who fled Austria from the Nazi-type of fundamentalists, was my personal and then training analyst and showed me my own inner fundamentalist again and again. Professor Houston Smith has been an inspiration and a demonstration of how to live an open-minded life. And my friend Phil Cousineau, who landed in New York the day 9/11 happened, became my colleague and soul-brother on the subject when a couple of days later we lectured together to a spellbound and attentive audience in Woodstock on the perils of the fundamentalist mind.

One of my oldest friends, the Reverend Dr. George Dole, not only steered me to valuable resources but gave me a valuable metaphor: "There is a place in the sea where the ocean roils and heaves due to subterranean geologic shifts. In regard to religion we are in a place like that." Dr. Frank Boyer has been a kindred spirit, helping me understand the texture of the historical fundamentalist mind. Bonnie Sgarro made the considerable resources of Bard Library as well as her own research skills available. Richard Smoley believed in this book, as did Lorraine Kisly, who was its agent. Carolyn Bond is one of the finest editors with whom I have worked (meaning that editing this book was an exquisite crucifixion and valuable alchemy), and Sharron Dorr, the publisher, has lent great insight and thoughtful support. Karl Pribram, Len Ochs, Siegfried Othmer, and Elmer Green have all participated in deep conversations on the neurological chapters. Swami Agnivesh; Drs. Willie Yee, Richard Brown, and Patricia Gerbarg; and Sri Sri Ravi Shankar have all contributed to perspectives on how religion can function in a healthy way.

I hope this book does some small justice to the gifts I have received from all of my teachers and friends—and from the eternal Spirit who can only weep or smile, or perhaps enter deep meditation, at our interminable folly.

INTRODUCTION

The bull is horned, massive, and powerfully intent on his single purpose. Facing him is a vaulter, nimble and athletic, preparing not only to evade the charge but to spring above it. But there are no guarantees, and it is a dangerous game.

This image, taken from the ancient Cretan frescoes of bull vaulting, comes to mind as I contemplate the theme of this book. Yes, you've got the metaphor: fundamentalisms are massive, truculent, single-minded creatures, belief systems of immense collective force, charging around in our social arena and also in our minds. Some are religious, positing events beyond all natural laws and commanding us to believe in them. Others, equally monolithic, are scientific and opaquely materialistic; but heretics beware—a scathing dismissal or an academic pillory could be your punishment. The bull's horns are the horns of our modern dilemma: the standoff between literalistic fundamentalism and metaphoric, symbolic thinking—the subject of this book.

In the explosive evolution of a planetary culture and the information superhighway, strange new antipathies and alliances have formed. Across national and cultural boundaries, and even within communities, people scowl at each other, dismiss each other's belief systems, brandish Bibles or other holy books—and sometimes, just as quickly, brandish weapons. Rhetoric becomes polarized and paralyzed. If you fail to vault elegantly above the warring ideologies you will surely get trampled or impaled.

What skills, what training, should an author bring to such a perilous encounter? I offer two, and they are found in the analyses and structure of this book: on the one hand, my years as a psychology professor and neurotherapist, teaching about and working clinically with consciousness and the brain; on the other, my long apprenticeship with mythologist Joseph Campbell, researching and writing books on mythology and shamanism. These universes of discourse may seem far apart, and most self-respecting professionals might refrain from listing *neurotherapist* and *mythologist* together on a resume. Yet the subject at hand—the myth-susceptible human brain that gets caught up in rigid, obsessive, and destructive ideas—calls for a conjunction between exactly these realms of knowledge.

My desire to write this book manifested after the events of 9/11. As a lifetime New Yorker, I felt personal outrage at how out of control things could get when cultures collide, how even the wisest among us stand like deer in the headlights of an impossible vehicle of doom. Now what do we do? What good is psychology—or anything else we know? Could anyone have seen this coming?

As I mused on the catastrophe, my memory flashed back to a quarter of a century ago. It was some time in 1975, and I was driving the great mythologist Joseph Campbell along the curvy roads of upstate New York on our way to a lecture he would be giving that evening. Along the way, the topic turned eventually to the state of the world. I remember commenting that most modern people seem a little schizophrenic because they don't know what to believe—there are just too many options. On the one side are centuries of hidebound belief that even the believers know is outdated and, on the other, a secular modernism that doesn't seem to believe in anything but the gods of chance.

We were driving past talus slopes under the beetling limestone cliffs of Rosendale, New York, and Campbell had been looking intently at the rocky debris. Suddenly he said something about standing on the "terminal moraine" of thousands of years of mythologies, and that we shouldn't be surprised if the ground seems to be shifting under us. Then he added, in words I can't forget, "The fragments of the gods are all around us."

As I wondered what he might have meant, I got that old *frisson*, the shiver up and down the spine that happens when a life-changing idea comes one's way. For a moment I wondered: Do these fragments emit a kind of spiritual radioactivity? Do partial gods walk and talk in our dreams, or judge us in our nightmares? Can god fragments themselves be insane?

Just as walking on a tumble of broken limestone rock is risky and demands our full attention, so making our way through the huge fragments around us—the broken cultural belief systems, unloved and worn-out deities, and phantoms of our own fears of transition and change—promises to be risky footing. I feel sympathy for our frightened, changing civilization.

That conversation with Campbell led to fifteen years of research on the topic of personal mythology, finally published in *The Mythic Imagination* (Bantam, 1990). The substance of the book is that, in the absence of a monolithic single religion such as Christianity offered in the Middle Ages, the modern psyche, trying to cope with the resulting alienation and dissociation, looks into the unconscious for guiding myths and images. I hadn't realized, until 9/11, how profound was the alienation and dissociation of the entire modern world—how the world itself seems to have lost its soul and is trying to find it—and thus how dangerous it is to have the volatile fragments of the gods lying around us. The situation could lead to both individual and group psychosis. It was, in fact, only three years or so after that conversation with Campbell that about nine hundred Americans followed a man with darkly messianic delusions, the Reverend Jim Jones, into the jungles of Guyana and died in a horrible mass suicide.

Recently, dozens of books taking positions on the dangers of misunderstood religion have been published with titles such as *The God Delusion*, *The Jesus Machine*, *The End of Faith*, *When Religion Becomes Evil*, and, in a different vein, *Why God Won't Go Away*. Authors, and even cartoonists, have been put on notice to watch what they say about Islam. Articles in popular magazines and scholarly journals alike are giving major coverage to issues of science and spirituality. *Newsweek* magazine has a thoughtful weekly section called "Beliefwatch." It usually takes a Jim Jones or a David Koresh, whose curious messianic delusions are examined later in this book, to prompt serious psychological or neurological investigation into what drives people to the extremes of religion. In this book, however, I am proposing that we do a sort of *preventive analysis* of how myth and culture affect the daily functioning of our central nervous system and, vice versa, of how dysfunctional nervous systems lead to rigid or destructive religiosity, before the next mass suicide, misguided rapture, or other hallmark event in the name of some offended god is headlined in the news.

If you think I am writing to ease my own anxiety about the world's problems, you are probably right. The dozens of books and hundreds of articles I read for this project, while sometimes reassuring me, have left me with no doubt that something large and dangerous is afoot in our half-conscious world. It goes by the name of fundamentalism. I believe there are new ways of looking at it. I am eager to share something useful I have found—a new way to approach fundamentalism by revealing it as something inherently human, *something we all do*. It is a psychological habit, related to our longing to reduce the awesome complexity of the world to a few simple rules. Being a habit, it can be addressed. I believe that as a species we are in a *genuine developmental crisis*. The world has become the ultimate dysfunctional family, caught in a bad dream of mis-communication and violence. In this sense, this book is wake-up reading, to be taken with your morning coffee, to shake off the nightmare from which we are all struggling to awaken in this dream-shrouded morning of humanity's childhood. The florid public examples of fundamentalism may be there just to awaken us to something pervasive in humanity that is definitely in need of transformation.

Let me offer a preview of the following pages. Chapter 1 looks at the problem of warring fundamentalisms with both a psychologist's and a mythologist's eye and examines Joseph Campbell's "prophecy," written in the 1980s in his *Inner Reaches of Outer Space*, about what happens when clashing fundamentalisms try to work out their dynamics.

Chapter 2 takes the issue straight into the human nervous system to show how physiologically vulnerable we are to dualistic and absolutistic patterns of thinking. Certain parts of the brain do seem to respond to reli-gious imagery, especially ritual, and to the sense of something as sacred. This chapter reveals the peril that looms when a nervous system already susceptible to dichotomies and rigid thinking (the hardware) is compro-mised with bad mythology (the software).

The third chapter looks at how religions have exploited certain vulner-abilities in the human nervous system—susceptibilities to authority, to obsession and ritual, and to "dissociation," the ability to cut off parts of our functioning and hide from ourselves. A psyche divided against itself is vul-nerable to manipulation and ideological thinking.

Chapter 4 investigates Campbell's "fragments of the gods" idea and con-siders what it is like to live on an archetypal talus. The inner version of the mythological problem is the fragmentation of the personality, and the personality's desperate attempts to achieve unity at all costs. Some fragments are problematical, like the naive hero, which leads people into childish idealism and fantasy, rather than the soul growth and realism we find with the mature understanding of the hero. Another dysfunctional fragment, because so easily projected on others, is the malignant image of the Antichrist, a collective manifestation of repressed shadow elements.

Chapter 5 takes the duality problem into cultural history and particularly the history of Western religion. We go from the ancient Middle East, through Europe and England, to America, where a new continent birthed strange religious forms never seen before, such as Mormonism and the Jehovah's Witnesses. These novel hybrids nonetheless hold onto ancient (Middle Eastern) beliefs, such as the expectation of a messiah (or his second coming) and a promised millennium of peace. Wonderful-sounding, and entwined with the perennial human need to return to paradise, such a belief, held literally, may imperil the whole world.

The sixth chapter offers a summarizing look at Islam and its own struggles with dualism and patriarchal patterns. Islam's history has been marked by internal schisms from the beginning and by battles between sects trying to out-fundamentalize each other, as in Christianity. The Wahhabist variety of Islam, born in Saudi Arabia, is one militant outcome of this polarizing tendency. We also look at the early historic events that underlie the *Satanic Verses* controversy, which had to do with Islam's repudiation of a feminine element in its own mythology.

In chapter 7, I take the heat off the religious fundamentalists and turn my gaze to secular fundamentalisms, including scientism, medical fundamentalism, psychotherapeutic fundamentalism, skeptical fundamentalism and (oh, yes) new age fundamentalism. Examining these systems shows us that *it is not the content of a belief but the way it is held* that make it a fundamentalism.

Chapter 8, "The Five-Minute Fundamentalist," opens up the idea that fundamentalist thinking is an inherently human habit we all engage in when we are least self-aware. It can also be managed by skillful means involving self-awareness. I share some personal features of grappling with the inner fundamentalist and offer some hopefully useful exercises for revealing this metamorphic but dangerous psychological character through self-observation and mindfulness.

Chapter 9 is titled "Natural Religion." Here I differ from the deconstructionist writers who say religion is ridiculous and should be discarded. Alongside the pathological religious forms prevalent through history are authentic, natural forms of religion that blossom in human lives without the hypocrisy, bombast, and coercion of the fundamentalist legacy. There is something perennial about the human desire to reach out to a living and responsive universe and find meaningful connection, love, and creativity. When that happens, and your bliss is embraced, in Campbell's words, "Doors will open for you that you didn't even know were there," and you may once again find yourself at home in the universe.

My hope is that you the reader will draw from this work both an awe of human creativity and imagination and an awareness of just how fragile these faculties are—and how easily subverted. I hope to engender an awareness of how old cultural habits as well as new cultural crises feed into fundamentalist thinking, making us more desperate for simple answers in a changing world. And I hope to inspire you to think, *we are they*, instead of, *it's us against them!* whenever you meet a fundamentalist, whether a religious or a scientific one. Only in this spirit can we move forward as a unified, healthy humanity, our exquisite diversity yielding not conflict but dialogue and the alchemy of mutual understanding.

- 1 -

THE PHANTOM RULERS
OF HUMANITY

The fire threw up figures
And symbols meanwhile, racial myths formed and dis-
    solved in it, the phantom rulers of humanity
That without being are yet more real than what they are
    born of, and without shape, shape that which makes
    them:
The nerves and the flesh go by shadowlike, the limbs and
    the lives shadowlike, these shadows remain, these shad-
    ows
To whom temples, to whom churches, to whom labors and
    wars, visions and dreams are dedicate. . . .

—Robinson Jeffers, "Roan Stallion"

The world is currently facing an array of crises unlike any before in
human history pertaining to the use of natural resources, distribu-
tion of wealth, health concerns, and just how the members of the human
family might get along together on planet Earth. It's a time when clear thinking is urgently called for, yet some people are starting holy wars, fighting to
the death over ownership of the places they call sacred, calling each other
"the Great Satan," and asserting a divine mandate for whatever they do—
from acts of violence to accumulating great wealth. Others, with seeming
joy, anticipate the end of the world, believing that in the near future the
heavens will open, divine figures will appear and enter the stream of history and, in the Mother of all Battles on the fabled plains of Armageddon,
good will once and for all win a decisive victory over evil.

Why does humankind relentlessly involve supernatural forces and players
in history? It has been so ever since the Iliad, since the Old Testament, since
the Bhagavad Gita. The answer has to do with the story-making capacity of
the human mind. Especially when human emotions are stirred, when people

feel vulnerable or frightened, rationality no longer suffices. People look for reassurance to events and realities beyond the ordinary human scale. Their frame of reference, in other words, becomes *mythic.*

Modern interpretations of myth seem to equate it with fairy tales or superstitions, if not patent falsehood, but myth is grander than that; if it lies or exaggerates on the outside, there is a deep perennial truth on the inside. Myths are universal stories that convey deep experiences of whole peoples and cultures. You can tell that myths are older than religions because they are there right at the beginning of things, when God walked in the Garden in the cool of the evening and serpents whispered to the mother of us all. Myths also give rise to rituals, as when an immortal event of ancient times, such as Passover or the Christian Eucharist, is celebrated symbolically. The myth says: *Do this in remembrance of me,* and the celebrant, through the ritual, is united with the God and the sacralized beginnings of things. Whenever we're concerned with the highest truths of life or life's most transforming experiences, we are in the realm of myth.

Mythic thinking, however, is not reserved only for solemn rituals and myths of origin; it is also found psychologically in the worlds of childhood and in dream and emotion. It inflates things so they are larger, more absolute; their dramatic potential is enhanced. The dark basement of the house we grew up in rustles with ghosts; that patch of woods becomes the forest primeval, with unknown creatures in it. Our parents can shift from godlike sources of all good things to fearful tyrants, witches, and monsters. We all remember our child's world, dimly or clearly, and though we gladly put many aspects of it behind us, we still return to that world regularly in night dreams and daydreams. We also find mythic thinking in our novels and on the big screen with Luke Skywalker or Harry Potter. And it is there whenever we become highly charged with emotions and try to grasp at big pictures and ultimate meanings. "The latest incarnation of Oedipus, the continued romance of Beauty and the Beast, stands this afternoon on the corner of Forty-second Street and Fifth Avenue waiting for the traffic light to change," wrote Joseph Campbell in his classic *The Hero with a Thousand Faces,* published in 1949. Everyman, though he seldom seems aware of it, is immersed in mythic thinking.

Myth draws its psychological (and sociocultural) power from what are known as archetypal *elementary ideas,* a concept first introduced in the writings of nineteenth-century German scholar Adolf Bastian.[1] Elementary ideas can wield power over the mind of any person anytime, anywhere. They include such archetypal forms as the Myth of Paradise, the Hero's Journey, the Earth Mother, Gaia, the Wise Old Man, the Wise Old Woman, the form and attributes of God (conceived of as a person rather than a presence), the Messiah, the anti-Messiah, the Evil One, the End of the World. Each mythology skillfully interweaves the elementary ideas with folk ideas. The former give an ineluctable dignity to the culture; the latter provide spice, flavor, and uniqueness to the eternal images and cosmologies. The folk ideas are drawn from local customs, idioms, geography, and support the community. They provide social *orientation* and a sense of belonging to something. The archetypal elementary ideas open the psyche and the spirit to wonder and awe, and give helpful hints and *guidance* through life—an example being the hero's journey, with its themes of separation, initiation, and return. Both orientation and guidance are necessary to human living, but while our orientation shifts as we evolve over time and encounter changing times and cultures, inner guidance and the maturation of the human soul through a lifetime are perennial issues.[2]

LIVING OUR MYTH CONSCIOUSLY

When the power of mythic imagery gets tangled up with literalism, we have something called *fundamentalism.* Fundamentalism takes the luminous and mythic, whose realm is meant to be metaphor and symbol, and imprisons it in matter and in history. Given the natural preeminence of the divine in the human psyche, all else pales before the realization, on the world's stage and out in history, of God's supernatural intention. Mythic imagination reified in this way can turn ordinary people into "God's chosen people," unfruitful deserts into "the Promised Land," and municipalities with heterogeneous histories, such as Jerusalem, into "our" holy city. Well now, you may ask at this point, are you talking about religion or mythology?

3

Good question, I respond. In my experience, humans easily confuse the relationship between these two, especially when the fundamentalist mindset is attempting to ground mythic forms in historical facts. After the great cultural Enlightenment of three to four hundred years ago, the clear light of rational thought was supposed to illumine our vision, and mythic thinking was expected to gradually fade into the dream world of humanity's abusive and tormented childhood. But we are finding, as Campbell and the depth psychologists of the twentieth century warned, that these old thought forms do not simply disappear. They stay around and when threatened, engage in maneuvers of self-preservation, as it were, like any living creature threatened with extinction. They try to bend the minds of their holders to keep them alive forever. Consider for a moment the reaction of Galileo's inquisitors to the idea of a heliocentric, rather than earth-centered, universe. Consider the reaction of fundamentalist Christianity to Darwin's theory of evolution. Consider the reaction of conservative Islam to the secularism of the modern world.

MIT theorist and psycholinguist Noam Chomsky has demonstrated that there is a faculty in the human mind capable of receiving the "generative grammar" of whatever language a person is exposed to as a little child, so that within a few years he or she becomes a fluent native speaker. This language is likely to remain the person's primary language for the rest of his or her life. In most right-handed people, the left hemisphere of the brain receives these linguistic imprints. The same phenomenon is true of mythic images, or *mythogems*. Like morphemes, or units of verbal meaning, the mythogem is a unit of mythological meaning. The idea of a garden at the beginning of time, like the Garden of Eden, is an example of such a mythogem, as are elements of the narratives around the lives of saints or saviors—including their "virgin birth," a theme not at all limited to Christianity, and even the very idea of God as "a being in the sky." The neurological organ for the imagery and emotional meaning of mythogems is probably, for most people, the right hemisphere of the brain—while the names and verbal lore are stored in the left (more about this in chapter 2). The myths and rituals of all cultural forms, including religion, are all-too-easily imprinted on young psyches, a fact which has prompted questions regarding the ethics of doing so—is religion too powerful and too peril-filled a thing to be foisted on children?

The idea of the sacred seems to come to us instinctively. Religious historian Mircea Eliade says human beings generically understand the difference between the *sacred* and the *secular*; we build a *frame of reverence* around symbolic elements presented to us in ritual contexts. These mythogems take on a different order of experience than secular reality. The elaboration of those sacred stories, images, and ideas into a systematic, time-honored form creates a religion. In the process, an enormous amount of motivation and emotion are interwoven with the lore and imagery of the religion's core myth. These crystallized forms accompany most of the world's population through the stages and trials and tribulations of life in their own emotion-impregnated vernacular. These forms in some cases become so meaningful that people are even willing to enter into holy conflict and risk death for the images, names, and ideas that comprise them. We see this, obviously, in some strict forms of religious fundamentalism today.

We are wired, if you will, for mythic thinking. It has a neurological basis in our brains and is ingrained in our cultural and deep psychological patterns. Myths fit into our psyches the way a neurotransmitter fits into a receptor site on a neuron, or the way digital code is recognized by a computer's processor. As the eminent American psychologist Jerome Bruner has said, not until we tell a story about our experience can we make sense of it.[3] For Aristotle, a myth was just a good story or a drama, but one that held power because of its effect on the mind.

Furthermore, such is the nature of the human brain and psychology that even when we eliminate all mention of a God or gods—anything supernatural whatsoever—from social discourse, still the human mind will make a religion of communism or free-market capitalism, or make a deity of Chairman Mao or a priesthood of politicians. It is even willing to make a fetish of scientific objectivity itself in the form of *scientism,* a hybrid view of reality cobbled together from Newtonian physics and tenth-grade science. All fundamentalisms are not religious or mythic. Many are secular and materialistic. It is not the *content,* in these cases, so much as the absolutist *style* of conviction and expression that betrays their fundamentalist nature.

5

We neglect myth at our peril. A horrific, not-to-be-forgotten example is Nazism, with its swastika symbol, sacred blood, and sacred soil—an apparent resurgence of archaic, warlike Germanic Wotanism. Hitler, himself steeped in mythology, knew he needed a scapegoat. He once confided to a friend that he didn't know what he'd do without the Jews, for anti-Semitism was the only cause that would unite his contentious Fascist buddies. Hitler also proved that myths, such as the genetic or cultural existence of an "Aryan" people, a "master race," require no basis whatsoever in fact. They only need to grab people's minds—and they are very good at grabbing minds.

Incendiary nationalistic evangelists and ayatollahs of our time may not be students of mythology or depth psychology, but they do exploit the same elemental principles: plucking mythic puppet strings that reach down into irrational human centers of belief, emotion, and behavior. Profound cultural collisions are unfolding before our wondering eyes, and religion and mythology are found everywhere in the mix, alongside modern technology. Islamic terrorists can contemplate using the secrets of the atom to shift the ancient concept of holy war to a new scale, and televangelists can rebuke and frighten millions about their souls in TV jeremiads not even old Jeremiah could dream of. Ancient actors in modern dress sometimes look terrifying.

In *The Hero with a Thousand Faces* Campbell not only lets us know that, like it or not, we all are on a mythic journey, he urges that it is far better to live the myth consciously than succumb to it in projected form. In a personal psyche, the healthy approach to dealing with "content" that is associated with fear or anxiety is to examine the content, try to understand it, and only then take action. An unhealthy approach, such as paranoia, for example, projects the fearful content onto others and, if strong emotion accompanies the process, takes immediate action. On a social or cultural level, the healthy approach would have been Hitler entering into a dialectical process of discussion with the Jewish people and coming to a compromise on their issues. The unhealthy version is the unfortunate history we know, in which massive paranoia was allowed to rule and genocide was the result.

PSYCHOLOGY AND MYTH

Sigmund Freud was one of the first to link psyche and myth. Freud based his early model of psychology entirely on the Oedipus story, sometimes called "the family romance," in which the male child wishes to possess his mother and kill his father. (Outspoken early psychoanalytic feminists forced Freud to consider the equivalent for girls, which he named "the Electra complex," marked by antipathy between the girl and her mother and a secret romance with daddy.) According to Freud, the primordial influence of the "family romance" accompanies us through life, as young men long to be reunited with their mothers and young women to be loved and cherished by their fathers. The god ruling Freud's early psychology was Eros—desire—based on sexuality. As he moved into the second half of his life, however, Freud seemed to realize he had based his psychology on only half a myth. In a conceptual move astonishing to his well-indoctrinated followers, in his book *Beyond the Pleasure Principle* (1920) Freud suddenly introduced a new player onto the psychological stage: Eros's brother and eternal counterplayer Thanatos, the lord of death. The harder the struggle of life (short, brutish, and nasty in Thomas Hobbes's phrase), the sweeter the desire to return to the womb or to paradise and the cessation of struggle.[4] We find the signature of Thanatos in the heaven-bound visions of Islamic martyrs, who embrace personal annihilation as a religious privilege, and fundamentalist millennialists, who seem exuberant about the end of the world.

Among Freud's students there was universal agreement of the power of myth on the psyche. In their work each one focused on a different aspect of the hero myth: Alfred Adler on the inexorable human will to power, Carl Jung on the underworld journey that leads to rebirth, Otto Rank on the myth of the hero as encapsulated in the human birth process. Anna Freud and Melanie Klein studied the displacement of primary love for the mother onto symbolic objects and the terrible resentment of the infant/hero when disappointed—myths of matricide and the genesis of sadistic aggression. Wilhelm Reich thought all myths, as well as the very "character" we play in time and space, are stored in the dynamisms of the body. Social philosopher Herbert Marcuse based his pessimistic commentary *Eros and Civilization* on the dichotomy between the life and death instincts. Myth permeates psyche, said Freud—and his followers echoed him—and the worst danger of all is to repress and hold back the energies of the "gods" as they move in us.[5]

Jung, Freud's most famous psychoanalytic protégé and renegade, during one of his last filmed interviews in the late 1950s with the threat of nuclear holocaust hovering over the world, pauses and looks straight into the camera. He positions his fingers upward as if holding a string. "The world," the old wizard says ominously in thick, Swiss-accented but impeccable English, "is hanging by a thin thread. That thread is the psyche of man." This was his plea that we begin to think psychologically. In his autobiography Jung notes that at one point he realized his "task of tasks" was to find out what myth he was living; everything else was secondary.[6] Jungian psychology invites each person to discover his or her own myth, or risk being seized by one unconsciously.

In the post–World War II period, with the world still reeling in the wake of a genuine fascist coup, Else Frenkel-Brunswik and T. W. Adorno did studies on anti-Semitism, ethnocentrism, the authoritarian personality and why we are so susceptible to demagogues and the mass psychology of fascism. Their psychological research on charismatic leaders and their willing followers has proved invaluable. During this time Hannah Arendt wrote her penetrating memoirs of Europe during the Holocaust, Eric Fromm and Eric Hoffer showed how pervasive is the human urge to set aside rationality and practicality in the service of a cause, and Stanley Milgram showed us that, alas, fascism, in the form of willingness to capitulate to authority, lurks in every human soul.[7]

By the middle of the century, coming at the same problem from the angle of mythological scholarship rather than psychology, Campbell's *The Hero with a Thousand Faces* hit the bestseller lists. The book starts with an analysis of a modern dream to show how Freud's Oedipus mythology can work unconsciously in the psyche of someone who has never read Freud or studied the myth. The book obviously touched some kind of vein. Shortly after this success Campbell commenced work on a four-volume opus titled

The Masks of God, which detailed the myriad ways world culture conceives of the divine. In the 1970s he published one of his most accessible books, a simple little summary entitled *Myths to Live By*,[8] which let us know that we live with, in, and among myths, and we live best by doing so consciously. The alternative is nothing less than compulsion and pathology.

During this time and the two decades that followed, many others became fascinated by the connection between myth and psyche. In the eighties, Feinstein and Krippner published their influential *Personal Mythology*, Rollo May wrote *The Cry for Myth*, Sam Keen and Anne Valley-Fox published *Your Mythic Journey*, Jean Houston wrote *A Mythic Life*, and my own *The Mythic Imagination* came out in 1990. These books invited the modern seeker to mine Campbell's "terminal moraine" of the great myths for patterns still meaningful enough to inspire our own lives. None of us anticipated the tremendous response to the television series *The Power of Myth* with journalist Bill Moyers interviewing Joseph Campbell, nor the enormous success of the book *The Power of Myth*, edited by Betty Sue Flowers and published by Doubleday, which sold a million copies.[9] A great many people responded to Campbell's underlying message that myths offer rich matrices of meaning to the meaning-hungry modern soul.

CAMPBELL'S PROPHECY

Beware the man whose God is in the sky!

—G. B. Shaw

Toward the end of his life, during the mid-1980s Joseph Campbell abandoned his labors on the monumental, multivolume *Historical Atlas of World Mythology* to write, in a relatively short time, an oddly titled little book, *The Inner Reaches of Outer Space: Metaphor as Myth and as Religion*.[10] He finished it in 1986, saw it in print by early 1987, and passed away on October 30, All Hallows' Eve, that same year.

The Inner Reaches of Outer Space is, in a sense, Campbell's last will and testament. It never became as popular as *The Hero with a Thousand Faces*, which was still on best-seller lists fifty years after its original publication.

However, *Inner Reaches* is Campbell's letter to the next generation. His scholar's mind saw an inescapable sociocultural and psychological trend forming—the dangerous one we find ourselves in now—and he prophesied. In this section I endeavor to summarize his prophecy and the thinking that led up to it. Hopefully, now, twenty years later, it may reach more receptive minds and hearts.

Campbell was disturbed about the condition of the world—he was troubled to see humanity still drowning in unconscious mythologizing and to see archaic collective mindsets lurching toward a technologically dazzling but ecologically and socially perilous future. As a mythologist who had traced humankind's mythic development as far back as the cave-bear shrines of the old Paleolithic, then through the massive ritual court burials of the Neolithic Levant to the bloodstained pyramid altars of Mesoamerica and the centuries of holy wars under the icon of a tortured man on a tree, Campbell was not one just to romanticize myths. He knew humanity's roots are not only deep but dark. "Myths," he wrote, "hold and give form to energies that are the essence of life itself, and which, when unbridled, become horrifying and destructive."

This is not the Campbell of the seemingly blithe "follow your bliss!" He knew that these raw and dangerous energies are held in check on the psychological level by the mythic narratives, images, and emotions woven into the child's socialization process, from baptisms and circumcisions to Bar Mitzvahs. On a sociocultural level, myths reconcile the individual psyche to the culture, and in fact support the culture, extolling membership in it— for instance, identifying as "a chosen people" with a special mission entrusted by God. In fact, some traditional societies' name for themselves translates as "the human beings," "the real people," or "the holy people." This kind of affirmation gives a wonderful "rapture," if you will, to the in-group described as chosen. The myth empowers them and makes them special; all their doings are blessed by the highest authority there is. But the same myth and vocabulary may describe other people—especially neighboring groups with whom they have an adversarial relationship—as other than human, as "heretics," "unbelievers," or "infidels." This can lay the groundwork for conflict, or for holy war.

Campbell's words in *The Inner Reaches* are chillingly prophetic: "In the old Near East . . . contending armies of the only three monotheistic monads of the planet (each dedicated to a notion of its own historically conditioned idea of "God" as having been from all eternity) . . . are threatening the whole process of global unification with the adventure of their scripturally prophesied Armageddon."[11]

The Abrahamic religions—Judaism, Christianity, and Islam—all of which claim Abraham as their patriarchal ancestor, bear all the imprints of tribal religions of nomadic peoples, Campbell points out. Nomads, moving around under vast skies rather than settling in one place, typically worship a sky god. Examples include Indra of the Vedic Aryans, who moved into and overtook the Indian subcontinent, and Zeus of the Dorians and Ionians, who invaded Greece. Consider the character of Yahweh as he systematically and repeatedly invites his people to invade, slaughter, and dominate the settled communities of other folk existing peacefully nearby—as Campbell writes, quoting from Deuteronomy 6:10–12—"taking captive their women and children, and usurping their cities and houses 'which you did not build, and houses full of all good things, which you did not fill, and cisterns hewn out, which you did not hew, and vineyards and olive trees which you did not plant.'" It is not uncommon to find sky gods talking to their fierce nomadic Indo-European or Aryan constituents in such a way. This kind of directive is underscored with the theological, metaphysical warrant (again from Deuteronomy 6:12): "And when you eat and are full, then take heed lest you forget the Lord, who brought you out of the land of Egypt, out of the house of bondage." It is a powerful psychological boost to be told that the people whose lives you are destroying and property you are occupying are "corrupt sinners who worship abominations for gods."[12]

The God of the Old Testament gives explicit instructions to destroy the altars and icons of the nonbelievers, especially their little clay and stone goddess statues called Asherahs. In other words, not only is our god better than your god (or goddess); he is, in fact, the only real God, and he doesn't want yours—no matter how lovingly prayed to, venerated, worshipped— to exist. Thus not only are the subject people (which may include the women of one's own people) dominated, but the spiritual core of their culture is smashed. Monotheistic male chauvinism seems to lead inexorably to *mythoclasm*, or mythic genocide. Horrible as they are, such rationales are familiar to the historian on every side, having been used to justify crusades, colonizations, and forced conversions all over the world—most often among less technologically advanced people.

The problem is magnified when the world as we know it is expanded beyond the local and even earthly proportions to a cosmic scale and that same warmongering, judgmental deity is conflated along with it—which is what Campbell alludes to in the title *Inner Reaches of Outer Space*. There was a time when the follower of one of the Abrahamic religions could point to a city on earth as the center of that religion's universe—Jerusalem or Rome or Mecca. But we no longer live in a time when the center of the universe can be such a place. Over the past few centuries our horizons have expanded beyond the local and ethnic to the planetary—the spectacle of the solar system with its wheeling planets and, beyond that, the breathtaking void of deep space. The center now is nowhere and everywhere.

Moreover, when the Earth is viewed from outer space, there are no visible boundaries or demarcations. Nothing in outer space confirms the centrality of any group; all of us are riding the global spaceship, floating in its azure mantle wrapped in clouds, together. Viewed from the scale of what we know now, making one's theological navigation dependent upon landmarks such as the Holy Land—Jerusalem, Mecca—is exposed as a childlike ethnocentric projection. We are now invited to think on a larger scale.

Whatever the size of the world as we know it, we assume that our God rules over it. Now that our horizons have expanded tremendously, we think that what is in fact our local god is in charge of the whole thing. Campbell wondered, then, what happens when Yahweh, the Middle-Eastern tribal deity, gets promoted to no less than the Cosmic God, ruler of everything. Likewise, what happens when the gentle, historical, Jewish Jesus gets promoted to the Cosmic Christ, to whom all beings, Christian or not, owe their salvation? Surely, Campbell thought, some *mythic megalomania* would be at hand, and the risks would be no less than with any other kind of megalomania, whether individual or collective.

MYTHIC DEMOCRACY

Campbell would gently, patiently explain to his audiences—including the believers, the theologians, and clergy—that in fact dozens of world traditions have the motif of a fall from paradise, or a place of perfection devolving into a world of imperfections. Many have mythologies of a "great flood" after which the world had to be reconstituted, or from which a progenitor saved himself and a few other beings. So, also, stories of the loss and reattainment of a holy land and its sacred features are universal mythogems, since most mythologies sacralize and develop sacred narratives about features of the landscape. The river Jordan, Mount Ararat, where the Ark came to rest, and the Temple of Jerusalem are only the sacred places of a few among many world traditions who have their own sacred groves, springs, and mountains. Jesus, before he was ever cosmicized by that brilliant PR man Saint Paul, seems to have been a wise and compassionate Jewish teacher, as Bruce Chilton has shown so beautifully in his book *Rabbi Jesus*. And even when he is seen archetypally, Jesus is not unlike Osiris, Tammuz, Mithras, and other dying-and-reviving gods or heroes of antiquity, all of them beloved, all followed with a similar heart-based fervor.

Some listeners, of course, resented Campbell's expansive, beatific vision. There is a difference, they argued, between *those*, er, mythologies and *our* religion, which is a codex of revealed truth that can be neither disputed nor compared. Religion cannot be compared to mythology. Even as academic subjects, religion and mythology are taught separately in universities and institutions to this day. Thus we are prevented from being able to stand outside our own acculturation and see that our religion is simply one among the many windows through which humankind looks to perceive and understand the divine.

The reverse is also true: what we designate as mythologies often were, or still are, religions. What we now call Greek mythology was once an elaborate religious system that informed state ceremonies and determined central architecture, such as the Parthenon, a temple to Athena. India, alongside its long history of lofty metaphysical subtleties, has narratives about cosmic deities, such as the austere Brahma (the Creator) meditating on a lotus arising from the navel of Vishnu (the Preserver), who is dreaming the world, and Shiva (the Destroyer), seated on a tiger skin, his matted hair tangled with snakes, who can incinerate the world with a glance of his third eye. Psychologically and mythically sophisticated, Hindus understand that one Truth can have many metaphors. My wife and I once rode with a Tamil taxi driver, careening wildly between the overloaded buses and bullock carts of Madras. I noticed icons on the dashboard, not unlike those sometimes found in American cars. Jesus was there, but also dancing Shiva (Nataraja), a little praying Hanuman, the meditating Buddha, and, swinging giddily from the rearview mirror along with lots of prayer beads, a picture of Guru Nanak, the founder of Sikhism.

"My," I said, "you belong to a lot of religions!"

"In my business, Baba," the dark-skinned man said, turning around completely—still at full speed—and flashing us a bright smile, "it doesn't pay to take any chances!" He twirled back to look at the road, just in time to narrowly miss a lumbering bullock cart, and we all laughed heartily.

MYTHOLOGIES IN COLLISION

Campbell was afraid the world would fall into turbulence if people didn't understand that *all* religions and myths are based on metaphor, and that the working of metaphor is meant to produce a psychological effect. Myths read literally, on the other hand, lead to a mental and emotional condition very similar to pathology—inflation within the psyche produces paranoia, along with righteous certainty. Myth is meant to lead the mind by implication, not by certainty or a fanatical attitude.

Religions that cannot see their stories as allegorical destroy the transparency of vision that authentic spiritual consciousness requires. And when we do not perceive other religions as transparent as well, we perceive them as false, as deceptive imitations. Thinking in terms of petrified images and myths leads inevitably to the conclusion: "Our reality trumps all other realities—our God is the true God."

Insight into this phenomenon is the reasoning behind the separation of church and state, wherever such political wisdom is found. Thomas Jefferson understood the difference between the Biblical narrative as a wisdom text and as mythology, which is why he edited the supernaturalism out of his Bible—absolutist myth and politics don't mix well. The state functions best as a rational enterprise run by cool heads and optimistic hearts. At its worst it gives a supernatural warrant for conflict with others whose belief systems happen to be different.

Joseph Campbell was in his eighties when he wrote *Inner Reaches of Outer Space*. He had seen George Lucas's *Star Wars*, which used ideas from his own *Hero with a Thousand Faces*. He knew that as we push the boundaries of our reality into deep space—as well as downward into the atomic structure of matter—we carry our myths and mythic susceptibility right with us. They accompany us into a world of nearly instant communication with a variously educated population of higher numbers than the planet has ever sustained, where we are guaranteed to have a certain number of visionaries, prophets, and terrorists trapped in their own peculiar myths. We are in a "free-fall into globalism"—a phrase of Buckminster Fuller that Campbell, who knew and admired Fuller, often quoted. The unit of social identity can no longer be the isolated group, the "only true religion," culture, or civilization. It is one world, as seen in the view of the astronauts from outer space. Our mythologies, Campbell insisted, can never be the same again.

Though he died in 1987, Campbell anticipated the shifting of cultural tectonic plates that would accompany the millennium. What he felt as premonitory whispers and tremblings are now emerging in full convulsion. Myths are in collision. These used to be small, local temblors along the familiar religious dichotomies: Catholic versus Protestant, Hindu versus Buddhist, Jewish versus Muslim.

But Campbell knew that the issue, at once broader and more profound than these familial bloodlettings, is the basic one of whether the universe is living or dead, meaningful or meaningless, spiritual or secular. He would often tell a rather charming story about overhearing an argument between a ten-year-old boy and his mother in a diner. The boy talks excitedly about evolution and dinosaurs, and his mother counters with "Don't be too sure about all that stuff; that's not what the Bible says." The boy wraps up the discussion with a triumphant: "But mom, they found the bones." The emerging struggle of our era is the conflict between science and spirituality. The tectonic plates that are moving are larger than any others in recorded time.

Thus we find the Creationists against the Darwinians, the astronomers versus the astrologers, even the anthropocentric "myth of progress" neoconservatives against the nature-based conservatism of the deep ecologists. The "old guard" of each fundamentalism is terrified that their very world, their cherished reality, is fraying and blowing away in the inexorable winds of change. Right now, in post-scientific and technological places, the change is clearly in the secular direction. So a countermovement is mounted that tries to cling to the venerated old values, sometimes with a fierce death grip. People get worked up when their sacred ideas are threatened—or they perceive them so.

WHEN RAPTURE GROWS PERILOUS

Joseph Campbell said on dozens of occasions that there is a kind of rapture, bliss, or intoxication that comes from vital contact with myths. The mind slides easily into mythic thinking as if falling under a spell. In the positive sense, he would say, when you are "following your bliss," or what moves you the most deeply, the journey is joyful and revelatory. The psyche finds an echoing resonance in the world through the medium of the myth.

But this mythic intoxication has a dark side as well. It emerges when people take a myth literally, particularly a myth of destruction and renewal. Such stories when treated as metaphor lead us to transformation and rebirth within. But when they are concretized and interpreted in history, we have, for instance, the mythogem that is at the opposite historical end of the mythogem of the Garden of Paradise: the Battle of Armageddon and the End of Days, which evokes such fascination for the millennialists among contemporary American Protestantism.

These two myths are based on the Bible but extracted freely from the prophetic books of the Old Testament, some passages in the New Testament, particularly Matthew 24 and 25, and the visionary allegory called the

Book of Revelation. The whole story is described in more detail in chapter 5, but the gist is that Christ predicted his own return and these other biblical sources confirm the same event. His return will be preceded by the arrival of an Antichrist figure, and a great battle will take place in which Christ triumphs and the devil, the Antichrist, and their minions are cast into a burning lake.

It sounds bad, but only for the enemies of Christianity. Good and loyal Christians may benefit in either of two ways—revealing that there are really two mythologies about this important happy ending. Even in the midst of the end-times battle, 144,000 believers (there is some quibbling about the number) will be snatched up out of the fray to "meet the Lord in the air." This is the celebrated Rapture. The other Christians and their descendants get to live in the *millennium,* a thousand-year-long, blessed and "perfect" rule of Christ as an earthly king. Millennialists are those who are preparing, in various ways, for these events to happen literally and in our lifetime. Naturally, if you wish to be among the raptured, you must lead a flawless Christian life—the worthy moral behind the perennial myth.

However, the psychological issues this prophetic account raises are the real peril of this second, millennialist kind of "rapture." The healthy kind of mythic rapture, said Campbell, uses myths instructively to shape and guide a useful life. The mythic and natural worlds are brought together in a meaningful, synergistic, and useful way. In the unhealthy variant, myths are used coercively and as a scare tactic to bring about moral reformation. And in this case, the literal fulfillment of the myth (and followers are asked, nay, commanded, to believe it will be fulfilled) is the complete annihilation of the world as we know it and the capitulation of any accumulated human wisdom to a divine authority—and thus a reattainment of childhood.

The *deus absconditus,* or hidden god in this story, seems to be our old friend Thanatos, Death. The perilous part of this rapture is the myth itself, dangled in front of us like a bauble, an illusion that never happens despite its many predictions through the centuries. In old medieval and Japanese folk plays, the face of Death was sometimes concealed under the mask of a beautiful woman. Similarly, two mythologies have here made a dangerous covenant: Paradise Lost and the wish to regain it through the Rapture.

Modern life is stressful and challenging, and the complexities of existence have multiplied with the growth of the technology that was supposed to simplify things. Scientism as a belief system emphasizes our mortality and essential meaninglessness in a vast materialistic universe. The cultural melting pot confuses us with its babble of competing voices. It is apparent that many people long for the womblike simplicity of the millennialist belief system: I came from paradise and I shall return to paradise. Thank God I can stop struggling and grappling with all these contradictions and paradoxes. Daddy will fix everything and make it right. All I have to do is obey him in everything.

A journalist reported overhearing a conversation between two of the top al-Qaeda planners—they were laughing sardonically about the naïve and illusion-prone young men they "sent to Allah" in the Trade Tower attacks: "By the time those kids found out there was no garden and no seventy-two virgins waiting for them in heaven, it would be way too late for them—oh well!" It is not a very long step from this to the Reverend Jerry Falwell telling his parishioners not to buy cemetery plots because the Rapture (the "uppertaker" not the "undertaker," he said) would be happening in his own lifetime—which came to an end just as this book was going to press. If enough people join with such destructive mythology and visualize Armageddon as their personal gate to paradise, then it's worth wondering if there is such a thing as a self-fulfilling prophecy. By the time they bring about the war that is supposed to precipitate the Rapture, elect or no, it probably won't be much better for them than it was for those poor Arab kids. These are the dangers of literalized mythologies.

Clearly, the childlike wish-fulfillment mythogem of the Rapture blinds adult responsibility of all kinds. That is why Secretary of the Interior James Watt could laugh at the "greenies" preaching sustainability and say: Let's cut down the last tree so that Christ will come again—an odd philosophy for a public official in charge of the state parks and the nation's environment. And why should we afflict ourselves with annoying delusions of long-term planetary stewardship? We needn't bother to care for the Earth or ensure a future for our children and grandchildren through healthcare or environmental measures because we're going to be taken up to heaven, and it will all disappear. This approach is not likely to produce a sustainable culture, nor help its participants find their own mature humanity.

Public religion may hold up myths of the gods that are splendid and irresistible, but dark deeds are done in their names. This is why it behooves us to look for Jeffers's "phantom rulers"—the shadows of the bright, shining sky gods lurking beneath their thrones. It is these mishandled myths and the dark, demonic potentials they hold that shadow our one-sided religions. It is now known that President Ronald Reagan enthusiastically favored the Frankensteinian "Star Wars" defense initiative because he believed it was the only kind of weapons system big enough to fulfill the Armageddon prophesies—which he thought would happen in *his* lifetime. Once again, it is downright scary when reality imitates myth and people are trying to "get the jump on God" by literally bringing about biblically prophesied events. The historical chapters that follow (5 and 6) depart from my neurological and psychological analyses to show just how disastrous is the wake of fundamentalism expressed throughout history.

Twenty years have passed since Campbell wrote his visionary and premonitory warning. The events of which he spoke are now upon us: the Great Mythoclasm, the shattering of mythological dynasties and traditions, is indeed happening, and unfortunately people are dying and cultures are growing a toxic hatred, rather than toleration, for each other. At the end of *The Inner Reaches*, Campbell again leans on a theme that persisted throughout his writing and his lectures: that the key is the way of the artist, who knows how to play transparently with the same forms the fundamentalist finds opaque. The fundamentalist faces what Campbell termed "the fragments of the gods" as if they are figures in a wax museum, whereas the artist—and I would include in this category the social artist and the cultural creatives of this world, God bless them every one—works with them as in a beautiful collage. In this way, mythology remains alive enough to evolve with the culture, not stay frozen in time.

I now take a step that is in a different direction than where the expertise of my mentor lay. Yet I hope to show that no account of the genesis of fundamentalist thinking could be complete without understanding its roots in the human brain.

THE NEUROBIOLOGY
OF BELIEF

I believe I have a soul, but it is mostly made up of little robots.

—Daniel Dennett

This chapter takes religious beliefs into the body, where they work some of their strongest wonders—and mischief. The human body and its nervous system are unmistakably implicated in mythology—the underworld, the experience of paradise, and the hero journey all have analogues within us. We have unconscious catacombs where consciousness ventures at its peril, pleasure centers that let us believe all is fulfilled for us, and records of our encounters with danger and our emotional life. There are even special physiological sensations built into our nervous system pertaining to contact with the supernatural: we experience a *frisson*, or shiver up the spine; our hair stands on end or we get "goose bumps"; the heart starts thumping or dilating; we naturally grow quiet and listen deeply when we step into a space we know to be holy. The sacred registers in our systems as an emotional as well as physiological energy, triggered by the symbols, signs, places, and names we have learned to associate with sanctity.

Joseph Campbell took seriously the role of the body and the nervous system in mythology. He thought of the genes, neurons, and organs as "playing against each other," as the hardware that receives the imprint of the software of language, mythology, and culture. In other words, it is our learning history, imprinted on neurology and physiology, that shapes our personality and beliefs. He lightly called this idea "Campbell's Law" and said he knew it from firsthand experience as a Roman Catholic altar boy in his youth. "Once a Catholic, always a Catholic," he would quote, for the sacred iconography and ritual, imprinted since the earliest childhood, had an emotional effect no matter what the conscious mind intended.

Neuroanatomy and spirituality is, in fact, one of the hot publishing topics of the past decade. Books like Andrew Newberg and Eugene D'Aquili's *Why God Won't Go Away: Brain Science and the Biology of Belief* and James Austin's encyclopedic *Zen and the Brain* argue neuroscientifically that the religious or spiritual impulse can be found among the complex structures of our brain.[1] In this chapter I make my own excursion into religion and neuroanatomy, but hopefully without the reductionist fundamentalism so common among my scientific colleagues. I do not wish to reduce God to nerve cells or imply that spirituality is simply the outcome of pathological brain states. God is not a product of the equipment with which we try to apprehend him (or her) any more than the electronic structure of a radio creates the program we receive on it. Rather, I wish to open the view—which some will find new and others very old—that there is an exquisite *correspondence* between the structure of our brains and the religious and mythological forms that flow so readily through them. We are wired for religious experience, as well as for a myriad of other human functions such as curiosity, sexuality, territoriality, and sociability.

Our behavior partly depends upon how we are hardwired, but our experiences and what we think and do also shape our nervous system. I see evidence of both in my clinical work of helping people recover from the aftereffects of head injuries, which I discuss in *The Healing Power of Neurofeedback* (2006). People who have suffered psychological deprivation or abuse as well as those who have experienced physical trauma to the head or have chemical imbalances or seizures can become, despite their best intentions, moody or explosive, anxious or depressed, insomniac or obsessive-compulsive. On the other hand, as people's nervous systems become balanced, and especially when they take an active role in their own healing, what is best described as a "natural spirituality" unfolds, characterized by an ease and flexibility of functioning and an instinctive empathy, charity, and reverence for life. If damaged neurology can produce some of the dark delusions this book discusses, healthy neurology often produces a positive mysticism that envisions the universe as a sacred process, as we shall see in the last chapters.

AN OVERVIEW OF THE BRAIN

Our nervous system bears the imprint of our evolutionary forbears. The model of the human brain that emerged in the 1930s, through the original work of Karl Pribram and popularized by his colleague Paul MacLean, was called "the tripartite brain." The brain's understory was termed the "reptile brain," since all the essential life functions we share with lizards and dinosaurs are coordinated there: primarily arousal, appetite, aggression, eating, and sleeping. We find a swelling at the top of the spinal column alternatively called the *medulla* or the *brain stem,* including the *reticular activating system* and the *pons.* The *cerebellum,* nestled beneath the "newer" areas, helps give us the grace and effortless coordination that characterizes the movements of snakes, fish, and reptiles. On top of the reptile brain sits the "old mammalian brain," also called the "limbic system" because of its many branches. This includes the organs that regulate our emotional life, some of the more significant being the *hippocampus,* the *cingulate gyrus,* the *amygdala,* the *hypothalamus,* and the various nuclei of the *thalamus* and the *nucleus accumbens,* otherwise known as the pleasure center. The mammalian brain is the center for emotional qualities we share with, say, our pet dog: affection, social behavior and affiliation, sexuality, jealousy, and shame. Like the reptilian brain, this part of the brain is not easily controlled voluntarily, as anyone can testify who has tried either to fabricate or suppress an emotional reaction.

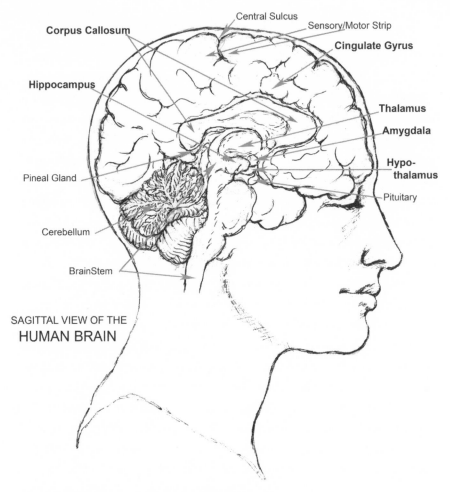

Corpus Callosum

Central Sulcus

Sensory/Motor Strip

Cingulate Gyrus

Hippocampus

Thalamus

Amygdala

Hypo-
thalamus

Pineal Gland

Pituitary

Cerebellum

BrainStem

SAGITTAL VIEW OF THE
HUMAN BRAIN

FIGURE 2.1: SAGITTAL VIEW OF THE HUMAN BRAIN
The sagittal section (seen as if sliced through center and viewed from side) shows interior
details; note especially the hippocampus, cingulate gyrus, amygdala, thalamus, and
hypothalamus of the limbic system.

At the top of the neurological tree lies the part that makes us truly human—the exquisitely complex cerebral cortex or outer part of the brain—
the "grey matter" comprised of billions of chaotically arranged, undedicated
neurons awaiting the imprint of experience. (Animal brains also have a
cortex, but it is proportionately much smaller.) The cortex is broadly divided into two hemispheres, left and right, each of which is comprised of
various lobes. These include the *frontal lobes,* involved in "executive func-

tions" such as planning, sequencing, and organizing, as well as regulating emotions; the *parietal lobes*, where new experience is matched with old; the delicate *temporal lobes*—located above the ears and reaching around to the back of the brain—which have both auditory and visual areas and are intimately involved in language, music, art, and emotional expression; and the *occipital lobes*—located at the back of the head—which interpret our complex visual worlds (see figure 2.2). If the cortex with its billions of modifiable neurons is the locus of our ability to learn, to think and imagine, and to anticipate the future, it is also vulnerable to lies, illusions, and delusions. The cerebral cortex receives the imprint of the complex worlds of our families and societies of origin. It is our greatest glory and also, as we will see later in this chapter, the instigator of our worst problems, especially when imprinted with cultural forms that are themselves pathological.

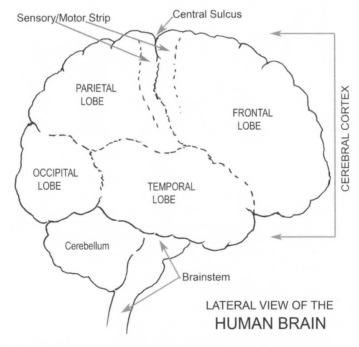

FIGURE 2.2: LATERAL VIEW OF THE HUMAN BRAIN
The lateral view, seen from the right side of the cerebral cortex, shows the conventional regions of the frontal, temporal, parietal, and occipital lobes. (The cerebellum is shown here only for orientation; it is not part of the cortex.) Acting as a behavioral control center, the sensory/motor strip is where information is received and acted on voluntarily.

The left and right hemispheres of the cortex are connected by the corpus callosum, a slender bridge of just a few million neurons—while billions reside in the hemispheres themselves (see figure 2.3). This lateral duality, along with the vertical and developmental regions just introduced, makes our brains exquisitely sensitive to internal divisions. Areas of the brain can become damaged or walled off, resulting in problems that manifest psychologically but are really grounded in the neurons' fragile yet exquisite choreography.

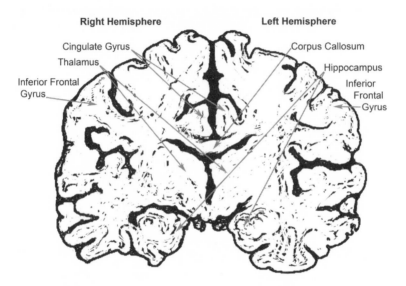

Right Hemisphere   **Left Hemisphere**

Cingulate Gyrus   Corpus Callosum
Thalamus   Hippocampus
Inferior Frontal   Inferior
Gyrus   Frontal
Gyrus

FIGURE 2.3: FRONTAL VIEW OF THE CORONAL SECTION OF THE HUMAN BRAIN
Sliced through the center and viewed from the front is the only way to show these organs buried deep in the brain. Note especially the corpus callosum that connects the two hemispheres. The view is from the front, as if we were facing the person, so the expected order is reversed: the left hemisphere appears on the right, and the right hemisphere on the left. The nucleus accumbens is not visible in the drawing because it lies in a more frontal plane than the "slice."

The brain is a neurochemical organ, so not only structure but also energy and chemistry matter. Physical brain structures can be read through standard neuroimaging techniques: MRIs, CAT scans, and PET scans. These can show damaged tissue, the presence of tumors, and areas of bleeding, such as an aneurysm, or blockage, associated with stroke. They also can register activity through blood flow (HEG) or glucose or oxygen consumption. The electroencephalogram, or EEG, my own area of interest and expertise, reflects function more than structure; that is, it shows how electrically measurable pulsations ripple through the cortex of the brain as it accomplishes its myriad tasks.

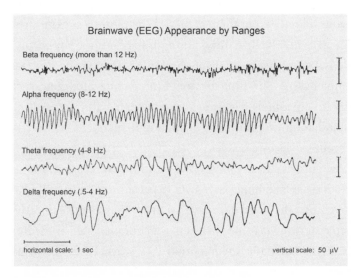

FIGURE 2.4: BRAINWAVE (EEG) APPEARANCE BY RANGES
Brainwaves are conventionally measured according to *frequency* in Hertz (Hz) cycles per second and *amplitude* (v, microvolts, or millionths of a volt) at the scalp. Ranges show the spectrum from slow (delta) to fast (beta). In a living EEG, all may appear simultaneously at different locations and successively or overlapping at a single locus on the International 10-20 map (a referential system for locating brain sites).

Topographic EEG brain maps reveal energy patterns. When we are asleep or depressed, slow frequencies predominate; when we are excited or over-aroused, fast ones take over. Simultaneous fast and slow frequencies, in which the energy of the brain flips back and forth among the frequency domains, are sometimes found in people diagnosed as bipolar. EEGs can reveal areas of *coherence* (neurons energetically stuck together, usually a pathological condition) or *comodulation* (neurons fluctuating together, as in meditation as well as some pathologies). When we look at topographic brain maps or qEEGs, we see areas locked together, functioning as if a single unit (see figure 2.7, page 37).

The brain has marvelous storage capacities not only for cognitive information but also, with the aid of the hippocampus, a limbic organ shaped oddly like a seahorse, for emotional memories. This organ helps form memories, positive or negative, that you don't have to rehearse or use rote exercises to access (your award at summer camp, and your terrible humiliation at the same camp later that summer—they happened when you were ten and you still remember them at fifty). When fear or anger is present, the amygdala gets involved. A tiny, almond-sized and -shaped organ, the amygdala is a specialist in dualistic thinking. It throws the cerebral cortex into a simpler mode and probably helps in extreme situations, such as determining if someone is friend or foe, or whether to fight or flee. This is also the mode of ultimatums and snap judgments.

The brain works by cascades of stereotyped information, which means that our own inner states—habituated emotion, expectation, and cognitive interpretation—play a huge part in our experience of the world.[2] Psychologists have coined the word *apperception* to emphasize the subjective factor in our perception. This is how projective techniques such as the Rorschach test or the TAT (Thematic Apperception Test) work. Each person interprets the ink blot or ambiguous picture in his or her psychologically unique way, which reveals much about the person to the astute clinician.

Neurologically speaking, in instances of heightened emotion our socially acquired rational, social, and ethical principles are easily overridden by more biologically primitive states. This is why dominance and territoriality, which probably originate in the reptile brain, are also found in the highest levels of human social interaction. (Have you ever noticed how many science fiction and fantasy movies cast the megalomanic, cold-hearted, power-crazed bad guys as reptiles?) Former vice president Al Gore, in fact, includes an intelligent section on neuroanatomy and politics in his recent book, *The Assault on Reason*. His discussion echoes a truth long known in neuroanatomical circles—that input through afferent (incoming) channels to the brain in a state of fear hit more primitive structures like the amygdala and trigger fight-or-flight or primitive thinking. When the person is calmer, the information passes instead through the ascending tracts of the thalamus, which receives it in a more rational state. Politicians of fear count on the amygdala to keep people stupid and polarized in their thinking.[3]

Even deeper, though, below the reptile brain, we have the plexi and ganglia of the autonomic and peripheral systems—the forms of which are most fully developed in mollusks, who have not a single brain but many, the starfish being an example. Here is found a truly schizophrenic babble of primitive voices as neural structures, physiological organs, and hormones announce their separate needs. (In dreams this kind of inner disharmony may present as a mob, or as animals fighting or a family arguing.)

Most human beings are in fact terrified by their own plurality, the "little robots" in the soul of which Daniel Dennett speaks.[4] The introspective and thoughtful—that is, evolving—human being learns to negotiate and achieve some agreement among the cacophony of inner voices and needs. Yet, as Eric Fromm and Eric Hoffer pointed out in the 1950s, humans also have a perennial need to escape from freedom, to be spared the awful responsibility of choosing and possibly making the wrong choice—thus the equally ingrained inclination to think monolithically, to find one emotionally attractive point of view and stick to it. This is the limbic brain's effort to run for safety when there's reason for fear. In the coming discussion we will see how people use myth and spirituality to strive for an inner unity by submitting to a single, superordinate power.

The Low Energy Neurofeedback System (LENS) created by Len Ochs, Ph.D., is a form of brain wave biofeedback. It provides us with a Power Spectrum, which presents all the brain wave ranges on a moving graph. As we look at the spectrum, we may see a "power hump," meaning that the brain is stuck in a certain frequency range (see figure 2.5 on page 30). The task of the neurotherapist may be to break up the concentrated dominance of such a hump, thereby freeing the brain to be more flexible (see figure 2.6 on page 30). Flexibility includes the ability of the brain to switch readily among its states rather than staying frozen. Because the amplitude (in microvolts) is so high in the brain in figure 2.5, all the person's energy is involved in one approach. (As Abraham Maslow put it, "If all you have is a hammer, everything looks like a nail.") The brain in figure 2.6, with its much lower microvolts, has its energy (see white bar) distributed across the spectrum. This person would probably be more able to multiprocess, or to smoothly and readily assume the state appropriate to the demands of an activity.

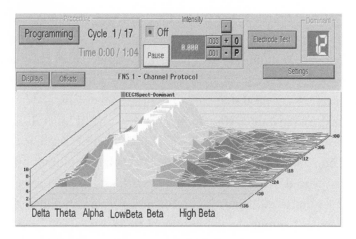

FIGURE 2.5: EEG POWER SPECTRUM: THE RIGID BRAIN
An earlier version of The LENS Power Spectrum captures a 3-D image of the "single-track mind" of a fifty-year-old woman stuck in an anxiety pattern, manifested by the ridge or "hump" in alpha (8-12 Hz); the white bar indicates power or "dominant frequency." While the bar is stuck in one position here, in a healthier brain it is free to move flexibly (see figure 2.6 below).

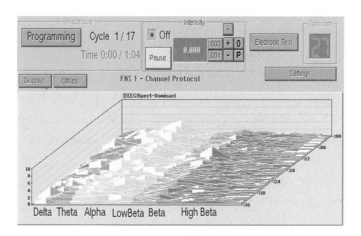

FIGURE 2.6: EEG POWER SPECTRUM: THE FLEXIBLE BRAIN
In the more flexible brain of a fifty-year-old man, notice that the white bar indicating dominant frequency moves freely through the spectrum and all amplitudes are low (below 4 v).

It is a sheer miracle that the whole thing works as it does, and that we can dance and sing and read and love and meditate, shifting fluidly from one state to another. Clearly molded by its environment, the brain becomes healthy with varied and interesting stimulation as well as lots of positive encouragement and good emotions, while it withers with neglect, anger, excessive punishment, or intimidation. The stuck brain of the fundamentalist is probably no *fun* for the fundamentalist, but even less fun for everyone else.

THE BRAIN'S DUALISTIC NATURE

Since the eighteenth century, science has debated about the many inherent dualisms woven throughout the human brain and nervous system— the differential functioning of the cerebral hemispheres, the competing demands of the higher (cortical) and lower (limbic) regions, the division of the autonomic nervous system into *sympathetic* (activating, vigilant) and *parasympathetic* (quieting, conserving) branches. Our brain chemistry is also dualistic, with *excitatory neurotransmitters* and *inhibitory neurotransmitters.* Even the energies of the brain, as recorded in the EEG, can be divided into *low frequency* and *high frequency*, and their regions as *coherent* or *chaotic.*

These dualities are probably not a surprise to most people. We need polarities in order to modulate our attention and behavior in response to environmental cues. Sometimes we need excitation and sometimes rest, sometimes intellectual and sometimes emotional intelligence, sometimes solitude and sometimes community. The key to health seems to be *fluidity,* which shows itself as versatility, flexibility, and the ability to move easily between states as the environment requires. In this model, *stuckness* and the accompanying rigidity are the enemy—and any social or religious program that locks up the nervous system into just one among its many states, or polarizes it into opposites, is pathological.

Possibly the most important of the neurological dichotomies, as well as the first to be explored systematically, is the bilateral functioning of the cerebral hemispheres. It was during the 1840s (ironically, the same decade of cultural and spiritual ferment that birthed the British and American millennialism discussed in chapter 5) that a Scottish neurosurgeon named A. L. Wigan did an autopsy on a man and found one hemisphere of his brain completely missing. During his lifetime, however, the man had seemed to speak and think normally. Wigan concluded that the hemispheres of the brain must be neurologically identical; otherwise, we would know from a person's behavior or cognition when one was missing. Though later research would prove Wiganism—as it came to be called—incorrect, Wigan did inadvertently provide clinical proof of neural plasticity, an important concept in modern theories of how our brains adapt to changing environmental exigencies. The remaining half of the man's brain must have fulfilled all the functions normally performed by two hemispheres. The example also demonstrates indirectly that most people have more brain tissue than they ever use.

In 1864, the neurologist Hughlings Jackson began to note that different kinds of aphasias, along with various perceptual and behavioral deficits, accompany damage to the left or right hemisphere. Observing that damage to one side of the brain was related to problems on the opposite side of the body, he proposed that the crossover is symmetrical, that is, the left half of the brain handles certain functions on the body's right side, and vice versa. This principle seems almost common knowledge at this point in time, but it was revolutionary then. However, Jackson also maintained that language resides in the right hemisphere—a theory later shown to be wrong, at least for most people.

In the early twentieth century, the idea that one brain hemisphere is "dominant," corresponding contralaterally with the person's dominant hand, became accepted. Ninety percent or more of the population, both male and female, was estimated to be right-handed and thus left-hemisphere dominant, and cerebral dominance was considered genetically inherited. Moreover, since most of the psychological tests (as well as academics itself) favored left hemisphere skills, such as reading, writing, and math, lesions or strokes to the right hemisphere were regarded as cognitively inconsequential. Neurophysiologists Strong and Elwyn wrote in 1943: "In man the higher control functions are vested principally in one cerebral hemisphere, the left one in right handed individuals . . . the dominant hemisphere . . . lesions of the other hemisphere producing as a rule no recognizable disturbances."[5]

Recognizable is the key word here. Not until the middle of the twentieth century were nonverbal learning disorders and their connections to right-hemisphere damage acknowledged. Skills like reading faces, finding places, following a map, even dressing correctly, turned out to be managed mostly by the right hemisphere. Clinical cases also showed that many musical abilities are stored in the right hemisphere, though some are stored in the left. Roger Sperry and Michael Gazzaniga presented further evidence of differential functioning from their studies of "split-brain patients" (epileptic patients whose right and left hemispheres had been surgically separated by cutting the *corpus callosum*, the "bridge" between them, ostensibly to prevent seizures from spreading from one hemisphere to the other).[6] Though the split-brain patients could apparently function normally, they exhibited "two different spheres of mentality." Later we will see how polarized mythologies render us "schizophrenic" in a similar manner.

In *The Psychology of Consciousness*, published in the 1970s, Robert Ornstein showed how subtle yet pervasive are the mentalities belonging to left and right hemispheric dominance. Summarizing the neurological research to date and combining it with cultural observations, Ornstein suggested that we live in a left-hemisphere dominant culture in which reading, literature, mathematics, and the sciences and disciplines based on them (called *propositional*, or intellectually proactive) are valued. Less valued are the creative arts, music, and the imagination (called *appositional*, or complementary), which are associated with the right hemisphere.

The growing recognition of modern intellectual culture's hemispheric bias occasioned a small revolution in the 1970s and 1980s, especially among "creative types." The hegemony of left-hemisphere values was critiqued as leaving the culture rigid and soulless. People began taking up all kinds of artistic explorations, such as drawing, music, sculpture, and dance, to bring in the missing element that some called creativity and others called "soul."[7]

Eventually, gender categories were added to the mix, buttressed partially by the observation that in many cultures the right hand and its lore are identified as masculine and the left as feminine. The left, "male" hemisphere became suspiciously associated with rigid rules and intellectual dominance, "bean counting," and everything that is analytical about modern society. The right hemisphere became associated with the repressed—but soon to be liberated—feminine, along with creativity, imagery, feeling, and even environmentalism. When the left is too dominant, we get the computer nerd and the soulless character Data in *Star Trek*, ran the theory. When the right is too dominant, we get the mad visionary and the disheveled artist. Values such as good and evil were also layered onto left and right, further polarizing our mythologies about the most advanced part of our brains.

THE BREAKDOWN OF THE BICAMERAL MIND

In the 1970s Julian Jaynes, a distinguished Princeton psychologist, wrote an influential book with a cumbersome title: *The Origin of Consciousness in the Breakdown of the Bicameral Mind.* Jaynes defines the bicameral mind as a two-part mind, or brain, that functions as a single unit—as distinct from a brain with two hemispheres operating separately but joined by a bridge. Attributing the conscious mind to the left hemisphere and the unconscious to the right, he suggests that in a bicameral mind there is no division between conscious and unconscious. He argues that in the early days of settled civilizations, around the third millennium BCE, the human brain was still bicameral. This is why in the records from that era—Sumerian and Babylonian documents and even Homer's telling of the Trojan War—we find kings and prophets hearing "the voices of the gods" in the form of auditory hallucinations. The gods thus intervened into human history, commenting on and dictating policy on whether to go to war, build fortifications, store up food, and so on. Something resembling modern consciousness was enabled, Jaynes says, only when this early, bicameral stage of the human mind "broke down" into two tenuously linked but separate spheres of mentality.

Jaynes speaks of his own perception of auditory hallucinations and argues that this phenomenon is a regression to bicamerality. It is present in a fairly high percentage of modern people (perhaps brain-injured or even "brainwashed"), many of whom find their way to asylums and psychiatric hospitals—especially since in modern society they are unlikely to get a job as state oracle. Whether or not you find merit in Jaynes's theory, he presents massive scholarly evidence for a divided human brain that fails to differentiate where its ideas come from, and hence exhibits the mental susceptibility to "supernatural" influences.

Not all theorists suggest that the conscious and the unconscious are located in the left and right hemispheres, as Jaynes does. However, psycholinguists, led by Noam Chomsky in the 1960s, have shown that the capacity for receiving, storing, and using an instinctive generative grammar for a verbal language—be it Chinese, English, or Eskimo—takes place primarily in the left hemisphere. Comparably, the right hemisphere's generative grammar, made up of the mythogems discussed in chapter 1, is mythological and emotional. The right hemisphere receives and makes use of stories with emotionally loaded images and ideas and revelations, and these patterns may be imprinted just as deeply on its neurons, as the patterns of language are on its counterpart. In other words, there is some evidence that the right hemisphere understands mythic narratives: heroes, gods, and stories about them.

Piaget and other psychologists of mental development have shown how all infants pass through a stage of undifferentiated oneness with things, called "magical thinking," in which they do not discern the difference between their own thoughts and outer reality. Such thinking is not so very far away in the adult mind, either. How many of us knock on wood, cross ourselves, or, if we are athletes, observe little pregame rituals? When modern adults are helpless, regressed, depressed, or elated—in other words, when analytic thought is pushed aside by stress or emotion—magical thinking comes readily to the fore.

During the early stages of cognitive development, children tend to attribute godlike power and infallibility to their parents. Some adults attribute the same kind of powers to their tribal leader, political leader, or guru. In the 1950s, Eric Hoffer commented in *The True Believer* that "remorse and a sense of grievance seem to drive people in the same direction"—that is, toward mass movements, fanaticism, and submission to an ultimate authority.[8] As they visualize, or believe in and worship the form, symbol, or book of a god, they may readily drop their ordinary personal agendas to do that god's work. If they join with others in a common place and customary form of worship, repeating the god's name while visualizing his image or icon, the magic is sealed. A collective movement—lots of people doing and saying the same thing together—creates a powerful, persuasive force.

A COMMUNICATION PROBLEM

If the whole spectrum of human mentality is packed into these two rather innocent-looking hemispheres sitting side by side, the question arises: Can they talk to each other, even dance together, or do they sit as if with their backs to each other, operating as separate worlds?

The compelling neurological fact is that strung between the approximately five billion neurons, stacked in many layers, that make up each hemisphere is a slender bridge of communications—a mere thirty million whitish, myelinated neurons that comprise the corpus callosum.[9] Think of the entire population of New York and the entire population of New Jersey arrayed on either side of the George Washington Bridge. Under ordinary circumstances traffic passes over this bridge every day—New York and New Jersey are in ongoing communication.[10]

Similarly, in a healthy brain, communication flows easily across the corpus callosum, giving us the cortical duality that creates the richly textured experiential world we live in (see figures 2.1 and 2.3, pages 24 and 26). Consider the flatness of monaural music compared with stereo, which creates a three-dimensional sound image such that you feel as if you're in the concert hall with the players. Consciousness is like this, too. The world is the liveliest in stereo. In a healthy person, hemispheric dominance shifts between left and right hemispheres many times per minute, or even per second. Or sometimes the two hemispheres may be beautifully synchronized, creating the "symphony in the brain" that Jim Robbins writes about so well.[11] As consciousness scans our experiential world, intellectual meaning and emotional meaning morph and shade in and out of each other. We listen to people's words and to their tone of voice at the same time. One hemisphere is tracking the sequence and the logic of what they are saying, the other is evaluating its emotional meaning *for us* (emotion usually personalizes things). The neurological complexity that makes sense of our world—for even one second of living experience—dwarfs technological miracles such as voice-recognition software.

But back to our bridge metaphor. What happens if, at rush hour, too many vehicles try to get across the George Washington Bridge at once? Traffic across the bridge slows, and gridlocks form at some intersections (visible in an EEG as brain waves in one area of the brain slowing). And what about accidents (physical or psychological traumas) or drunk motorists or over-zealous cops (brain arrhythmias or mini-seizures)? Under these conditions, how much can New Jerseyans know about what's going on in New York, and vice versa? Impairment of the flow of communication between the two hemi-spheres disrupts their synchronized balance. One may dominate while the other is blocked or "repressed." In EEG terms, this condition is called "hemi-spheric asymmetry"; and, in figure 2.7, we can see the neuronal coherence that accompanies it. It is a condition that has profound implications for how we can psychologically wall off whole universes within ourselves.

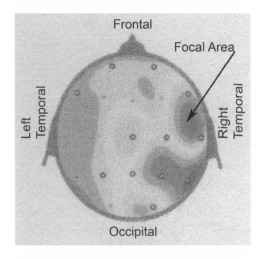

FIGURE 2.7: qEEG BRAIN MAP: ASYMMETRY AND COHERENCE
This view from the top down shows hemispheric asymmetry with a focal area of high activation in the right temporal region, from which unhealthy coherence has spread, primarily affecting the right hemisphere. The "q" stands for "quantitative"; qEEG maps are usually "data-base referenced" so that abnormalities can be detected on the basis of statistical comparisons to many other people who match the subject. (Some distinguishing detail is lost in grayscale image.)

The right hemisphere has been romanticized and glorified as the neglected yet gifted artist within us. Yet the recent EEG work of Richard Davidson and his colleagues has shown that the right frontal area of the cortex, holistic or not, is also a consistently pessimistic thinker. When activated and at the same time cut off from the left hemisphere (due to some jam-up on the corpus callosum), it can precipitate toxic clinical depressions. The left frontal area, bean-counter though it may be, in most people is consistently more cheerful and optimistic.[12]

So if you are taught from childhood to be suspicious of others, to regard the world as dangerous and full of Satan's work and ourselves as sinful, and if hell is repeatedly described in graphic terms with God above frowning in judgment, all those emotionally loaded images are more than likely stored in the right hemisphere of your brain. Meanwhile, the left hemisphere, cheerful parrot of everything it is told, may hold a Pollyanna view of the world that is in constant danger of ambush from its darker counterpart. This is a neurological model for the brittle optimist who falls into a black hole of depression when his or her shallow view of "the bright side of things" is disrupted.

But what if you are a secularly socialized modern person, brought up in conventional, print-oriented schooling and skeptical about religion? You are probably left-hemisphere dominant. Unless you engage in art, poetry, dance, music, or creativity of some other kind, your right hemisphere may be just as repressed as that of your religious counterpart, except that maybe you are susceptible to fixation on secular armageddons—human-caused and ecological catastrophes. Or perhaps your negative emotions only surface through nightmares or periodic emotional upheavals.

Or if your inner darkness rises up in reaction to your blandly conventional upbringing, you might become a full-on Goth with death's-head tattoos, multiple piercings, and a penchant for the dark lyrics of heavy metal. At least you would be honestly expressing the atmosphere of your neglected or persecuted right hemisphere. But even Goths with dark imaginations don't seem to seek the end of the world with the same kind of fanatical fervor as their God-fearing Christian millennialist counterparts. The difference is whether the darkness is on the surface or buried in the unconscious.

THE FREQUENCY-CONFUSED BRAIN

In the field of neurofeedback, it was discovered years ago that certain brain-wave frequencies not only go along with certain states of consciousness but also emerge from particular kinds of experiences and injuries. *Delta*, the lowest-frequency brain wave (.5–4 Hz), corresponds to deep sleep but also appears in the brain waves of people with deep depression or a serious brain injury. Delta corresponds to the lowest levels of consciousness, the "unconscious" of Freud and Jung. *Theta* (4–8 Hz), the brain wave frequency right above delta, is very much present in epilepsy and attention deficit problems (see figure 2.4, page 27). It is in this state that images held in the unconscious come to life as dreamlike forms that invade liminal consciousness. Thus it is probably the state in which the voices and presence of Jaynes's archaic gods were perceived. Many of the reported visionary experiences of mystics and evangelicals alike, in which the Lord or an angel appears and gives instructions, most likely took place while the brain was in the theta state.

Hypnotists, as well as psychologists studying how people are influenced, will repeat the same simple message over and over again to the listener at a slow, theta-wave pace and in a suitably solemn or dramatic tone. Hypnosis thrives in the theta state; illusions, dreams, and substitute realities can be created by dipping down into the substories of the brain. This is the realm of the magician and the bard—but it is also exploited by revival-tent preachers and charismatic demagogues.

The higher brain wave frequencies are *alpha* (8–12 Hz), usually associated with a kind of cognitive "idling" or neutral wakefulness, and *beta* (low, medium, and high, 12–28 Hz), associated with focused attentiveness, mental effort, and even high anxiety and hypervigilance. These are less interesting for our purpose than the "unconscious" (delta) and hypnagogic (theta) states that hover between sleep and waking. But, as we will find, these states also can be manipulated by the psychologists of fear.[13] There are, then, both *places* in the brain (the right hemisphere) and *energetic conditions* (theta brain waves) that are susceptible to religiously flavored images and ideas from the social environment.

The parietal and temporal lobes of the right hemisphere are where we store our constructs about how the world is put together. Because the emotional and mythic impressions held in these areas of the brain are nonverbal, they tend not to be very accessible to the conscious mind. If you are reared with a cosmology that portrays the natural world as inherently evil—as the result, say, of Eve's sin and God's displeasure—that ingrained prejudice is hard to undo. If exposure begins early in childhood, the conditioning may become deep and almost irreversible. Even if after attaining adulthood and thinking one is finally free from such conditioning, a person may still be susceptible to its convoluted magic. Certain humanistic thinkers have seriously questioned whether emotionally-loaded negativistic ideas of God and the self should be taught to children before they reach the age of critical thinking and questioning. I tend to agree. As a psychotherapist, I have seen people engage in lifelong struggles for their very selfhood because of cruel ideas—not to mention humiliating punishments—meted out to them in parochial schools. Although people can change a lot and learn many things, those deep nonverbal prejudices are hard to outgrow.

As mentioned, though generally more cheerful and optimistic than the right, the left hemisphere is also a wonderful parrot. If you have fed it the entire Qur'an or Bible, it can remember it. It is not inconceivable that verbal productions of the left hemisphere may compensate for or console fears held in the right. That is, you have nice things to say to yourself when serious social and economic realities and moods of black despair overwhelm you. Some of the sayings, many of which are quite beautiful, are also associated through automatic Pavlovian conditioning with states of acceptance or pious resignation.

We are leading to a scenario in the brain that is hypothetical but plausible: The right, more unconscious cerebral hemisphere—which is naturally pessimistic and vulnerable to depression, particularly in delta or theta conditions—can also function autonomously and willfully. An activated right hemisphere partially dissociated from the left can give rise to the experience of dealing with a separate being (God, angel, or demon). When stimulated into black-and-white thinking from beneath by the amygdala, it can easily dwell on catastrophic thoughts and images and end-times scenarios. And, as they arise, across that slim phone line of the corpus callosum the left hemisphere can respond with poetic words from the Revelation of St. John—sacred words that make the terror of the world comprehensible.

It does not take much for the right hemisphere to rev up another emotional notch when the left hemisphere's rhetoric waxes warlike. *Cast down the unbelievers? Do righteous battle against the spawn of Satan? When do we get started?* The mythic imagination does not flinch at violence, as long as good is going to win over evil and the catastrophe will be followed by the dawning of a new day. Thus, in the prediction of Armageddon, the bloodbath stops with the glorious apparition of the Savior. The elect are lifted up to him, while the rest perish in a lake of fire.

Meanwhile, the optimism of the left hemisphere may be confined to certain anointed rituals—which, in keeping with the left brain's literalism, must be followed to the letter: Only after the sacrifice of a spotless red heifer will Yehovah give his blessing to the reconstruction of the Temple and send his Messiah. Only after the Antichrist and his hordes are defeated at Armageddon can the millennium come. Right-brained obsessions and compulsions, along with a left-brained literalist reading of a promise made in God's name by wild-eyed prophets of long ago, are some of the ways fundamentalist religion and unbalanced brain neurology conspire to make black magic.

CONVERSION PSYCHOLOGY

As we have seen, when the cerebral cortex is beset with urgent signals from the amygdala, it goes into either/or thinking. It believes some kind of extreme decision is called for. The demagogic evangelist unknowingly relies on this brain mechanism when he engineers a conversion. *Your old self is hopelessly sinful and out of control. You know this from experience. You have only two options—to suffer in hell or to throw yourself on the mercy of the Lord.*

The evangelist himself was probably converted in the same way. He will tell you: "I was down and out (with drink, gambling, whoredom, or whatever), but the Lord reached out his hand to me. I once was lost and now I'm found." For most humans, hearing this is pretty powerful stuff. *His story is my story. I will come to Jesus just as he did.* Similarly, a black man in an American prison knows he has only a few chances left and that he has a bad proclivity for drugs, wine, and women. *I will convert to Islam because it offers complete submission to the will of Allah—I can't afford to make any more mistakes.* He also finds there a sense of dignity he is not offered in his own culture. In the eyes of Allah, he has joined the rank of the saved, the faithful. Indeed, the new leaf that some people turn over with conversion can be impressive, and the change in them can be genuine. But there are psychological consequences.

If you wish to induce a state of compliance in your would-be constituency, it is clearly an advantage to frighten them. First induce the amygdaloid fear response, and then offer them a loaded choice: be saved or be damned; convert or die. The rhetoric is often strong, especially among the evangelicals. *You are not only sinful, you are powerless, and you are damned to an eternity of suffering by an almighty God. All power belongs to God. Only he—through me—can save you.*

However, pointing out personal failure and offering a limited choice may not be enough, in which case the adrenaline of the fight-or-flight response must be added: The end of the world is coming! The righteous judge is coming right now, and he doesn't like your confused mind or your wimpy wobbling. He wants your soul. And if he doesn't get it, his eternal adversary is waiting outside the magic circle to claim it. So shut up and let us tell you what to do!

Melodramatic as this scenario may be, it is the stock-in-trade of conversion psychology. Its compelling nature and the neurology that supports it are the reason why the millennium keeps getting predicted, even when it forever fails to arrive. It is also one good reason why God is so often depicted as angry. He seems to get especially worked up when human beings are indulging the procreative proclivities he laid on them. It's reverse psychology at work: make people appear absolutely terrible and worthless to themselves and before the image of a displeased God—then offer them only one way out.

THE EFFECTS OF TRAUMA

We are pursuing one more link in the neuropathology of fundamentalism in this chapter, and it is a particularly painful one: trauma. We can think in terms of a continuum ranging from the physical blows of traumatic brain injury (TBI) to the trauma of seeing others, including loved ones, dismembered or killed (post-traumatic stress disorder, or PTSD). One is a physical, the other a psychological, blow—which is the meaning of the word *trauma*: a blow of whatever kind.

In our clinical center at Stone Mountain we have treated dozens of victims of accidents, the 9/11 tragedy, the Vietnam War, and both Gulf wars, as well as those with more mundane problems such as finding a loved one dead after a heart attack. In these cases, a change in brain function has occurred—perhaps because the brain is trying to protect itself or reestablish equilibrium. Concurrently, the client may be experiencing depression, anxiety, or panic. Sometimes there are eidetic replayings of the incident, reliving it in vivid photographic detail again and again—also called "flashbacks." People develop insomnia, hypervigilance, and loss of appetite or other gastrointestinal disturbances. They may suffer from nightmares or migraine headaches or other seizurelike activities. They may have spells of *absence*, as the French call *petit mal* seizures.

Traumatic brain injury may announce itself in an EEG focally, that is, in what we call "hot spots" or "bull's-eyes" (foci) of very high-amplitude but low-frequency delta and theta waves, or in areas of coherence we call "rugs" that are spread throughout major areas of the brain (see figure 3.1, page 66). Other areas, related to but now cut off from the area of injury, may go into high gear, as if getting ready for the next trauma, producing areas that are extremely uncomfortable and agitating *hi-beta* (22–40 Hz, the highest frequency usually recorded in clinical neurofeedback—see figure 2.4). Traumatized people may fall into extremely uncomfortable mixed states, such as agitated depression.

"Shell shock," an old name for PTSD, is now commonly used to describe TBI problems caused by being near a bomb or artillery shell explosion—a quarter mile often being near enough. The victims may show no visible signs of injury, but they nonetheless have all the symptoms of TBI. If they also lost friends or loved ones in an explosion or violent attack, they may show symptoms of PTSD, which include a proclivity for dissociation, or psychological "splitting," and for trancelike states. Combine background problems like these with nutritional lack and continuous stress from urban upheaval and the relentless desert sun, and you have a neurophysiological recipe for the *shahid martyr*. After all, what's he got to lose? And God is hopefully better than the Israelis or the Americans at keeping promises.

A similar phenomenon is at work in our own soldiers when they return from the theater of action. From my own experience, such people are highly at risk. They are often prone to alcohol and drug addiction. They are also emotionally volatile and very suggestible. When their rage or addictions get out of control, they really do need strict rule systems or controlled residential programs to keep them from self-destruction. Until recently, it seemed that little could be offered to traumatized veterans besides multiple medications and years in VA hospital psych wards. But now recovery programs involving less traditional approaches, including Alcoholics Anonymous, the Native American sweat lodge, and neurofeedback, are beginning to prove helpful for many.

Joseph Campbell's first published work, an essay titled *Where the Two Came to Their Father: A Navajo War Ceremonial* (published in 1943, two years before World War II ended) was based on conversations between medicine man Jeff King and researcher Maud Oakes. What so impressed Campbell was the Native American wisdom on how both to send warriors off to the soul-wrenching zone of war and to help them return from it, using psychologically efficacious myths and ceremonies. By comparison, our own society is the "primitive" one, as evinced by the terrible psychological casualties of the Vietnam War. In the ensuing years, many more veterans have chosen to die at their own hand or through self-inflicted catastrophes of alcohol or drugs than died in the actual war.

With damaged nervous systems, volatile and panicky emotions, and no simple answers about why people have to go through such overwhelming experiences, it is easy for veterans to become bitter and disillusioned, as well as prey to simple answers. It is also one zone where violence clearly breeds violence.

Physical injury to the brain has long been associated with anomalous experiences—that is, seeing angels or aliens or having out-of-body or pre-cognitive experiences. A few years ago at a professional symposium titled "Traumatic Brain Injury and Anomalous States,"[14] I presented a paper based on Vietnam veteran cases, in which I also told the story of Edgar Cayce, probably the most famous American psychic and healer. When Cayce was four, he fell off a porch and impaled himself through the top of the head with a large nail sticking out of a board. It was rural Tennessee in the early 1900s, so they just poured turpentine into the hole. It did not get infected, and it sealed itself up in a few days. A few years later, Cayce began to have anomalous experiences involving clairvoyance and the occasional visit from an angel.

Paleontologists have often wondered about the holes they find knocked in Paleolithic skulls, and there is some consensus that this widespread practice, called *trepanning* or *trephining*, was deliberate. Various explanations have been put forward, including that it was done to cure headaches or—more consistent with the shamanic worldview—to let evil spirits out. No one truly knows, but I can offer a simple suggestion: Perhaps it was done to "make" a shaman, someone who participates in anomalous experiences. You crack a little hole in their head and they gain a greater-than-average chance of being able to converse with the spirits and see the future.

Neuropsychiatrists and brain theorists have observed the connection between epilepsy and mystical states, particularly temporal-lobe epilepsy, which is very different from *grand mal* (the falling-down-and-convulsing type of epileptic seizure). Often there are strange, elaborated delusions and hallucinations that resemble paranoid schizophrenia. The experience almost always has religious or spiritual dimensions, which has prompted some theorists to propose the temporal lobes as a possible locus for the experience of God in the brain. The temporal lobes are also not far from—and right adjacent to—the deep limbic structures, particularly the amygdala, hippocampus, and cingulate gyrus. Epilepsy of the limbic system causes extremes of emotion, marking whatever cognitive content is present as overwhelmingly important. It's not surprising, then, that people can enter a "mystical frenzy" so intense that their life is transformed.

The neurotransmitter *dopamine* also plays a part in these experiences. Dopamine also participates in the delusions of advanced parkinsonism and in schizophrenia. When a flood of self-induced dopamine accompanies an experience, the person is overwhelmingly convinced that the event is real, even though other people, or even common sense, would contradict this conviction. People with injured, imbalanced, or religiously imbalanced brains flooded with dopamine thus have all the requisites for thinking their delusions are real and require action—leading to the extreme and fanatical behaviors that have occurred in most eras all over the world.

Furthermore, injured brains, already prone to anomalous experiences, can easily be manipulated by authoritative figures with an agenda. Religious or cultural programs that emphasize rigid patterns of belief and polarizing philosophies set up dissociation in the brain, and dissociation in the brain creates polarities in our experience. One of the major "splits" is the one between the hemispheres. When either a trauma or a powerful mystical experience happens to a psyche that is already "divided in its own house" and used to a negative outlook, it can assume the baleful forms we find in paranoia and delusional thinking. The person may perceive the universe as a *bad* place that is "out to get me," and it becomes easy to "project the negative" onto others. If the person's religion then encourages him to attack the "evil ones" and the nonbelievers, we have a recipe for violence.

WHY GOD WON'T GO AWAY

The brain is, for better or worse, our hardware for experiencing both outer and inner reality, including the spiritual realm. If my computer's hardware is damaged or not running well (the traumatized, neglected, or undernourished brain), it messes up every software program I try to run. And if the software is also poor (a rigid or authoritarian belief system), the problem is compounded. On the other hand, with smooth-running hardware and software, I can download music and factual information galore, even spiritually inspiring ideas. The same is true with the brain. Let's say the body is healthy and flexible, nutrition is adequate or superior, the nervous system is used to periods of intense concentration and also relaxation (sleep and dreaming are normal), and the cultural inputs from religion are not fear- or guilt-laden but rather are affirmative about the miracle of life we're all a part of. It's not likely that the person will live in expectation of an imminent Armageddon (see figure 2.6 on page 30 and discussion in chapter 8).

Suppose this person wishes to enter a state of meditation, prayer, or deep spiritual reverie. The literature on mysticism agrees that the first requirement is to quiet the body and still the mind. It is also useful to slow or regulate the breathing and sit with eyes closed or half-lidded to reduce distraction. In *Why God Won't Go Away*, Newberg and D'Aquili discuss the deep neuroimaging techniques they work with, which they feel is paving the way for a new science of neurotheology. Their research underscores the fact that mystical experience is more likely to occur in a sequestered environment where input from the external world is limited. Research by Richard Davidson and his colleagues on advanced meditators reveals the same thing: as sensory input is reduced and the mind is stilled, the brain of the meditating lama or monk begins to show regularized theta activity.

The work of my friend and colleague Lester Fehmi is also relevant. Fehmi's specialized technique is an EEG-based synchronization of the left and right hemispheres—the very opposite of the hemispheric segregation we see with pathological dissociation.[15] He also incorporates a process he calls "Open Focus," a method of freeing consciousness from its habitual narrow purview. As the brain experiences *phase synchrony* of its EEG patterns, a unified field of well-being occurs. Ordinary tasks become easy, and something like the "flow experience" described in Zen and attributed to moments of peak performance supervenes. Mystical experiences are also known to happen in this training. Originally a skeptic, I had an undeniable mystical experience while using Fehmi's method, as did Jim Robbins, author of *A Symphony in the Brain*. In such a state, one slips into a benevolent symbiosis with the universe. For me, the universe felt sentient, as though it was as aware of me as I was of it. Thoughts about God came easily, as did a resolve to live with compassion for all beings and with mindfulness of the spiritual dimension.

The evidence says, then, that we meet God best in the silence, when all our verbal chatter has quieted. The same human brain that, through exposure to fear, sin, and guilt, has the capacity to pray for Armageddon in order to be united with its God can, in this other, perhaps more natural modality, find God in the small, loving moments of everyday life.

AUTHORITY, RITUAL, AND DISSOCIATION

To be in possession of an absolute truth is to have a net of familiarity spread over the whole of eternity. There are no surprises and no unknowns.

—Eric Hoffer, *The True Believer*

The end result is a true *antimimon pneuma*, a false spirit of arrogance, hysteria, wooly-mindedness, criminal amoral-ity and doctrinaire fanaticism, a purveyor of shoddy spiri-tual goods, spurious art, philosophical stutterings and uto-pian humbug, fit only to be fed wholesale to the mass man of today. That is what the post-Christian spirit looks like.

—Carl Jung, in Lindorff, *Pauli and Jung*

"Brains are biologically expensive and risky," writes ecologist Paul Shepard. "Flexibility in behavior and a capacity for imagining reality do not usually outweigh the disadvantages of making bad decisions and the time learning takes. Flexible behavior puts a huge array of choices before the individual with the proportional likelihood for terminal error. Brains are especially vulnerable to developmental impairment due to mal-nutrition, disease, traumatic experience, and injury, and they require large amounts of energy and investment of parental care and protection for a long time. The range of *psychopathology increases with brain complexity*."[1]

Indeed, we human beings seem to be neurotic precisely because of our complexity. We are just beginning to appreciate the stresses of being a mod-ern human—managing a primate-style physiology and nervous system, with its archaic impulses and its outrageous dreams, while living in a soci-ety that itself seems a crystallization of our pathology, lurching at the very edge of loss of control and not resembling any social configuration ever seen before.

Some argue that religion is the source of our present-day pathologies and we would be better off living entirely without it. I disagree. Religion contains timeless inspiration; it pulses in sacred music and informs great art and literature. At its best, it lifts the human spirit beyond daily materialistic pursuits to perceive that we may be on a spiritual adventure after all. Moreover, as we have seen, religion won't really go away, even if we try to rid ourselves of it. Spirituality and religious experience have a resonance, if not a basis, in the human nervous system, and the tendency to think mythically, which is the functional basis of religion, is equally ingrained in the human psyche.

In fact, our pathologies stem from taking sacred images and ideas literally, instead of letting them point us to the ineffable for which they are metaphors and symbols. And, as we have already seen, they rest in unhealthy neurological patterns associated with dysfunctional ways of thinking and processing experience.

In this chapter we take a look at three features of human neurology and psychology that can lead us to pathological places and, especially when exploited by unscrupulous people hungry for power and control, to individual tragedy and collective downfall. These are: the human readiness to honor and submit to authority, the biological power of ritual and patterning, and the ability of our dualistic nervous systems to dissociate. Each of these has a positive function psychologically, as well as a basis in our neurology. Each in its own way contributes to our very survival. Yet each is also vulnerable to distortion and pathologizing, especially in proximity to religion. People universally seem to rank the sacred higher than the ordinary doings of life, and so value systems and behaviors supporting a healthy psyche and well-being can become distorted in religion's name. An extreme example is the case of the Branch Davidian tragedy that took place in Waco, Texas in 1993, which we consider at the end of this chapter.

HUMAN SUSCEPTIBILITY TO AUTHORITY

> But man, proud man
> Drest in a little brief authority,
> Most ignorant of what he's most assured,
> (His glassy essence), like an angry ape
> Plays such fantastic tricks before high heaven
> As makes the angels weep. . . .
> —Shakespeare, *Measure for Measure*

When it comes to the study of human social behavior, sociobiology, which compares animal and insect social organization with that of humans, and sociology, which assumes that culture and patterns of social learning are uniquely human, don't often agree. But whatever the cause—genetic similarity or similarity of social patterns—both human beings and other primates are universally hierarchical and authority-oriented. Freud noticed the tendency in what he called "the primal horde" of prehumans for a dominant male or a few dominant males to rule the roost, and he used it to justify his Oedipal theory. The desire to "kill the father" is focused on the "alpha" male, who monopolizes the females. The females may have a hierarchy of their own but are usually subservient to the dominant males.

But compared with humans, other primates are real pikers when it comes to hierarchies. Human societies become infinitely hierarchized from the simplest to the most profound. Each village has its chief and elders, each corporation its president and board. Our human attention is relentlessly attracted upward through the hierarchy to the alpha male, and we are disdainful and inattentive toward those we see as lower than ourselves. We may even declare those at the top infallible, as with the Pope, or omniscient, as some gurus are believed to be. And when a figure like the Judeo-Christian and Islamic God is placed at the very top of the hierarchy, everyone and everything becomes subordinate to him.

We are, moreover, hard-wired with what are called "mirror neurons." First identified in the 1980s and 1990s by Giacomo Rizzolatti and associates, and also called "The Parma Group," these are the "monkey see, monkey do" receptors that enable us to become socialized by imitating first our parents and later our peers. (Mirror neurons—which appear in some species of monkeys and in humans—are concentrated in the inferior frontal gyrus of the left hemisphere, not far from the major language areas of the cortex, and develop early, before twelve months of age. There is a secondary area in the parietal cortex, which also seems to contain our self-image. Mirror neurons are probably involved in simple acts as when parents and infants mimic one another's facial expressions or play reciprocal games such as "pattycake."[2] (See figure 2.3 on page 26; the inferior frontal gyrus of the brain is a major area containing mirror neurons.)

We strive to imitate primarily those above us in the hierarchy. When God is at the top of the hierarchy, it's natural to want to align with him and, along with that, imitate him. In its positive expression, this is—quite literally in Latin—*imitatio Dei,* the "imitation of God" well known in religious texts. One models one's life on that of Christ—or Muhammad or any other great religious figure—as if he were "living through you." In its negative expression, however, imitating God appears as patriarchal posturing and theological demagoguery. The desire to "ape" God seems to be almost irresistible to people whose hierarchically oriented, primate-based nervous systems are disturbed.

Imitatio Dei is indeed dangerous business. It can drive men mad—as it did the Roman emperors Caligula and Nero, who, as rulers of the greatest empire of the day, had themselves appointed as gods. Both emperors died violently and as a consequence of the excesses they enacted in their state of untrammeled "divinity." Mental institutions the world over are filled with people who claim to be God, or to talk to God or Jesus Christ or some other prophet.

Comedienne Lily Tomlin once quipped on an NPR radio show: "Why is it that when we talk to God, it's called 'prayer,' and when he talks to us, it's called 'schizophrenia'?" Fifty years ago, in one of the most daring gambits in psychology, social psychologist Milton Rokeach did an experiment he probably couldn't get away with today. He put three paranoid schizophrenic inmates of Ypsilanti State Hospital in Michigan, each of whom thought he was Jesus Christ, together for several months. They lived and ate and communicated while he recorded and took notes. Rokeach was testing the limits. He wanted to see if the men's stories would crack when confronted with the fact that the world considered them mental patients, and with the ultimate contradiction of three Jesuses existing at the same place and time. The apocryphal story is that they worked it out: one became the Father, one the Son, and the third the Holy Ghost. But in fact each man remained as mired in his delusion as before. This aligns with the experience of every mental health professional who has tried to argue a paranoid or schizophrenic person out of his or her delusions. They seem to be wired into the neurology. It's not about logic, and no amount of talking can bring about a cure.

The claiming of spiritual authority, usually by men, is endemic in human affairs. The aptly named American fundamentalist Dwight Pentecost states: "God has assigned authority and demands submission to authority in four areas: in the civil realm to magistrates to curb lawlessness, in employment to the master or employer, in the Church to the Elders, and in the family to the husband and father."[3] At its best, if the male person in authority is wise, just, and loving, with a generous eye on the well-being of those under his jurisdiction, there can be safety, protection, and true growth and thriving. However, if the "alpha male" lacks this development of character, suffering and diminishment can occur all too readily.

In *The Chronicles of Narnia* C. S. Lewis describes a sinister ape who sets up a bogus religion in Narnia based on a "false Aslan." Aslan is the kingly lion who, in Lewis's magical land of animals, represents the Christ principle. But the selfish ape, eager to wield power, sets up a donkey draped in a lion skin as a substitute and then bullies and manipulates the animals into worshipping this caricature—an ugly and sad spectacle Lewis uses to teach us about inauthentic religion and the dangers of religious hierarchies.

In authoritarian structures there is a ready differentiation between good and evil, as if these are absolute qualities instead of subjective judgments. Codes of dress, prescribed forms of behavior and speech, and the veneration of authoritarian figures as "good" without examining the nuances of their values (including putting political figures on a pedestal without considering their voting record) are typical. Other groups tend to be viewed simplistically and are often feared. The authoritarian mindset even shows up with respect to appreciating art. Abstract, paradoxical art or artwork that otherwise challenges one's perceptions is generally shunned. The preference is for romanticized popular art, which may express what is longed for but rarely conveys the complexity of real human situations. Sentimental art forms often indicate a mind or culture drowning in easy, simplistic solutions for complex problems.

In authoritarian systems, the top dog gets to bite your ears off, but you don't dare do it to him. Sociological studies have shown that in fundamentalist families where this model prevails and the primary male sets himself up as the absolute authority, instances of familial abuse are much higher. The abuse is more pronounced when the patriarchal heavy-handedness is accompanied by bigoted social attitudes, xenophobia, literal belief systems, and a willingness to settle issues by force—and, of course, an amplified sense of righteousness: *This is for your own good!* The abuse is less, however, when the patriarch and his family go to church regularly. Evidently, frequent exposure to Christian ideals and still higher authority figures is a mitigating influence.[4]

After the great Swiss developmental psychologist Jean Piaget laid out his stages of cognitive development, which show how a child's conceptual and moral worlds are in constant flux and growth, his work was taken up by cognitive psychologists such as Lawrence Kohlberg. Kohlberg's own model of developmental stages expands on Piaget's, and part of his theory concerns how one construes authority. According to Kohlberg's theory, once higher stages are attained, there is seldom sliding back—except under emergency or traumatic situations. Conversely, however, no one can maintain their highest level at all times.

LEVEL ONE (PRE-CONVENTIONAL)

1. Obedience and punishment orientation
2. Self-interest orientation (*What's in it for me?*)

LEVEL TWO (CONVENTIONAL)

3. Interpersonal accord and conformity (*The good boy/good girl attitude*)
4. Authority and social-order maintaining orientation (*Law and order morality*)

LEVEL THREE (POST-CONVENTIONAL)

5. Social contract orientation
6. Universal ethical principles (*Principled conscience*) [5]

It is not hard to find elements of Kohlberg's level 1 in fundamentalist rhetoric. Pat Robertson's and Jerry Falwell's immediate public interpretation of the World Trade Center disaster was that it was God's punishment for allowing evils—such as liberals and gays—to pursue their agendas "in our Great Land." From this level of development, everything is about crime and punishment. Then there is the desire to please (level 2): "If I have been a good boy or girl, then God, the best among parents, will include me among the Elect at the Rapture."

In Kohlberg's model, surrender of one's will to an absolute authority is a less developed, more primitive stage of cognition than the ability to make one's own decisions and face their consequences. Only at the higher stages, 5 and 6, do people fully participate responsibly in the social contract in a democratic way.

Stanley Milgram's famous experiment on cruelty and authority illustrates this elegantly. In the experiment, the actual subjects were told to deliver shocks of up to 450 volts to people called "learners," who were seated in another room, whenever the learners made mistakes. Remarkably, very few subjects were willing to disobey the psychologist-authority. Most of them went ahead and delivered what was supposedly the full 450 volts. The learners, of course, were not actually shocked but were stooges of the experimenters, coached to scream and beg for release as if they were receiving electric shocks. Afterward they fell silent, so the subjects couldn't even tell whether they were still alive. Most of the actual subjects explained: "I did it because you [the authority figure] told me to." This, of course, is the same rationale that surfaced during the Nuremberg Trials: "I did it because my commanding officer [or the Fuehrer] ordered me to."

Only a handful of the subjects were willing to defy authority in the interests of the learners' well-being and would not deliver at least some of the shocks. Most of these people said something like: "I refuse to take part in something that hurts another human being." "I am going to treat them as I would like to be treated." On Kohlberg's scale, being willing to question authority, especially when it seems unjust or ridiculous, represents the highest stage of moral development, which is based on abstract reasoning using what he calls "universal ethical principles."

Unfortunately, many adults are emotionally and cognitively still at lower stages of Kohlberg's scale, even though they hold high positions in social or institutional hierarchies. Such people tend to believe that authority— one's own or another—should be followed blindly, and so they manipulate others, who are often stuck at the lower stages themselves. It is easy to see, then, how manipulation of psychologically immature people by religious authority is possible. Those who know well how to use beliefs, rituals, and symbols can influence, even command, millions of people. They, in turn, are lorded over by people in positions above them, and the latter are under the thumb of others further up the ladder, creating the kind of multilevel authoritarian hierarchy all too familiar in churches and religious organizations as well as some business scenarios and families, as Pentecost indicates.

The whole enterprise is based on such specious assumptions that you would think it would fall apart like a house of cards. But the assumptions are interlocked and fit together into the worldview of the believer, who questions neither the parts nor the whole. When someone does question, they are usually told they are wrong to ask.

On one of the monthly Joseph Campbell "round table" evenings at the Center for Symbolic Studies here at Stone Mountain Farm, a participant brought a friend I shall call "Ella." Ella had never heard of Campbell but was very moved by his inclusive statements about world religions in the video from the *Mythos* series we showed that night. The discussion following the film turned to how religions can be destructive as well as positive. Ella, who shared that she was eighty-five years old, told us a story from her childhood that became the centerpiece of the evening.

When she was growing up, Ella and her family attended a black Southern Baptist church in Georgia. Though the family lived "on the wrong side of the tracks" they went to church every Sunday, dressed in their finest. After church the pastor would sometimes come over to their house, poor but immaculately clean, for dinner.

Something about the preacher's sermons was puzzling for the ten-year-old Ella, and on one of these occasions she asked him about it.

Sometimes the preacher said Jesus was loving and kind, and just wanted to "gather the little ones" onto his lap or into his bosom. You couldn't imagine a kinder friend. But at other times the preacher would get worked up, threaten the congregation, and say Christ would come with terrible wrath and anger, killing the sinners with his "terrible swift sword" and tossing them into the fires of hell. How could those two Jesuses be the same person? And which one was right?

There was silence at the table, and then the preacher got mad. He glowered at Ella and told her not to ask the "wrong kind of questions." After he left, she got a good slapping around from her mother, and later, a beating by her father. Somehow, it became hard to sit through that minister's sermons after that, and the whole subject of religion soured for Ella. When she came of age she left the church, never to return.

One day she saw an ad for the Rosicrucians in *Popular Science* magazine. She got some books and then was able to find some meetings of Rosicrucians (some probably puzzled, some delighted, to have a person of color in their mostly white, esoteric spiritual community). She had now been a Rosicrucian for many years.

"They're tolerant," she said, "and they say there is some good in all religions. That's what I went for. Then there are all these study guides. It's very psychological, very spiritual."

That evening it was evident to the empathic group that Ella had suffered a form of abuse by spiritual authority—yet ultimately she found a path of her own.

What do we do with the bright child who has reached the stage Piaget called "formal operational" and is able to perceive and process logical consistencies and inconsistencies in the world around them? Of course they will start by questioning their parents, their preacher, and other authority figures. How else will they learn to look for inconsistencies or imbalances in others or in themselves? Fundamentalist authoritarianism, however, keeps its adherents in the lower stages of moral development in order to sustain its hierarchical structure, creating a self-perpetuating ceiling on their personal growth. Ella's pastor couldn't take her to the next stage of moral or intellectual development because he wasn't there himself!

WHEN RITUAL GROWS RIGID

Ritual is one of life's efficiency systems. Why learn to do something over and over when it can be programmed? Ritualized behavior tends to promote survival, since if a certain response produced a positive outcome once, it's likely to produce it again. Because these patterns are handed down from one generation to another, they often carry meaning for a species. We see this phenomenon in animals in mating rituals, in yearly migrations to ancient breeding grounds, and in the way position in the social hierarchy is acknowledged—for instance, by averting the eyes or head (perhaps a precursor to bowing) as a signal of submission among primates and dogs.

Human cultures and social institutions of all kinds generally favor ritual, since it supports conformity—whereas novelty and creativity, while appreciated in certain contexts, tend to be treated with suspicion. Writer and scholar Thom Hartmann offers an elegant hypothesis in this regard.[6] He points out that we are descended from many, many generations of Paleolithic *hunters* and proportionately fewer generations of Neolithic *planters*. Hunting and gathering cultures tend to be organized in smaller groups, like tribes, with a minimum of hierarchy, and hunting itself requires flexibility and individual creativity, whereas settled agricultural cultures tend to develop larger, more stratified communities organized around water and land rights, which means a more hierarchical social organization and more conformity.

As human social organization evolved to city-states, kingdoms, and nations, conformity was clearly adaptive. However, if Hartmann is right, the genes of those old Paleolithic mavericks—we call them "cultural creatives"—who were inclined to break the rules and discover new things continued. Both kinds of genes are in all of us today, albeit in different proportions. Yet the social prejudice remains that conformity is "good" and unconventional innovation is "bad." Especially in times of stress, novelty and creativity can appear fearful, and familiarity can seem the only safe haven. The conservative position tries to find security in old social forms and ways of thinking—reducing complexity and subtlety to simpler, often dualistic, structures that are often mythologically justified. In a complex, relativistic world, it can be comforting to have a simple model, bolstered by religion, of what is good and what evil.

Perhaps not surprisingly, patterned behaviors tend to be held in our neurology. The structure in the brain called the *cingulate gyrus* helps us ritualize the small action patterns of life (see figures 2.1 and 2.3, pages 24 and 26). Tucked into the cleft between the two hemispheres, it is considered part of the cerebral cortex by some neuroscientists, and part of the more primitive and instinctual limbic system by others. The cingulate is associated with the learning-prone cortex and easily takes in rituals and also enacts them. Teamed up with the "monkey see, monkey do" mirror neurons, the cingulate has us, rather automatically, take on rituals from our families and cultures of origin. We all have little internal neurological mechanisms that remind us: "brush your teeth," "feed the dog," "lock the house," and so on. Normally, these are useful functions to help us develop routines and manage our responsibilities. But washing the hands ten times a day or checking the locks ceaselessly is another story.

In religion, the tendency for ritual is brought to a fine art. The moment you enter a sacred space, you bow, remove your hat or take off your shoes, or touch your lips with holy water so that nothing defiling may pass them. This principle is carried to a high level of observance, for instance, among Orthodox Jews. I admire the care and attentiveness they must learn properly to observe a Sabbath, not to mention a high holy day—and doubt I could do it myself. Kosher rules govern not only foods but also cooking and eating utensils, the timing of ritualized services, the people with whom one associates, and more. These observances hold power for many Jews who were brought up with them even if their personal beliefs have since wandered far from orthodoxy, which demonstrates the grip these patterns have on the psyche. Ritual is *orthopraxis*—literally, "straight practice" or behavior. It is, if you will, the enacted correlate of *orthodoxy*, straight, or straightened, belief. When Muhammad introduced the idea of the *salaam*, or full-length prostration, to his tribe, the haughty Quraysh, they would have none of it—prostrate yourself like common *fellaheen*? No way! But now the humility-instilling posture is practiced five times a day by faithful Muslims throughout Islamic countries.

I am not saying that religion is made up only of conditioned reflexes. Rituals are necessary, but not sufficient, conditions for an encounter with the sacred. Often-repeated rituals bind, through repetition and thus association, the conditions under which the experience of the sacred occurs. Monks and anchorites meditate for decades, priests pray in high holy places, children kneel by their beds and open their tender thoughts to God's all-good, all-wise presence. The spiritual infusion that often results can be strong medicine indeed. Philosopher-psychologist William James called the experience of Spirit *noetically true.* The majority of humankind—our little Western secular enclave aside—endorses that life is a spiritual experience, no matter how varied the inflections. I believe, as Carl Jung urged, that spirituality (mostly) improves mental health. It is often comforting and offers a way of relating to the unknown and invisible things about life. It does seem to change lives, and often it wakes us up, as it were, for the better. The problems occur when people confuse the symbolic props and ritualistic actions that got them to the experience of God with God—not unlike mistaking the telescope for the sparkling reality of the star it allows us to see.

It is sad to see how much organized religion trades on symbols and props; it also counts on the obsessive-compulsive tendency in people, with the many beads that are told and Hail Marys and Hare Krishnas that are repeated. Counting and obsessively working over the details of something, even something as culturally important as the Bible, can be considered dysfunctional if it interferes with a person's ability to hold down a livelihood, make practical decisions, or lead a socially productive and balanced life.

Some of these problems seem to be rooted in dysfunction of the cingulate gyrus. Psychiatrist and neuroscience researcher Daniel Amen has published extensively on problems he believes originate in the cingulate gyrus. He says an over-aroused cingulate can produce worry or anxiety, obsession (getting stuck on thoughts), compulsion (getting stuck in behaviors), oppositional behaviors and arguing, cognitive inflexibility, holding onto hurts from the past, and even road rage.[7] Cingulate disorders frequently register on what psychiatrists call the "obsessive-compulsive disorder (OCD) spectrum." Dr. Amen says cingulate problems "may not reach the intensity or cause the dysfunction of a full-fledged obsessive compulsive disorder, but [they] can nonetheless erode a person's quality of life. . . . Cognitive inflexibility and rigidity may not send you to the therapist, but they can make your life unnecessarily gloomy."[8] You might say that in cingulate pathology, our formerly tractable and useful inner "servants" take over and begin to comment on and interfere with everything we do.

One of the generic cingulate symptoms is what Amen calls "the automatic *no*." A person can begin to define himself or herself by what is *not okay to do*. No to dancing, card playing, and drinking; no to literature, education, and the arts; certainly no to sex and to birth control, and maybe to abortion; no to nutritional aid to babies born out of wedlock; and no to preschool programs for children of single parents. I think you get the drift.

As mentioned, another cingulate problem is road rage. I would like to expand the category to include theological road rage: people becoming incensed that there are other belief systems—imagine that! Other, different people are on the spiritual path or "road," too, and in their own vehicles and driving their own way—the very idea! I'll (theologically) run them off the road if they don't behave!

The cingulate is not far from the amygdala (see figures 2.1 and 2.3, pages 24 and 26). When stress and anxiety irritate both organs, innate but dormant inherited patterns favorable to obsession can be set in motion. The amygdala is the organ that throws people into simple dichotomous thinking, such as: "Should I fight or take flight?" It contributes to their becoming stupider the more frightened or angry they get. According to leading EEG researchers, in some people who get into this state, there is a "hot spot" in the right orbital pre-frontal cortex that correlates with constant dark, pessimistic thoughts, irritability, and rage.

When the symbolic contents of one of the world's religions are conjoined with cingulate problems, the person may become obsessed with recurring thoughts about his or her moral uncleanliness, past sins, fear of temptation by the devil, or relationship with a hard-to-please God. People suffering from disorders somewhere on the obsessive-compulsive spectrum can be "beside themselves" if something is out of place—"Just think, there are infidels with their feet on holy soil!" "Just think, there are atheists teaching in our colleges!" "Just think, fetuses are being murdered!" A person with a full-fledged OCD condition cannot rest until the thought-about thing is resolved. They may drive their families or those around them crazy with harping on the same topic *ad nauseam,* or with repeated requests to wash their hands, pray with them, or do some other ritual over and over. Someone with a lesser degree of compulsiveness may still experience a persistent need to "fix" whatever is wrong—destroy the enemy, claim the Holy Land, convert the heathens.

While the cingulate is a locus, a deep cleft in the brain, where all kinds of mischief may brew, there are also larger cortical patterns that indicate a stuck brain: neurological rigidity can be found in large areas of *coherence*, signifying a brain that cannot change what it is doing, even when asked to. Certain areas of the brain can be slowed way down or sped way up, and stay that way no matter what activity is being asked for (so you toss and turn all night, and then sleep through class the next day) or stay in a permanent state of distraction. There may be hot spots of high activity or even seizure-like foci (see figures 2.7, page 37 and 3.1, page 66), while the areas around them look like military blockades or neurological no-man's lands because they are so neurologically suppressed.[9] This is because the brain also has its own tranquillizers and inhibitory neurotransmitters. It is capable of shutting down whole wings of its own functioning. Even though old Dr. Freud wasn't able to look at EEGs, his concept of repression is similar to what these EEGs show. When there is something too uncomfortable or painful to admit to consciousness, the brain walls it off. Whole areas go dim, while others compensate by revving up—but not in a healthy, fluid manner. In this way, certain mental and emotional patterns become instituted as familiar habits and ways of thought. It's not that old dogs can't learn new tricks; they may just be so locked into their old ones that new tricks are not an option.

According to Dr. Len Ochs, the discoverer of the Low Energy Neurofeedback System (LENS), when repetitive and outworn patterns *are* broken, new frequencies and comodulations with other parts of the brain become possible. Sometimes a tremendous amount of energy is released. People start new projects, their creativity opens up, and they don't feel stuck any more. A healthy brain is always a flexible brain, just as the healthy body is a flexible body.[10]

An old Viennese gentleman once gave me a quintessential definition of neurosis: You discover that something doesn't work and you keep on doing it. Or, in Ochs' words, "You redouble your effort while you've forgotten your aim." This seems to be one of the real stumbling blocks to genuine problem solving. *The old way has to work at all costs!* In fact, the solution you're searching for may lie in an entirely new modality. Many human discoveries and inventions have happened by stumbling upon the new, not clinging to the old.

And what of our ability, nay, our need and privilege, to make mistakes? This is generally how human beings learn—we try it one way and fail, then try another way and maybe it works. Think of how a child learns to walk, or to feed himself or herself. There is a lot of trial and error, and a lot of awkwardness, on the way to grace. Many people won't try new things because of guilt or aversive social conditioning. They have heard too many "no's," so they are afraid to make mistakes. If this one single fear could be cured, who knows what creative human potential could be unleashed?

In their thoughtful book *The Spirituality of Imperfection*, Ernest Kurtz and Katherine Ketcham urge that we don't really begin on the spiritual path until we have encountered our own woundedness. Learning to accept flaws in ourselves also leads to accepting flaws in others. "Spirituality begins with the acceptance that our fractured being, our imperfection, simply *is*: There is no one to 'blame' for our errors—neither ourselves nor anyone nor anything else. Spirituality helps us first to *see*, and then to *understand*, and eventually to *accept* the imperfection that lies at the core of our human *be*-ing. Spirituality accepts that 'If a thing is worth doing, it is worth doing badly.'"[11]

Ironically, the all-American game of baseball quietly offers us this very wisdom. Kurtz and Ketcham quote Commissioner of Baseball Francis T. Vincent Jr. in the dedication to their book: "Baseball teaches us, or has taught most of us, how to deal with failure. . . . I also find it fascinating that baseball, alone in sport, considers errors to be part of the game, part of its rigorous truth."

This issue is urgent because American millennialists and ascetic Islamists alike seem to fuel their fire with rants about the imperfection of the world, as if it were fallen, perverse, devilish, and at odds with its own Creator. The only remedy, since the Creator is all-powerful, is propitiation of this undeniable authority figure—and a catastrophe that must chasen and cleanse the fallen Creation. Joseph Campbell used to recount the Buddhist scholar D. T. Suzuki's response when he was asked what he thought of Western religion. "Let's see," the diminutive Japanese philosopher said, "Nature against Man, Man against Nature. God against Man, Man against God, God against Nature, Nature against God. Very funny religion!"

Original peoples could be wiser than Western theologians in this respect. Many of their religions accept that trial and error are part of the natural order of things. The Native American traditions, for instance, often include a trickster whose role is to undo or undermine the works of the Creator (often a sky god in the best Indo-European tradition), thereby introducing a theme of humility and humor. In the spirit of *imitatio Dei*, such traditions imply that human beings, too, are sometimes so obtuse that they have to be *tricked* into humility—which then leads to genuine spiritual growth and greater consciousness.

In contrast, consider the following statement from Religious Right champion Ann Coulter, a devastatingly nihilistic gloss on an originally sacred narrative: "God gave us the earth. We have dominion over the plants, the animals, the trees. God said 'Earth is yours. Take it, rape it, it is yours.'"[12]

To those Christians who feel obsessed about bringing an end to this sinful world, I say: Relax and you'll realize you are part of an ever-flowering mystery that's been going on since time began. Your own master said: "Consider the lilies of the field; they toil not, neither do they spin, yet Solomon in all his glory was not arrayed like one of these."

DISSOCIATION AS A PSYCHOLOGICAL
AND SPIRITUAL PROBLEM

By now it should be evident that the human central nervous system, because it relies on opposite and complementary functions, is like the proverbial two-edged sword. Its beautiful complexities, such as the left-right hemisphere interplay, bring depth, texture, and emotional meaning to our world. But the same complexity can be our downfall, as in self-initiated inner splits where we wall off certain areas of our functioning and act as if they simply didn't exist. Freud called this practice "denial" if the dissociation was more deliberate and "repression" if it was less so. In either state, something troublesome or inconvenient is excluded from consciousness. We now know far more neurobiology than Freud ever did and can describe the precise mechanisms of the process.

As I was constructing a brain map of a client recently I remarked on how highly functional she seemed in almost every area. Her brain looked flexible, energetic, able to multitask. But in the right temporal lobe there was a "hot spot" or "bull's-eye," a little storm of anxiety. Since we were in a clinical situation, I asked her if she had been abnormally worried about anything recently. She responded, "Well, yes." The day before she had watched a deeply disturbing news report. A group of Iraqi soldiers had come to a small community where both Sunni and Shi'a sects lived together, usually amicably. The warriors broke bread with some of the people and were quite friendly and polite. Then they crossed a river to an adjoining community and began shooting down young boys in the street who were playing. They were kids from both communities, Sunni and Shi'a, together, and they shot them all.

After telling me the story, my client, who has an eight-year-old boy herself, suddenly broke into convulsive crying. "How could they do that?" she wailed.

"Dissociation," I said flatly. "It's how people can kill other people's kids and then come home and love and cuddle their own. It's also how people

65

can espouse a religion of love, then turn around and authorize attacks on civilians of another nation and still sleep well at night. It's how we cut ourselves off from ourselves, and it's a human epidemic."

The human mind is very, very powerful. It can create high technology and the music of Mozart, and it can make little firewalls in its own circuitry and hide from itself in truly horrible ways. Most of us dissociate all the time, as we change mental states and social contexts. My client had a genuine reason for her "little storm." Real life sometimes taxes our very sanity. After her release, she felt better. A follow-up session a week later showed the site had quieted. Figure 3.1 below illustrates similar changes in the brain mapping of another client:

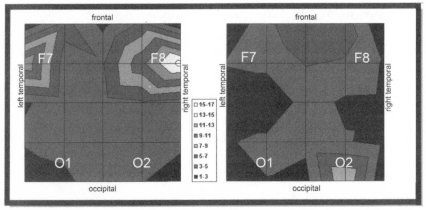

Map 1(left): Session Date 10/30/2001   Map 2(right): Session Dates 02/26/2002-08/20/2002
LENS Topographic Brain Maps: Delta Means by Amplitude, before & after treatment

FIG 3.1 LENS TOPOGRAPHIC BRAIN MAPS: HEALING A "HOT SPOT"
The LENS maps use a square graph format, but, like the qEEG, represent the head viewed from top down. Map 1, before treatment, shows a large delta coherence "rug" with two frontal "hot spots" at F7 (left) and F8 (right), indicating injury. In Map 2, several months later and after LENS treatments, the hot spots at F7 and F8 are gone and the delta rug is smaller. A new focal area has appeared at O2 (right posterior) which should, with treatment, subside in turn.

Dissociation may be a self-protective mechanism to keep the human brain from falling apart completely. We saw in chapter 2 how tenuous and vulnerable is the neural bridge between the cortex's hemispheres, and thus how easy it is for one hemisphere to split off from the other. With the variety of neurotransmitters we have at our disposal, we can use excitatory ones to agitate one part of the brain so it remains in fear or anxiety and then quarantine that area with inhibitory neurotransmitters. The chemical stimulants and inhibitors in turn affect the pulsing waves of energy that ripple through both the cortex and the structures that lie below it. It is on these waves that the fragile boat of our consciousness rides.

According to what is called "the law of state dependency," certain mental states of, say, arousal or torpor or intoxication or adrenalization are associated with certain modes of thinking and even certain subpersonality characteristics—simple examples being the grouchy persona some people wear before their first cup of coffee in the morning and how people's personalities change with a drink or two of alcohol. The brain waves visible in an EEG reflect these changing chemical and physiological states. Sometimes many waves are present in fairly high amplitudes at once. One way to guess what state the person is experiencing is to look at the dominant frequencies, the highest-amplitude waves. Of course the problem with any kind of neurofeedback therapy is whether the changes initiated in the clinician's office will hold on the outside. Sometimes they do so very well, and sometimes not so well.

Much of the time, certain brain rhythms and their associated states will ignore the others and try to maintain dominance, but there can also be shifts, as when someone suddenly becomes emotional or there is external danger. (You can see examples of the differences in rhythms in figure 2.4, page 27). What happened to my patient is comparable to what researcher Eugene Peniston and his colleagues found years ago in their work with Vietnam veterans and biofeedback. While the theta wave state could bring back traumatic wartime memories—and perhaps retraumatize the person—adding in soothing alpha waves (in what is called the "alpha-theta protocol") could help make the traumatic recovery and reprocessing more gentle. (See also the cases of veterans with PTSD in my book *The Healing Power of Neurofeedback*.)

Freud, trained as a neurologist, struggled to understand the almost instantaneous nature of personality changes people could go through in identity shifts. Neither the study of brain structures nor neurochemistry offered a good-enough explanation. The reactions were too global and quick. People's nervous systems can change in a trice. For instance, at a hypnotist's suggestion, someone may no longer feel the pain of a flame or pinprick, or they may feel a sudden pain or heat where there is no visible agency. But to the international neurofeedback community, whose work strangely lingers unknown to mainstream neurology, this is no mystery whatsoever; the sudden shifts correlate with the fact that the brain is a dynamic, ever changing energy field, only partially in our control.

In the more extreme cases of dissociation found in multiple personality disorder, or what is now called dissociative identity disorder, the divisions between one state and another are more marked. One personality has an allergy to nylon stockings, the other does not. One likes to drink strong alcohol, the other dislikes it intensely. The handwriting may be different. Even certain memories may be accessible to one personality but not to any of the others.

Changes of state and dissociation between states play a role in religion, too. Here again, the same mechanism that can operate for a person's benefit can also be misused and even contribute to pathology. People can influence their nervous system through gentle practices like prayer, meditation, yoga postures, breathing exercises, or Tai Chi to shift themselves into a state more receptive to spiritual influence. On the other hand, revival-tent preachers, who understand the manipulation, if not the precise mechanism, of these state changes, can engineer a crisis in which a person agrees—under divine guidance of course—to take on a completely different personality.

In the psychodynamics of conversion and self-reform, there is a strenuous attempt to cast out the old self and embrace a new, "born-again" one. Unfortunately, such newly minted personalities are not always successful at keeping the old personality at bay—as illustrated by the many cases of lapsed converts. Freud spoke of something he called "the return of the repressed": an impulse or thought forcibly pushed out of the psyche comes back to haunt the person as an obsession. The same process is operative in what is now almost a cliché: the charismatic evangelist who preaches family values on Sunday but during the week slips away from church and family into the arms of a prostitute (consider, for instance, the sexual vicissitudes of evangelists Ted Haggard and Jimmy Swaggart). Emotions can make us forget the contents of one hemisphere, or substitute a meaningful pseudo-memory for a real one. The same mechanism is involved in the classical "Freudian slip." The rejected, unaddressed subpersonality does what any good disenfranchised rebel does—goes in for sabotage. The "outer devil" is told, "Get thee behind me, Satan"—and the phrase inadvertently holds the truth. The old, disowned derelict aspect of the soul lurks behind or within. The evangelist smiles and approves his clean-cut, well-coifed image in the mirror while his finger dials the prostitute's number.

THE SINFUL MESSIAH

In his book *When Religion Becomes Evil*, Charles Kimball identifies five patterns or conditions that mark a belief system gone wrong: claims to absolute truth, blind obedience to authority, establishing the "ideal" time, believing that the end justifies any means, and declaring holy war. Kimball's patterns are evident in the story of the Branch Davidians of Waco, Texas, as well as in many of the fundamentalist religious phenomena studied in chapters 5 and 6. When the conditions are *all* met, you definitely have a recipe for religion "becoming evil." Kimball writes, "Understanding the factors that can and do lead people of faith and goodwill—wittingly or unwittingly—into destructive and evil patterns of behavior must emerge into being a high priority on the world's agenda."[13] A world consensus is emerging that spiritual leaders can be just as flawed as the rest of us, and more so to the extent that they insist they are faultless—or, even more tricky, that the God they represent and speak for is faultless, so they must be also.

Prophecies of such people are frequently known to fail. Pat Robertson, for example, claims he has annual meetings with God in which God tells him what is coming up in the next year. A recent article in the journal *Church and State*, examined the accuracy of Robertson's prophecies: "On Jan 1, 1980, Robertson reported that God had told him that the Soviet Union would in that year invade several Middle Eastern nations, seize the world's oil reserves, and throw the United States and Western Europe into economic chaos, sparking worldwide conflict. In 1981 Robertson predicted a global economic collapse between 1983 and 1985. He once predicted a Russian invasion of Israel and claimed that the USSR would collapse after the outbreak of World War III."[14]

How do true believers, including the prophet himself, deal with such failures? Social-psychological studies show that the more people have invested or sacrificed for an idea, or to be part of an organization with strong beliefs, the more reluctant they are to abandon it, even when the prophecy fails or the leader proves to be flawed[15]—or, as the following account shows, at the risk of death.

The Branch Davidians were an offshoot of the Davidian Adventists, founded in 1929 by Victor Houteff, an avid student of the Bible with a third-grade education. Having immigrated from Bulgaria in 1907, he settled in Los Angeles and became a Seventh Day Adventist. But he found the clearly radical, millennialist Adventists far too "lukewarm." After 1934, he started his own, more radical branch of Adventism, the term "Davidian" referring to the literal restoration of the Davidic messianic kingdom in Palestine. Houteff, equating himself with the Angel from the East in the Book of Revelation, believed his divinely appointed task was to gather the 144,000 truly elect and lead them to Israel to meet Christ at the Second Coming.

Houteff died in 1955, before any such event had occurred. His wife, Florence, then took charge of the group. Under her direction the Mount Carmel property was built near Waco, Texas—eighteen houses, farm buildings, and a large dairy. Florence became convinced that the 144,000 would be saved in April 1959, and about nine hundred Davidians arrived at the Waco property to prepare for the moment. Some expected Victor Houteff to resurrect from the dead and lead them to Palestine. But after the nonevent, the predictable disillusionment and squabbling reduced the community to less than fifty people by the mid 1960s.

Ironically, Vernon Howell was born in 1959, the very year the predicted salvation of the 144,000 did not happen. He joined the community at Mount Carmel in 1981. In 1985, in Pomona, California, he officially changed his name to David Koresh, allegedly because he was an entertainer (more on the meaning of the name shortly).[16] His two passions were the Bible and his electric guitar. He had memorized huge swatches of scripture and loved to debate the local church establishment. The Mount Carmel community at that point was in the hands of Ben and Lois Roden, who had declared themselves yet another offshoot sect called the Branch Davidians. After Ben died, Lois, astonishingly, tried to bring "the feminine face of God" to Adventism and started a magazine called *SHEkinah*, after the mystical feminine bride of God.

Koresh began a "marriage" with the lonely sixty-seven-year-old widow, quoting prophecy that "a prophetess would have a child by a prophet." (Later, confronted by an Australian film crew about this idea, Koresh joked that if he had gotten an elderly woman pregnant, he must indeed be God.) By 1983, Lois was proclaiming Koresh her successor, and he was claiming to have received guidance from the seventh angel in Revelation 10:7.

Lois's son George Roden, however, was not amused at these antics. He apparently suffered from Tourette's syndrome and, despite being a devout Christian, swore ceaselessly, amid bouts of rage, at what was going on between his aging mother and the young Koresh. He took to wearing a .357 magnum to Bible study meetings and threatening Koresh and his loyalists, which threatened to "branch" the Davidians even further.

Around this time, to Lois's displeasure, Koresh announced that he was told by God to take a (younger) wife. While Koresh was on a trip to Israel with his new wife, George Roden tried to marshal the community against him—but on his return, Koresh gained their loyalty again. Now declaring his own spiritual authority as Cyrus, the angel that ascends from the east (Koresh is the Hebrew name for Cyrus), the young man claimed messianic status and special contact with God. In one of his hours-long discourses to his flock he is recorded as saying, "That person Koresh, Cyrus, . . . that same person is going to be able to stand before Christ and explain to Christ why we are so bad the way we are. Let's face it, we are bad. . . . You reject Cyrus (Koresh), you reject God."[17] He also started "marriages" with several teenage girls, the youngest of whom was thirteen. Soon some were pregnant with his children, each of whom was expected to enjoy special spiritual status.

Koresh had centered his teaching on the Book of Revelation and the coming of the End Times, and considered himself the "Lamb" who could open the Seven Seals. Believing he had already opened four, he had to pause—according to the Fifth Seal, a period of waiting is required before the Sixth Seal can be opened, and apparently Koresh was waiting for that, and for a sign from God. In the meantime, a good Christian who was preparing for the End Times should be armed—hence the considerable arsenal amassed at Mount Carmel. The community apparently expected "a great war to take place in Palestine, in which they would fight alongside the Israelis against an invading United Nations force."[18]

Meanwhile, Koresh had gone further with strange rules concerning sexual behavior for his flock. From his messianic position as decision-maker, he made and dissolved marriages in the group (a couple might be astonished to find their marriage suddenly annulled by Koresh.) He also claimed the *droite de Seigneur,* the "lord's right," as it was called in medieval France, only it wasn't just for the *jus primae noctis,* or "the first night." While remanding most of his male followers to celibacy, he claimed sexual privilege among his female followers, married or not. He claimed throughout, however, that it was not at all about "lust"; he was simply obeying divine instructions. Koresh even set up sham marriages between group members to cover up the fact that he was polygamous with many of the women.

It was disaffiliated members who alerted the authorities to what was happening at the Mount Carmel compound. Marc Breault testified that "on 5 August 1989 Koresh gave a Bible study in which he stated that he was the 'Lamb of God.' As the Lamb of God he was entitled to have all the women and girls sexually. Only he had the right to procreate. Howell stated that he would give married couples time to adjust to this new 'revelation,' as he called it."[19] On February 27, 1993, the Waco Tribune-Herald began a series of articles titled "Sinful Messiah," in which some of Koresh's sexual rules and practices were reported, including the alleged polygamy. But it was on weapons charges that the agents from the Bureau of Alcohol, Tobacco, and Firearms (BATF) stormed the compound the next day.

Both Davidians and BATF agents were killed in the first exchanges of fire. Koresh promptly called 911. The transcripts of Koresh's conversation with Waco police lieutenant Larry Lynch reveal a great deal about Koresh's dissociated state of mind at the time. Indeed, his predicament illustrates many of the themes we've been discussing: denial, dissociation, obsession with religious things, misuse of authority by divine mandate, and failure on the followers' part to question authority. Whatever Vernon Howell's original psychological makeup, clearly his fundamentalist thinking had driven him mad and put himself and his community in serious harm's way. On the transcript Koresh begins by talking about the prophecies and the Seven Seals in the Book of Revelation. Lynch tries to direct the conversation to what has just happened, including trying to determine how many people in the compound are dead or wounded. Koresh insists on talking about the Bible. Lynch counters that this conversation needs to be about life-and-death matters. Koresh responds with a telling—and chilling—phrase: "Theology is life and death."

This was the beginning of the fifty-one-day standoff that eventually brought in the FBI, the media, and thus the attention of the world. Tabor and Gallagher in their book *Why Waco?* point out how little the FBI negotiation team knew about cults, the Branch Davidians in particular, or what they were facing. Some of the agents thought the Seven Seals were animals and couldn't understand why all the fuss about "the seals."

Koresh clung to his biblical narrative, his mind divided in the way we have discussed. People say that in person, talking about practical things, Koresh seemed sane, even articulate. But as the BATF tried sincerely to unravel what they considered a complex barricade and hostage scenario, Koresh continued to interpret the event in terms of the arcane secrets of the Seals. Myth trumped reality yet again.

Koresh believed the fifty-one days was the prophesied hiatus between the Fifth and Sixth Seals. While the eyes of the world were fixed on Mount Carmel, nothing seemed to be happening. However, inside the citadel, Cyrus, "destroyer of Babylon" (that is, corrupt Western civilization), pried and poked at the Sixth Seal of the Book of Revelation and began work on a manuscript about his theory. Koresh believed he was the only one "who could open the seals and thus show a way of repentance to our society." He stressed that Jesus had not fulfilled all the details of Biblical prophecy, whereas he, Koresh, at thirty-three years of age (about the same as Jesus at his death), would. And the days of Passover were approaching.

He finished drafting the first chapter on Sunday evening, the night before the devastating fire that destroyed the community. Ruth Riddle, a community member, typed it into a computer, and when the fire began, carried it with her as she walked to safety. In this text, Koresh emerges as a dazzlingly important semidivine figure, as a second Christ, described in Isaiah 46:11 as "a ravenous bird from the east" who would "execute my counsel from a far country." In the manner of most fundamentalists, when metaphoric thinking served his own purposes, he could do it brilliantly. Tabor and Gallagher point out that in equating himself with this mysterious bird—connected with the Angel of the East theme—Koresh plundered texts that had "nothing to do with prophetic apocalypticism" to piece together his own fabulous story. The same bird, he thought, was also "the right arm of Yahweh." Another passage from Isaiah, commonly understood as a rather moving metaphor for the process of human aging, "he took to be the tribulations of the end of history, not aging."[20]

For the FBI officials and SWAT teams, who were scratching their heads over the mythology, it did not help that the women and children still in the compound were declining to leave, apparently by their own choice. Among the latter were twelve of Koresh's children by various mothers of the community, as well as other pregnant mothers, presumably with his children. Koresh apparently commented at one point, "We don't expect you to understand, but these children are serious business." He presumably meant that as his children, they were semidivine and destined to play a part in the Armageddon scenario where he and the 144,000 Davidians would fight alongside the Jewish nation against the armies of the Antichrist. He certainly didn't want *those* children fed potato chips and soda by the corrupt "soldiers of Babylon"—as had happened with the children who had already left the compound with their mothers—so they all died in the conflagration on April 19. It was a true holocaust that killed the remaining members of the community, including Koresh himself.[21]

The Davidian incident meets all the requirements Kimball outlines: absolute truth claims, blind obedience, establishing the "ideal time," the end justifying any means, and holy war—in this instance, a mini-version believed to come before the great one. Another theme that warrants investigation in charismatic leadership is the persistent and almost automatic way in which the divine leader, be he a Joseph Smith, a Jim Jones, or a David Koresh, claims all the women by divine right. Koresh felt that because of his own high spiritual valence, other men were like females in comparison to him and thus properly his will should dominate theirs, as a man does a woman, and they should love him for it.

Lest it be thought that such things happen only in oddball Christian traditions, there is the story of Osel Tendzin, the *dharma successor* to Chogyam Trungpa Rimpoche, himself a sadly flawed teacher in the Tibetan Karma Kargyu (Black Hat) lineage who died of alcoholism in his fifties in 1987. Trungpa had founded the popular Tail of the Tiger Ashram in New Hampshire and the impressive New Age learning center, Naropa Institute, in Colorado. When the relatively young Rimpoche died, spiritual authority and responsibility for this empire landed in Tendzin's hands. Tendzin avoided the alcoholism trap that had engulfed his master but succumbed to an even more perilous rapture: Tendzin was bisexual and decided it might be nice to sleep with some of his followers of both sexes. However, he had already been diagnosed with HIV, as he knew full well. Tendzin died in 1990, and most of his partners died within a decade from AIDS. Evidently, Tendzin somehow believed that his spiritual privilege would protect him and his partners—or should we call them victims?[22]

I happened to be with the Dalai Lama when he was confronted with the news of this situation. He listened gravely and meditated on the problem overnight. The next day, visibly saddened, he spoke about it before an audience of over a thousand people.[23] What had happened was a very bad thing, he said, because it occurred when the spiritual seeker was the most vulnerable. The consequences of sexual abuse by a religious leader would sour her or him on all things religious, and thus impede further spiritual effort and growth at a critical time.[24] Disillusionment visits almost everyone so victimized, whether by lama, therapist, or priest—they become turned off to Buddhism, psychotherapy, or Catholicism. His Holiness recommended establishing a board of elders drawn from different denominations and groups to monitor infractions of this kind and to discipline infractions, just as professional boards do for psychotherapists.

It is clear that civil damages may be done to people under spiritual auspices. David Koresh unquestionably caused horrible damages among his followers and the families of his deceased followers. Hundreds of millions of dollars have now been received in compensation for the confusing of holy privilege with license to do what you wish. And what of millennialists? There were probably no millennialist malpractice lawyers around in the year 1000, when people divested themselves of all they owned to ready themselves for the Second Coming.

It's very likely that public, willful, and irresponsible promulgation of fundamentalist thinking has been implicated in millions of human tragedies. What, then, is the culpability around the daily and weekly promulgation of inflammatory rhetoric—and what if it drives a nation to war?

The human brain, along with its correlate, human consciousness, does indeed have all the vulnerabilities and weaknesses we have followed through these two chapters. In the final two chapters of the book we return to these vulnerabilities again, but with the affirmative message that we are an evolving species and that, besides our neuroses, we also have wonderful resilience, strength, and courage with which to overcome the rigidity and childish projections of fundamentalism and say "yes" to the challenges of human existence.

- 4 -

FRAGMENTS OF
THE GODS

Things fall apart; the center cannot hold;
Mere anarchy is loosed upon the world . . .
The best lack all conviction, while the worst
Are full of passionate intensity.

—W. B. Yeats, "The Second Coming"

An unforgettable moment in my early education was the afternoon class hour when my seventh-grade social studies teacher took the whole class from the realm of polytheism to monotheism in a single sweep of rhetoric. It was an unusual class for public schooling during the fifties. The teacher, reputed to be uncompromising and thorough, included culture and religion in a course on world history. We had studied the Greek and Roman gods and the ancient Greek origins of modern government. We even touched, in a cursory manner, on the nature-centered religion of Native Americans. But that afternoon she made it plain that the flow of human history was from a primitive belief in many gods to the civilized certitude that there is only one God. Humanity could not really grow up culturally and achieve modern forms of government until monotheism was firmly established. Protestant Christianity was the pinnacle of all human religious achievement, and America was the Great Society, Christianity's greatest triumph.

I was normally quite reticent in class and had been raised in a very Christian household, but I found myself raising my hand and questioning her reasoning. I guess my twelve-year-old brain couldn't wrap itself around how the idea of God versus the idea of gods could make one civic structure better than another. Something about this felt intuitively wrong. Even I was surprised by how passionate I was about the issue. The teacher's authority, of course, decided the debate, but the incident left me with disquieting questions that have lasted to the present.

Now I know that much more sophisticated theologians than my teacher have made the same point far better than she ever could, and I have read their arguments. They go like this: If one divine energy permeates the universe, recognition and proper worship of that real God (instead of the legion of antecedent "false gods") would unite humanity in common moral and ethical principles. God would be worshipped appropriately, human spiritual aspirations would be properly directed and shaped, and blessings would shower down upon humankind.

Arrayed against this optimistic theology, however, are the facts of history. Many, if not most, crusades, conquests, *jihads*, and even genocides have been enacted in the name of "the one true God." At the edge of a sword or the muzzle of a gun these wars feel no holier than others. The idea of a single energy underlying the universe that intends the good for all is a sublime concept, but it becomes dangerous if it is held by immature minds who mistake the metaphor for the thing it represents.

Joseph Campbell used to quote Meister Eckhart in this regard: "The ultimate leave-taking is of God for God." We have to leave aside our *idea* of God if we want to perceive God directly. Eckhart, the renowned medieval theologian, was always a hair's-breadth away from the stake because of his paradoxical, Zen-like pronouncements. However, he was also a genuine mystic, with direct experience. He knew that to move closer and closer to the living Mystery, we must continually outgrow our childish ideas and projections. Hubris lies in pretending to know ultimate things—on the basis of flawed evidence and our illusion-prone minds.

Much as we would like to believe that the simple monotheistic model instills virtue, it is not necessarily so. Perhaps the religious pedants got it wrong: It is not that monotheism leads to morality, but rather that most instinctively moral people think there must be a single underlying principle for all life that deserves our respect.

Many of the societies called "primitive" in the nineteenth century were as monotheistic as the Christians who came among them. They didn't mistake the little gods of the hearth and the forest for Wakan Tanka, the Great Spirit. But they didn't desacralize and objectify nature either. The term "animism," usually used in a demeaning sense, simply means the belief that the universe is alive with spirit. Which spirit someone focuses on is a kind of cultural Rorschach test.

CULTURAL NUCLEAR FISSION

Any god who is not transparent to transcendence is an idol, and its worship is idolatry.

—Joseph Campbell

The Great Mystery has always attracted human worship. In the process, idols are fashioned, be they images, buildings, or books. It is thus truer in an objective sense that man has made the gods than that God "made" man. For a time, such images, consecrated by groups of believers, compel worship. But these approximations of the divine, made, told, and written about by human beings, are also subject to mortality and decay. The human attention span and its creations morph and shift ceaselessly. The outworn forms, shells, or "masks" of God are set aside or left to decay or absorbed into new forms.

I believe this is what Campbell meant when he said to me, "The fragments of the gods are all around us," as I describe in this book's introduction. The qualities, personas, and forms usually associated with a story that humanity has created to approximate the divine are severed from their original contexts, and yet they are still with us. Such fragments often carry with them *mana*, the power or luminosity derived from association with the sacred, and believers regard them as absolute and eternal. This is also why they are dangerous.

In religions with many gods, it remains clear that no single form can represent the vastness of the divine. But in monotheism, the single sacred figure—here too only a shell, a human-created container—is confused with the essentially unknowable cosmic power itself. These fragments of monadic gods have been dangerous enough through the past millennia. In the twentieth and twenty-first centuries, however, the fragmentation has only been happening faster, and modern technology has made the risks greater, as Campbell's prophecy, discussed in chapter 1, forewarned. As we have seen in that discussion, myths hold energies "that are the essence of life itself, and which, when unbridled, become horrifying and destructive."

As traditional cultures wither before our eyes and groups heretofore isolated are invaded by the new culture of technology—television, airstrips, and tourism—the primordial energies previously locked up in their customary forms and rituals are cracked, and, as in the splitting of the nucleus of the atom, awesome energies are released. These energies can either tear apart or enrich the world. Or sometimes both.[1]

Sometimes these cultural entities remain translucent and adaptable to changing cultural and technological conditions. Some, however, resist change. They have undergone what I call *logosclerosis*, a "hardening of the categories," over time. Their meanings have become concretized rather than remaining transparent. And, according to Campbell, the job of myths is *always* to be transparent—that is, to point to a metaphysical truth beyond themselves.

Perhaps an example will make this idea clearer. When transparent, Christ's crucifixion can be seen, not as the sacrifice of God's son for a sinful humankind, but as the divine principle's willingness to partake of our condition, caught here in time and space—crucified among opposing forces. Christ-consciousness reaches down and suffers with humanity. This is a very different message than "he died for you sinners." The latter makes you fearful, obligated, and obedient. It blocks the psychospiritual insight that *divinity is crucified within us*—that we partake of the divine even as it partakes of our state.

Campbell said we should most fear those religions whose metaphors have become realities, that is, whose myths are taken literally. Paradoxically, the worship of graven images, or idolatry, so poignantly proscribed in the Old Testament, can include the idolizing of a book, like the Bible; a geographical place, such as Jerusalem; or a symbol, such as the Ark of the Covenant, the "Holy of Holies" of the temple. In Islam these become the Qur'an, a holy book; the Kaaba, a holy stone; and Mecca, a holy city—in a holy land—that must not be defiled by infidels. Regarded transparently, these texts and symbols instruct the spirit; regarded literally, they become foci for fanaticism and violence. (In Iraq right now the Shi'a and Sunni sects seem determined to desecrate each other's holiest mosques and shrines. When they do so, the violent energy of reprisal is like that of splitting the atom, as if they have attacked the very nucleus of holiness.) The more concretely such sentiment is grounded in a symbol, the more attractive it is to those who wish to break the tradition's spirit. And when whole traditions resist change, despite the fact that the times are changing, the more global is the destructive energy that is generated.

Fundamentalism of any stripe shows us that pieces of the gods are truly dangerous. Why? Because they are forms charged with divine *mana* but related to unconsciously. Worse, because they are literally believed in; instead of being transparent and therefore full of spiritual and creative implications, they have become opaque. Since they are taken as both powerful and literally true, the impetus is to play these ideas into history. This is the most dangerous part, because while in our psyches and our belief systems we can carry our funny ideas around to our heart's content without hurting anyone, when monolithic myths step onto the stage of history, a violent struggle ensues to see which one wins out.

The fragments of the gods may seep into a completely secular political figure, like Lenin or Chairman Mao, so that he appears to have divine or paranormal powers. They may inflow into a philosophy or a science or a school of thought. They may also appear in our fears and phobias, our fetishes and little shibboleths. These images may even show up in the psyches of people who have no idea or names for what they are experiencing; they know only that a *numinousness*, a power or a compulsion, seems to accompany the encounter. The feeling-loaded image may occur in a dream, a fantasy, an involuntary ritual, or a situation of everyday life. The most dangerous configurations seem to occur with dualism, as we explored in chapter 2, and in the dangerous mechanism of obsession, discussed in chapter 3.

RE-MEMBERING THE FRAGMENTS

If our images of the gods fragment into dangerous pieces, is it better to stay away from them entirely? The myths themselves say no. In fact, they advise us to take them symbolically into ourselves as a way to deepen and enrich our own journey.

Jesus said, offering the disciples symbolic pieces of himself to eat (bread) and a representation of his blood to drink (wine), "Do this in remembrance of me." The god, the hero, is saying: "Take me in" (use me psychologically) and "re-member me."

Consider the task faced by the Egyptian goddess Isis, looking for the scattered pieces of another archetypal hero, Osiris, her husband/brother, who has been dismembered and whose pieces have been scattered by his dark brother, Set, or Seth. For endless times in the morning of the world, the story goes, Isis roams the papyrus swamps collecting the pieces of the god she loved. At last, because of her love, he comes back to life, but in a completely new, transfigured way.

We may have a similar cultural and psychological task. The image of God, as we have seen, will always fragment or morph. Some of the pieces are more useful and instructive than others and bring the soul to life. Take, for example, the idea that Jesus rose from the dead. Whether this happened literally, as fundamentalists like to think, can never be proved. But the metaphoric idea that after we suffer the worst contradictions of our human condition (crucifixion) divinity arises within us anew leads us to the eternal psychological possibility of being "born again."

Renewal is a powerful archetype, one that calls for our continuous awareness and respect. It is older than Christianity—older even than Osiris. In the oldest strata of culture we find the idea that the shaman is taken apart by the spirits to become an instrument of vision and healing for the entire community. Only the reconstituted "twice-born" person can see into the future or discern the hidden causes of illness. In Neolithic times it was the "green man" who died yearly with the vegetation, was dismembered as the fruit was divided and consumed and the grain threshed, and was then re-born with the sprouting seeds in the spring. Osiris clearly follows in this tradition. Jesus also died on a tree, was ritually devoured, was put into the earth, and emerged again. Many mythologies throughout the world are interwoven with the cycles of death and rebirth in nature and with the concept of rebirth in the soul.

When a spiritual rebirth happens, the psyche is refreshed and renewed and the world is transformed—a wonderful feature about which "born-agains" of all traditions have remarked for centuries. But for the fundamentalist, the mythic embodying of an archetype and the accompanying inrush of divine *mana* associated with rebirth are attributed to a single figure, the Christ, who carries all the power of the transformation. Thus the fundamentalist himself can only be an evangelist, not an authentic spiritual teacher. Since he did not have to do the hard work required for genuine spiritual transformation, his own task is not to teach and guide but rather to convert others in the name of his particular God. Such is the formula for an extroverted society, where everything is projected outward. Moreover, in his view, only *his* way of getting there—the particular form of Christianity he embraces—is valid. Outside of his church there is no salvation.

Joseph Campbell hinted that the quest for an authentic wholeness is the next stage awaiting humanity as a whole. We cannot aspire to this new re-membering, though, unless we honestly confess our own inner plurality and fragmentation. Premature attempts to reach that wholeness by converting everyone to "the one true god" in fact hold us back from the daily inner inquiry that will allow us to find an authentic human spirituality—the real "god" everyone is so certain we must meet and know.

FRAGMENTS OF THE GODS, FRAGMENTS OF THE SELF

We think of ourselves as whole beings. We identify ourselves with a single ego, a single life story. But in fact this is a fiction, both neurologically and psychologically. Everyone alive has experienced their psychological plurality—the fact that in reality we are made up of "part-selves." All you have to do is listen to yourself to hear these characters, your subpersonalities, endlessly working out their relationships. One thinks only about food, another mostly about sex. One obsesses about social *faux pas*, another loves to have a few too many drinks and say wildly clever things.

So, one immediate question to ask yourself is: How do my part-selves get along? Am I "together," or do I seem "schizzy"? How well do I integrate my angel and my ape? How does my ADD self like the OCD one? How can I be so disciplined in some areas of my life and so profligate in others, how truly charitable at times and at others how selfish?

Somehow we manage to establish a working relationship among these part-selves. We are able to be civically responsible; we mostly restrain inappropriate impulses and delay gratifications. We also have a good time, make love with a consenting adult, and have elements of "right livelihood" in what we do. Life could even be defined as the dynamic interplay between these selves and their moods.

My book *The Mythic Imagination*, based on a sample of about three thousand dreams, presents abundant evidence that the fragments of the gods are alive and well in the modern human psyche. Dreamers as well as daydreamers find themselves in the predicaments of myth and fairy tale—climbing glass mountains, rescuing princesses, fighting monsters. They have shamanic encounters with spirits or helping animals, they undertake hero's journeys. Dreams routinely include what I call the "frame of reverence," in which the dreamer is invited to step across a line from the ordinary to the sacred. You find yourself in an abandoned chapel, at a sacred place in the forest, near a holy well waiting for a drink of water. The "ground" of the dream may show itself as alive—a theme I call the "living landscape." Suddenly, a road or a way down appears that you hadn't seen before, or a clearing opens in the forest and before you stands a majestic stag, looking at you with luminous eyes.

In those three thousand dreams were sacred figures from throughout history and culture—animal helpers, spirit guides, wise old men or women, Jesus (who appeared a number of times), the Buddha, even the lord of the underworld (at first glance a grim figure but, like the Roman underworld god Pluto, in the dream he held incredible wealth and possibilities). There were clear-cut initiations and rituals to be gone through, mazes and labyrinths, transformations and transfigurations.[2]

We need richness in our inner mythology so that the soul, or psyche, doesn't get caught in stereotypes and miss the deeper archetypal presences. We need plural images and textured stories because the soul is plural, and many images can capture its multiple transformations and metamorphoses. Rather than blazing goodness facing off against unspeakable evil, we need flawed heroes and complex villains worthy of redemption.

During the seventies, David Miller, a professor of religion at Syracuse University, wrote two influential books: *The New Polytheism* and *Gods and Games*. On behalf of depth psychology, and especially for the sake of the psyche, he was making a plea for the return of polytheism. The gods and goddesses exemplify parts of ourselves; they are parts of the archetypal psyche of humanity. Aphrodite can instruct us about love in ways that Jehovah cannot offer. Hermes is a quicksilver messenger who rules communication, double entendre, and even lies—which, like it or not, are probably an indispensable part of being human. Zeus is an authoritative sky god, like Yahweh, only he gets into mischief with the nymphs and often acts like a jerk. The struggles between Zeus and his wife, Hera, though full of divine wrath, also play like Olympian soaps, with lots of practical examples of male-female psychology.[3]

James Hillman, in his groundbreaking *Re-visioning Psychology* as well as later books, likewise pleads for a more polyvalent, flexible psychology. Ideas and mythic images, he says, are eyes for the soul. When we hold an idea or a myth in mind, it transforms our perception of whatever we behold—as well as how we think and feel about it. Polytheism instructs the psyche in many scripts and many viewpoints. Hillman was most concerned about the sophisticated fundamentalisms operative in psychoanalysis or behaviorism that actually conceal the soul from itself. Each paradigm shows you some features of reality not otherwise visible but blinds you to a whole realm of others. To be truly flexible, creative, and happy, Hillman suggests, the soul needs permission to move among many gods and their myths and symbols, and thus among many psychological perspectives.[4]

Christianity is notorious for the limited menu it offers the psyche. Many critics have pointed out that the Christian heaven is a sort of male bachelor pad, with the Father, the Son, and the Holy Ghost as roommates. Attempts have been made to bring in the feminine face of God—the mystical Shekhinah from Judaism; Sophia, or Wisdom, from the Greek Gnostics; and the Catholic coup that so outraged the Protestants: the assumption of the Virgin Mary to heaven. During the Middle Ages, the culture of the

Virgin became so strong that many of the great Gothic cathedrals were dedicated to her and became known as "lady churches." The officialdom in Rome was sometimes embarrassed at how much emotion seemed to flow toward a feminine divinity.

"As above, so below" says the Emerald Tablet of Hermes Trismegistus, a Neoplatonic proto-alchemical treatise. The person who insists on keeping a patriarchal God in heaven and a feminine deity at bay carries a similar pattern in his or her psyche. True, the Logos of masculine judgment, warriorhood, authority, and decisiveness has carried Western civilization a long way, but whether it has been the best way is debatable. Scholars have pointed out that in the Upper Paleolithic and Neolithic times, long before the Axial Age when the sky gods were the unquestioned lords of the universe, the Great Goddess ruled much of the world. The goddess-centered cultures were mostly about fertility, growth, nurturance, and sometimes, it is true, sacrifice. But overall, there seems to have been less systematic violence and less war.

A friend of mine, aware of my preoccupation with the subjects in this book, emailed to me the following excerpts from the online site *The Onion*. I quote them here, as they delightfully sum up the need for a multifaceted sense of deity.

JUDGE ORDERS GOD TO BREAK UP INTO SMALLER DEITIES

JANUARY 30, 2002, ISSUE 38

WASHINGTON, DC. Calling the theological giant's stranglehold on the religion industry "blatantly anti-competitive," a U.S. district judge ruled Monday that God is in violation of anti-monopoly laws and ordered Him to be broken up into several less powerful deities.

"The evidence introduced in this trial has convinced me that the deity known as God has willfully and actively thwarted competition from other deities and demigods, promoting His worship with such unfair scare tactics as threatening non-believers with eternal damnation," wrote District Judge Charles Elliot Schofield in his decision. "In the process, He has carved out for Himself an illegal monotheopoly."

The suit, brought against God by the Justice Department on behalf of a coalition of "lesser deities" and polytheistic mortals, alleged that He violated antitrust laws by claiming in the Holy Bible that He was the sole creator of the universe, and by strictly prohibiting the worship of what He termed "false idols."

"God clearly commands that there shall be no other gods before Him, and He frequently employs the phrase 'I AM the Lord' to intimidate potential deserters," prosecuting attorney Geoffrey Albert said. "God uses other questionable strong-arm tactics to secure and maintain humanity's devotion, demanding, among other things, that people sanctify their firstborn to Him and obtain circumcisions as a show of faith. There have also been documented examples of Him smiting those caught worshipping graven images." . . .

"God was the first to approach the Jewish people with a 'covenant' contract that guaranteed they would be the most favored in His eyes, and He handed down standards of morality, cleanliness, and personal conduct that exceeded anything else practiced at the time," lead defense attorney Patrick Childers said. "He readily admits to being a 'jealous' God, not because He is threatened by the prospect of competition from other gods, but because He is utterly convinced of the righteousness of His cause and that He is the best choice for mortals. Many of these so-called gods could care less if somebody bears false witness or covets thy neighbor's wife. . . ."

To comply with federal antitrust statutes, God will be required to divide Himself into a pantheon of specialized gods, each representing a force of nature or a specific human custom, occupation, or state of mind.

"There will most likely be a sun god, a moon god, sea god, and rain god," said religion-industry watcher Catherine Bailey. "Then there will be some second-tier deities, like a god of wine, a goddess of the harvest, and perhaps a few who symbolize human love and/ or blacksmithing."

Leading theologians are applauding the God breakup, saying that it will usher in a new era of greater worshipping options, increased efficiency, and more personalized service. . . .

"This decision is a crushing blow to God worshippers every-where, and we refuse to submit to a breakup until every possible avenue of argument is pursued," Childers said. "I have every confidence that God will ultimately win, as He and His lawyers are all-powerful."[5]

A FRAGMENT OF THE PATRIARCHAL GOD

When the fragment of a righteous male sky god is present in the psyche, the temptation to act it out is almost irresistible, at least for men. In a televised interview on spousal abuse among Mormon wives in (polyga-mous) households, one disillusioned woman put it trenchantly: "When God is male, why then, most males seem to act like God." Women are generally encouraged to cower abjectly before such a figure and simply obey. If, in the social sphere "power corrupts," and thus "absolute power corrupts absolutely," the same applies in the archetypal and psychological realms. That is to say, the God of Christianity, Islam, and Judaism is partial or lopsided—it's a god fragment because it leaves out not only the feminine but also the fallible and sometimes foolish aspects of the ruling sky-god archetype.

You don't have to be privately or publicly committed to patriarchy to carry such a figure unconsciously in your psyche, as my Jungian analyst pointed out to me years ago. Though my conscious values have always tended toward the egalitarian, including taking up the cause of women, I was raised with old-style patriarchs in the family, was trained by authoritarian athletic coaches, and served in the military for four years. In such contexts, *imitatio*

Dei is an inevitable problem. Men who find themselves in positions of authority are tempted to "play God."

I remember a member of my father's congregation at a small church in Orange, New Jersey, who for the sake of privacy I will call Mort. Mort was a high school teacher with a wife and two boys. My father had taken this man under his wing, even letting him read the scripture at the altar most Sundays. By conventional standards, Mort was a wage-earner and a responsible citizen. His main afflictions were righteousness and a penchant for fulmination when anyone crossed him. Disagree with Mort and you got an angry lecture complete with biblical passages, including, on occasion, biblical epithets meant for heathens or idolaters. He had no trouble telling me (at the time a Columbia University student) that I was in league with the *liberals*—he would use the word like a curse—and that my professors were in cahoots with the devil.

Although I appreciated the efforts of my far more middle-of-the-road yet politically conservative dad to help this tormented man, I cringed whenever the Sunday reading was from Leviticus or Deuteronomy. When Mort would come to the parts where horrible things were done to the Canaanites, he would wax into a fiendish glee at the evildoers being "smitten" or cast into Gehenna. His eyes would become beady and bright, and he would literally spit the harsh words and judgments into the air, leaving the startled congregation no doubt about how this man would act were he in Jehovah's place.

During church luncheons he would hold forth on world politics. Because they didn't convert to Christ, the Jews got Hitler. Did he think they deserved Hitler, I asked in some alarm. "Oh, yes," was the answer, "because they killed Jesus! Much of their suffering over the centuries is due to that."

Mort's wife Dorothy looked anxious and startled most of the time. She dressed plainly and modestly, and mostly kept her eyes on the floor while Mort was expounding. His children looked equally cowed; they didn't play freely like most kids. There was no doubt about it, little Jehovah was master in that house.

It was a most instructive and painful encounter. Going back to therapy, I vowed to work on how this archon operated in my own psyche—because

I could see the consequences, in spades, for what happened when he was played into life. And what about integration of this figure? It's a lifetime task.

Jehovah does have redeeming qualities. He inspired Moses and Aaron to lead the Children of Israel out of long captivity. Lots of immoral people might be even more so were it not for his commandments (which some think need to be chiseled in stone or set in concrete). We certainly do need rules, and we *are* better off when we don't kill, steal, covet, or commit adultery with our neighbor's wife. In the face of real injustice, judgment and decisive action are called for. This is the God of the Old Testament. On the other hand, Christianity often justifies its very existence on the fact that such an austere and frightening fellow requires some softening around the edges. Jesus is presented as a merciful and saving figure who offers to take on our sins and thus save us from his dad.

THE NAIVE HERO AND
THE HERO OF EXPERIENCE

Recently, however, the Jesus narrative seems to have gotten a little out of hand. The Jesus of the Gospels, for whom love triumphs over violence and who submits to the ultimate sacrifice to redeem fallen humanity, has been replaced by a superhero caricature right out of the comics. You can hear the scenario recounted in hundreds of pulpits around the nation—especially if the preacher has read too much of Tim LaHaye. It's Armageddon, Jesus is coming back, and, boy, is he "pissed" about how he was treated last time—no more Mr. Nice Guy! Now he is wielding a terrible light-sword, just like any self-respecting pagan sky god, and he is going to slay everybody who doesn't believe in him and cast them into the pit of hell forever.

The hero figure does indeed have a thousand faces, as Campbell said, but these are divisible into two major categories: the naive hero and the mature hero. The latter is an initiate, naive at the outset, but also usually endowed with qualities of curiosity and kindness, who ventures forth from the everyday world into a region of supernatural wonders. He makes allies, through spontaneous acts of compassion. He meets an insuperable obstacle or perhaps a deadly adversary. He may even succumb, suffer, and die, and perhaps takes a journey to the underworld. Allies whom he once treated kindly, however, come to his aid. He is reborn or metamorphosed, finds a treasure, and comes back to share it with his people—who may or may not appreciate what he is giving them.

This older, wiser inflection of the hero usually has a wound—both Achilles and Siegfried had a vulnerable heel. We might say Jesus had a character wound: he couldn't stop saying provocative, socially unwelcome things in dangerous places. Part of the authentic Christian journey, the "imitation of Christ," if you will, might call for each Christian to inquire psychologically into how his or her own wound leads to conflicts—"crucifixions." Likewise, by participating in the Eucharist, "eating the body and drinking the blood" of Christ, the believer is symbolically brought into direct contact with the wise, transformed "hero." These are psychological and spiritual processes that thoughtful people throughout the ages have found meaningful.

The naive-hero version of Jesus's story comes from a very different place. In this highly idealized narrative, he appears on the plains of Armageddon, endowed with preternatural skills and strengths, and overcomes his opponents by blinding displays of divine power (just like he *didn't* do before). Jesus as the naive hero interjects into the Christian narrative a very different kind of story, itself a weapon for conformity—a terror-inspiring Jesus meant to make *you* submit to authority.

Mythically speaking, the intent of the Gospel story is to lead us to a figurative dismemberment and death through which we are reborn, or resurrected, in a new way, just as the mature hero returns, renewed and wiser, from his epic journey. The story is transparent in that, by following it, we are led to a psychological and spiritual transformation of ourselves. In contrast, the concretized fragment of the naive hero is polarizing and incendiary, leading to "acting out" some childish drama. Fantasylike identification with an idealized invincible hero invites us to forget how vulnerable we are to literal human frailties.

The wisdom tradition says that though we are essentially fragmented beings, we can grow toward a wholeness that transcends "good" and "bad." "Let him who is without guilt cast the first stone," says Jesus in defense of

Mary Magdalene. But if we have tried to achieve a premature and thus false unity through identification with the naive hero, we can get no farther than placing ourselves on the side of the right or good—which leaves us face-to-face with all the evil and error "out there" as our projected enemy. Thus our fragments end up polarized, and we have already studied the perilous neurology of dualism. The next chapter will look at the enactment of dualistic agendas in history, but we move to an immediate example in the next section that shows just how figures of light have cast a shadow of darkness down through the millennia.

LET'S NOT WAIT FOR THE ANTICHRIST

> With this degree of incompleteness of the God-image, it was predictable that the dark side of the Christian God would appear elsewhere, as in the Antichrist.
>
> —David Lindorff

The Antichrist is a wholly mythical creature—meaning that he never walked this earth. He is traceable, however, to the Antimessiah of the Old Testament, who himself has roots in earlier Middle-Eastern mythical figures. Ancient Israel's penchant for historicizing myth was evident by the early second century BCE. While the faithful Jews waited for their Messiah, the Hellenized Seleucid emperor Antiochus IV blasphemed against Yahweh by trying to replace his worship, in Israel, with a god of the Greeks: Zeus Pater. The Jews decided Antiochus was an Antimessiah to be fought against and rejected at all costs. The Book of Daniel mentions the terrible figure of the "abomination of desolation," who would act as Antimessiah, invading the temple and desecrating the Holy of Holies. For both Jews and Christians, a later candidate was the emperor Nero, who ruled Rome right up to two years before the destruction of the Jewish temple in 70 CE and liberally persecuted early Christians.

Jesus never spoke of his opposite, but he would have been aware of the messianic prophecies in Isaiah, Ezekiel, and Daniel. Though I Thessalonians, probably the earliest Christian document (c. 50 CE) and probably authored by Paul, does not refer to the Antichrist, II Thessalonians, of more doubtful authorship, speaks of a "final enemy," a "wicked man" whom the Lord will destroy "by the breath of his mouth" and by his *parousia*, his "manifestation" or coming. Jesus did say, in what is known as the "little apocalypse" of Matthew and in Mark (probably written twenty or thirty years after Thessalonians), that his manifestation could not take place before a rebellion, when the Son of Perdition and the "enemy" would be revealed, and that there would be "false Christs and false prophets" (Mark 13:22).[6]

Though the Book of Revelation does not use the word *Antichrist*, its well-known Beast with Seven Heads, who morphs into various forms through the narrative, has long been considered a possible candidate. Early Christians believed that when Jesus returned, as he had promised, it would not be easy; he would probably face demonic opposition. The Apocalypse of John thus announces the arrival of a great enemy or opponent, who morphs into the figure of the Antichrist. (In later redactions, this figure reigns for either three-and-a-half or seven years and wreaks great havoc—the Tribulation. He is defeated after Christ's own appearance in clouds of glory. This proves to be the decisive event, initiating the beginning of the Millennium—a thousand years of Christ's reign on earth).

It was the early church father Irenaeus, in the second century CE, who managed to consolidate all of these images and narratives into one person—the Antichrist. The figure was proposed to be human, even as Christ was human. It was Irenaeus who introduced the idea that the Antichrist would be born a Jew and from the tribe of Dan—also considered the stock of the false Jewish messiah. (Scholars regard Irenaeus's five-volume *Against Heresies* as an accurate description, in the form of a critique, of the Gnosticism of the early Christian era, confirmed by details found in the Nag Hammadi manuscripts in the 1940s.)[7] Irenaeus deplored the dualism of Gnostic theology—even though his own writings initiated and perpetuated a mythic dualism between Christ and his opposite that would last to the present day.

It was a follower of Irenaeus, Hippolytus, who probably wrote the earliest treatise about this figure, called *On the Antichrist*. Hippolytus introduces him as the inverse of Christ, "for the Deceiver seeks to liken himself in all things to the Son of God. Christ is a lion, so Antichrist is a lion; Christ is a king, so Antichrist is also a king. The Savior was manifested as a lamb, so he too, in like manner, will appear as a lamb, though within he is a wolf."[8] Hippolytus then notes six ways in which the Antichrist will be a perverted imitation of Christ: 1) being of Jewish origin, 2) sending out apostles, 3) bringing together people scattered abroad, 4) sealing his followers, 5) appearing as a man, and 6) raising the temple (actually erecting a stone temple in Jerusalem). In most versions of the Christian Apocalypse, this temple, once erected, is then destined to be quickly destroyed.[9]

The myth thus attests to its own origins. It is a dark mirror image of the light image of Christ, like the Escher drawing in which Christ is standing up bright and tall, and underneath him, head downward, we see his identical dark twin. There is a similar figure in the Zohar, the Kabbalistic Book of Splendor. As a psychological image, it is splendid indeed. It tells us that for everything we desire there is a countermovement, and that each of our intentions has a shadow.

Once again, it is the fundamentalist tendency to render mythic fragments as literal historical figures that has created havoc with this myth. According to Bernard McGinn, in his cogent *Antichrist: Two Thousand Years of the Human Fascination with Evil*, apocalyptic eschatology, which tries to predict what will happen between now and the great unfolding of the end of the world, dates back to the original time of Christ. "The history of Antichrist can be conceived as one way of writing the history of Christianity, or at least the history of the hatreds and fears of Christians. The image of the totally evil human being has been molded by the personalities and deeds of many individual rulers and leaders—Simon Magus, Nero, Justinian, Muhammad, Frederick II, John XXII, Luther, Peter the Great, Napoleon, Mussolini, and so on—all of whom have come to be viewed as enemies of the good."[10]

Believers in the literal figure of the Antichrist might take note: If he is a single malefic human person, he couldn't possibly have been all those people. Seen metaphorically, however, he offers a wonderful excuse for each side to project ultimate evil upon the other. I say to fundamentalists: Don't wait for a historical *guy*, Jewish or not, or from the tribe of Dan or not. Look for the Antichrist in yourself or risk projecting him onto your neighbor—or, heaven forbid, having him projected on *you*.

Jesus was a master psychologist and a very inward man. When his message is literalized, it strays further and further from the Jesus of the Gospels. That is, it becomes "anti-Christ" in nature. It loses psychological subtlety and spiritual depth. Two books I would call to the reader's attention are Robert Jewett's *Jesus against the Rapture* and Barbara Rossing's *The Rapture Exposed*.[11] These studies show just how "Antichristian" some Christian fundamentalists can be. Understood as the systematic misinterpretation and manipulation of Christ's teaching, the Antichrist is among us now, even as he has been for the past two thousand years. Paul Ricoeur suggests that the role of such a figure is to make us think—particularly about the implications it holds for the psyche: "The legend of Antichrist can . . . function by revealing that ultimate human evil, even if we no longer view it as enshrined in a single personality, can include our seemingly ineradicable capability for religious self-deception."[12]

Psyches that are fragmented produce mythologies that are fragmented, and fragmented mythologies have schizogenic (split-producing) effects on brains and psyches. Dualism, polarization, literalism, turning the sacred and mythical into history or politics and away from psychological inquiry—these form the crucifix on which Christian humanity suffers, and on which, ever and again, religion seems to become fragmented.

– 5 –

DUALISM AND MILLENNIALISM IN CHRISTIANITY

> The Zen master says I should be "at one" with everything;
> but what if you feel "at two" with everything?
>
> —Woody Allen

Now that we have examined several neurological and psychological phenomena, including dualistic thinking, authoritarianism, obsession, and dissociation, it is worth examining how they have played out over time in the formation, the trials and tribulations, and ultimately the self-fragmenting of Christianity. Dualism was evidently very much abroad in the world by the sixth century BCE. The Jews were enduring persecutions and captivities, and their prophets were having to explain why a God who was all-good and all-powerful, and had chosen them as his favorite people, kept exposing them to sufferings.

The problems inherent in a polarized dualism must have been evident by then as well, as we find Heraclitus of Ephesus (ca. 540–480) warning of the dangers. The opposites, he said, cannot be divided—rather the universe is made up of the opposites in interplay. Without dark we don't understand light, without absence we cannot grasp presence, without evil we can't understand good. Heraclitus made it his life's message to show that "human desire inevitably is imprisoned within the structure of opposition."[1] Ignorant people strive only for what they see as "good" without recognizing that good and evil are inseparable. Lao Tzu, a contemporary of Heraclitus, likewise taught that dark and light, *yin* and *yang*, are intertwined, and the ego's attempt to treat them separately, or favor one over the other, is the source of error and conflict.

We might say that much of Western history for the last twenty-five hundred years reflects the actions of people who didn't understand Heraclitus's message. Their idea of what was good was often presumed worth going to war over, and violence in the name of good was evil if it was enacted by someone else, but not if by themselves (the opposite of the Golden Rule). In this way, through psychologically dissociated and projected evil, religion is implicated in most wars and violent conflicts throughout history.

Spiritual dualism seems to be the most pronounced in religions having an eschatological cosmology, that is, a cosmology concerned with the end of the world. Along with this belief comes usually a unidirectional time scheme with a great big beginning (the Creation) and a great big ending (the End Times). History does not repeat itself but rather is the proving ground for a continuing struggle between good and evil, directed toward a final reckoning in which good finally triumphs and evil is vanquished forever. Thus a linear, historicized scenario replaces the more fluid, cyclical interplay of opposites that Heraclitus (and the Taoists and Buddhists) emphasized. The psychology of irreversible linear history and a good/evil dualism seems to produce intense anxiety about one's role in such a universe, as well as a perpetual paranoia about evil and its insidious and seductive magic.

The cyclical view of history in Hinduism, for example, seems to encourage a "live and let live" philosophy. The Hindus believe that we're all on a great wheel of incarnation and in perpetual relationship to each other. Animals could be our relatives; we have inhabited their condition, and presumably they could have fallen from ours. This law of *karma* modifies Jesus's Golden Rule with a slightly different emphasis: Whatever you do to others will indeed come back to you.

Great wheel or eternal-return cosmologies seem to be older than the eschatological ones. The idea of metempsychosis, or the transmigration of souls, also characterizes the animistic and polytheistic religions, where "what goes around, comes around," including constant exchange between animal, human, and divine realms. Even the gods are subject to *moira*, the overarching Greek principle of fate or destiny. They also have multiple aspects. In Hindu myths, for example, Shiva is lord of both meditation and destruction. Sometimes he's the hero of the story and sometimes he's the troublemaker. (Attributing the gods with personality quirks and the ability to grow by working through them is a useful psycho-mythological approach. The myths tell us how the personas, the "masks" of the gods, play out on the mythic stage—and so how the human personality, our own fragmentary collection of masks, fares in life as well.)

When the image of God is monolithic and immutable, rather than metamorphic and capable of growth, the model for the human personality follows suit. If God is seen as judgmental and wrathful, so are the men who aspire to his image. If God is viewed as invulnerable and infallible, his vicars on earth will present themselves as the same. Rigid theology is thus paired with rigid psychology. People with a frozen notion of the sacred exalt a petrified god image and dread a literal devil that is mostly external—but even if his voice is heard within, he is *other* than the self. Thus polarized, such a dualistic mythology cannot grow and change with the times. There are psychological consequences to such a mythology.

THE ROOTS OF DUALISM

The roots of Western dualism reach back to the Zoroastrian religion of ancient Persia (modern Iran).[2] While some scholarly traditions date the prophet Zoroaster as far back as twelve to fifteen centuries BCE, he is generally believed to have lived in the sixth or seventh century BCE. His religion is grounded in a duality—the all-important difference between *asha*, truth, and *druj*, the lie. The universe is ruled by Ahura Mazda, the great Lord of Light, who is the sole possessor of *asha*. His counterplayer is the dark, twisted Angra Mainyu, the liar, who is nonetheless powerful and an almost equal opponent. History represents the great struggle between the forces of light and darkness, good and evil. Life will always contain both good and evil until Ahura Mazda, in a great battle at the end of time, binds and vanquishes Angra Mainyu and his minions. Once light has triumphed over darkness, all worship will flow to the Lord of Light, and he will bless his elect and reward them with eternal life.

Zoroastrianism contains other familiar themes and parallels with Judeo-Christianity: There is a Garden of Paradise, the soul is immortal, and a bodily resurrection will be followed by a Day of Judgment. Zoroaster is said to have been born to a fifteen-year-old virgin named Dughdov, who while pregnant with him shone with such a celestial light that demons were attracted and menaced her. She sought refuge in the house of Pourushasp, who became Zoroaster's earthly stepfather, as Joseph did for Jesus. One of Zoroaster's guardian spirits took the form of a plant, *haoma*, containing an intoxicating milky juice. More than once the prophet's life was saved by drinking *haoma*, and so his priests and devotees drank it, too—similarly to the way wine appears in many places in the Gospels and is drunk at the Eucharist.

After a life of preaching and teaching and performing miracles, Zoroaster was killed while at worship. Subsequently, he was venerated as the greatest prophet of God (Ahura Mazda) and a "conduit to the divine," as is Christ. Some scholars think that Zoroastrian themes entered Judaism during the Babylonian captivity in the seventh century BCE. The eschatological dualism of Zoroastrianism also shows up in Gnosticism and in Mithraism— Zoroastrianism's solar hero offshoot, with many similarities to Christianity. Later, it appeared in Manichaeism, born in the second century CE, the dualistic religion that first appealed to St. Augustine before he became a Christian. All of these traditions see life as a struggle between evil and good and between falsehood and absolute truth, the latter held exclusively by God and his righteous saints. Zoroastrianism continues in today's Parsi religion, with about two hundred thousand members worldwide, including the wealthy and influential Parsis of India.[3]

Dualistic Gnostic ideas permeated early Jewish sects such as the Essenes, the Nazarenes, and the Zealots. Hence they probably influenced Jesus and his wild visionary mentor, John the Baptist, as well. Once evil and good are absolutized and projected, there comes the problem of explaining how these absolutes play out in the world and in human life. The Gnostics described the presence of evil in the world as the actions of a twisted "god," or archon. The orthodox tried to explain it as an outcome of the struggle between God and Satan. Often the latter seems to be winning, as all the limitation and suffering in the world proves. But evil can never win out over good (so the dualistic story goes). So the struggle between good and evil is projected out to the end of time in a final battle, Armageddon, in which good finally triumphs. Thereafter Christ will reign as an earthly king for a thousand blessed years (the Millennium). Millennialists are thus those who await this final resolution—and who even hope for it in their lifetimes.

Because this idealized event is the only unequivocally *good* thing, all intervening time is shadowed, as it were, by evil, which is all too obvious in the world. The only choice is to commit oneself unreservedly to that good day at the end of time.

MILLENNIALISM AND MYTHOLOGICAL CHRISTIANITY

Matthew writes in his twenty-third chapter that Jesus, addressing a "multitude," had just denounced the scribes and Pharisees who sat in power in Jerusalem, calling them "a generation of vipers" and "whited sepulchers" who are "beautiful outward, but . . . within full of dead men's bones" (Matthew 23:27). Departing from the temple, he predicted that it would one day be thrown down, so that "not one stone would remain upon another" (Matthew 24:2). This was strong language, to say the least. Understandably, a little later, on the Mount of Olives, the disciples came to Jesus privately and asked, "When shall these things be? And what shall be the sign of thy coming, and of the end of the world?" (Matthew 24:3).

Jesus's s reply is so visionary, frightening, and prophetic that this section of Matthew has been called "the little apocalypse": "For many shall come in my name, saying I am Christ; and shall deceive many. And ye shall hear of wars and rumors of wars . . . all these things must come to pass, but the end is not yet" (Matthew 24:3–6). Jesus must have been aware, in that moment, of his similarity to the Old Testament prophets. He predicted that the terrible "abomination of desolation," spoken of by the prophet Daniel, would stand in the holy place, and a terrible suffering, or *tribulation*, would begin for humankind (Matthew 24:21). Then: "Immediately after the tribulation of those days shall the sun be darkened, and the moon shall not give her light and the stars shall fall from heaven, and the powers of the heavens shall be shaken. And then shall appear the sign of the Son of man in heaven; and then shall all the tribes of the earth mourn, and they shall see the Son of man coming in the clouds of heaven with power and great glory" (Matthew 24:29–30).

Shortly after comes the historically problematical passage: "Verily I say unto you, this generation shall not pass till all these things be fulfilled" (Matthew 24:34). Jesus evidently thought these things would happen in his lifetime or at least that of his "generation." (Others, including many fundamentalist literalists, have taken license to read "generation" metaphorically, to include everyone who has lived since then.)

Expectations of Jesus's s return thus began not long after his death, and twenty centuries later they are still going on—a belief that itself seems unwilling to die. And thus we have almost two thousand years of historical accounts about how people behave when they think the end of the world is at hand. Practical duties of life are tossed out. If Jesus is coming back and intends to "gather together his elect from the four winds, from one end of heaven to the other" (Matthew 24:31), you might try to ensure your place among them. (Some rather sad examples of this attempt are discussed later.)

Judaism had long been waiting for a messiah, as announced in its "prophetic" books, also incorporated into the Christian Bible as the Old Testament. While the prophets Jeremiah and Isaiah seem to focus on explaining to the Israelites why God was so upset as to let them fall into humiliating captivity, the prophet Ezekiel's visions—born, he says, "of a whirlwind and a fire"—are rich in mythic symbolism. But the "living creatures," as he calls them, who appear to him resemble no living being that ever walked the earth. In "the likeness of a man," Ezekiel describes them, but with "four faces . . . and four wings. . . ." They have feet like those of a calf but also like "burnished brass." They have hands like those of a man under the wings, with the faces "of a man and of a lion . . . and of an ox . . . and of an eagle." Their appearance was like "burning coals" and also like lightning. The sound of their wings was "like the noise of great waters, as the voice of the Almighty, the voice of speech as the noise of a host" (Ezekiel 1:1–20). Also in Ezekiel appears the fiery mystical Chariot, the Merkabah, with its wheels within wheels and eyes everywhere.

The symbols are both compelling and confusing and, like all archetypal symbols, invite interpretation. No wonder literalistic millennialists have had a field day through the centuries connecting them to historical figures and events.

The Book of Daniel is a hero tale showing how God helps his chosen ones. Daniel refuses the king's food and lives on gruel and water, yet appears more radiant, strong, and wise than those who feast with the king on his sumptuous fare. When the Chaldean wise men fail to interpret King Nebuchadnezzar's dream, it is Daniel who saves the day with his interpretation. Then Nebuchadnezzar erects a grand golden image and commands that "at what time ye hear the sound of the cornet, flute, harp, sackbut, psaltery, dulcimer, and all kinds of musick, ye fall down and worship the image" (Daniel 3:7). Those who refuse are to be "cast into the midst of a burning fiery furnace" (Daniel 3:11). Three Jews, Shadrach, Meschach, and Abednego, refuse to worship any god but Jehovah and are thrown into the fire. But when Nebuchadnezzar sees them walking about with an angel in the furnace unharmed, he reverses his judgment, now threatening to "cut into pieces" anyone who speaks against the God of the Jews (Daniel 3:29).

Nebuchadnezzar thereby qualifies himself as an early fundamentalist of extraordinary puissance. His beliefs seem amenable to manifestations of divine power. Dreams and their interpretation, magical rescues from lions and fiery furnaces, and "giving it back" to the captors of Israel make Daniel one of the most popular books in the Bible. The psychology of persecution persists right into Christianity. The theme is the same: the world is full of evil and oppression. God is on our side, but he's watching, so don't get him upset or he'll let the evil loose on you.

Unconscious dualism clearly can be inherited, in this case by Christianity from an oppressed and persecuted Judaism. The Book of Revelation of St. John was written not by John the "beloved disciple" but by John of Patmos, who was probably born after Jesus's death. The Jewish captivity was over, but now cruel Rome sat astride much of the Levantine world, including Jerusalem. John's Revelation is a visionary allegory, a moral parable in symbolic form. Like Daniel and Ezekiel, it can be seen as offering compensation for brutal and unfair social conditions, and as an explanation of sorts for how God could let such things happen to his "chosen people"—now identified as the followers of Jesus.

Ever since the early church fathers assembled the writings that form the canon now called the Bible, there has been hot debate as to whether the Book of Revelation should even be included in the New Testament. (Martin Luther, for example, thought it should not, as it has no relationship to the biographical story of Jesus that is the main subject of the Gospels.) Only in the peculiar contemporary enclave called Christian millennialism can you find the idea that Daniel, Ezekiel, the "little apocalypse" of Matthew, and John's Revelation are all talking about the same end-time events about to unfold now, two thousand years later, in a world unimaginable to the biblical writers themselves. Most religious scholars outside the millennialist camp are stunned into silence at such hermeneutical pole-vaulting.

JESUS BECOMES A COSMIC SACRIFICE

The apostle Paul, originally Saul of Tarsus, a literate, Hellenized Jew, never met the historical Jesus. The change of mind and heart that converted Jewish Saul into Christian Paul is well known. He was, in fact, enthusiastically persecuting the early Christians, when, in an epiphany that blinded his earthly eyes but opened his spiritual vision, Jesus Christ appeared to him and said, "Saul, why persecutest thou me?" In his eloquent Acts and Epistles, Paul helped to change Galilean Jesus from an inspiring but human teacher, murdered through the complicity of hypocritical Jewish elders and cruel Roman occupiers, into the Christ, which means in Greek "the messiah." In a conceptual stroke as brilliant as his conversion was blinding, Paul saw Jesus as fulfilling the law and the prophets of the Jews, yet starting a new religion that extended beyond Judaism to all people—a monotheistic religion that concerned the doings of the one God and so by definition became the one and only true religion.

The new religion still contained the Old Testament idea that God was angry and wanted to expose erring humanity to more tribulations, but, in this instance, it maintained that he would accept a blood sacrifice of atonement. The idea of God sacrificing his own son for humankind was a syncretic idea, combining the Old Testament story that God ordered Abraham to sacrifice his son Isaac to test his faith and images of the beloved "dying and reviving" gods of the Middle East, such as Osiris or Tammuz. Jesus was also mythically similar to Dionysus and Orpheus, whose mystery religions permeated early Christian times and places.

The universal religion Paul developed promised eternal life for believers, but because so much had been sacrificed for mankind, much would be exacted in return. It was a new inflection on an old contest for the human soul that began back there in the Garden, only now the religion of the sacrificed savior became the only conduit for human salvation.

For the early church father Tertullian, born about 155 CE, the literal truth of the Gospel is what separates the Christian from the pagan. For him, the pagan gods are clearly human inventions, whereas God as revealed in the Christian corpus is not. Tertullian also vigorously tried to clear the early Christians of the horrible crimes of which the Roman establishment accused them: incest, ritual infanticide, and cannibalism. He argued passionately for freedom of religion. It was Tertullian who famously said *Creo quia absurdum*, "I believe because it is absurd," and stated that Christ was, as foretold in the books of Daniel and Ezekiel, "an everlasting king of a universal kingdom."[4]

In *The Gnostic Gospels*, Elaine Pagels discusses how early Christianity eventually divided itself in two: on the one hand, the Gnostic-like variants, which focused on the inner life of the spirit; and on the other, the orthodox (*orthodox* means "straight-thinking") variants, which were being crafted by the early Church fathers.[5] The latter would, of course, become historical Christianity because monolithic, collective bodies of doctrine tend to survive over groups that tolerate individuality and divergence.

OBEDIENCE AND MILLENNIALISM

Irenaeus, who was the influential bishop of the city of Lugdunum (modern Lyons), a far-flung part of the Roman Empire during the second century CE, endorsed the orthodox position. Because Jesus had been "perfectly obedient" to God in submitting to his sacrifice, humankind must also be "perfectly obedient" to the religion of Christ. Just as the orthodox Jews must do, the Christian must obey the Ten Commandments and all other religious prohibitions and restrictions until he or she is disciplined enough to find his or her will in Christ. Christ's mercy, for Irenaeus, was extended only once. Christians who had doubts or wavered would be excised from the body of the faithful, submitted to judgment, and allowed to fall into the hands of Satan. For Irenaeus, either you were with Christ or against him.

Irenaeus thus helped imprint both the monotheistic legalism of Judaism and the dualism of Zoroastrianism into youthful and protean Christianity. Irenaeus did not like metaphoric thinking. He said of the early Christian Gnostics, for example, that they were creating "mythological poetry" and daring to compare their personal experience to the divine Word. Christ is not to be realized within; rather, he will come literally and in this generation, here and now. This, of course, is the root belief of millennialist Christianity to this day—all that has changed is the date!

Irenaeus also went against both Paul and the Gnostics in insisting on literal, corporeal resurrection of the dead—paving the way for fundamentalists through the ages to picture extraordinary scenes in which the last trumpet sounds, graves open, and people, dismembered for centuries or even burned alive, rise up to heaven in their physical bodies, their very molecules somehow miraculously reconstituted.

Irenaeus was probably the most influential early millennialist. All things written or spoken of in the scriptures would come true, including Christ's imminent return. He was so outspoken about it happening in his own lifetime that, after his death, the many places in his writings where he affirms the return were deleted. These original, rather embarrassing, passages were discovered only later.

So pervasive for the early Christian church was the expectation, and consequent disappointment, regarding Christ's imminent return that by the fifth century, St. Augustine took on the problem squarely.[6] A substantial and enduring church cannot be founded on repeatedly failed prophecies, he thought. Roman Catholicism then subsequently tried to free itself of millennialist tendencies, a trend that may well have contributed to relative stability of the Church (compared with its millennialist offspring) over the centuries.

The apocalyptic expectation, however, continued to haunt Christianity, disappearing when the prophecies failed but reappearing in the next generation. It surfaced at times of plagues and other disasters, when comets appeared, and at significant calendric events, the year 1000 being a case in point. Expecting that Christ would return exactly a thousand years after his own birth, people gave away their homes and lands and prepared for the End Times. Great expectations, of course, led to great disappointments. But, as we saw in earlier chapters, the delusional and obsessed human brain, even in the face of realistic disappointments, does not easily change. Sometimes an impetus emerges to help the expected result take place somehow anyway. If God is slow in bringing about his scripturally foretold prophecy, perhaps he needs a bit of human help.

FORCING GOD'S HAND

Ernest Sandeen, in *The Roots of Fundamentalism*, argues that the Crusades were one of the first grand exercises of "forcing God's hand"—a disturbing modern trend that also exists among the Christian Religious Right. The year 1000 was highly charged with expectations. Surely the prophesied events would come. But when the Holy Land still rested in Infidel (Muslim) hands, and it was apparent that Jesus was delayed in returning, the architects of the Crusades set out to help him. Surely God would respond in a supernatural manner, if they just set some armies marching and began taking back his holy city for Christendom. Thus we have the confusion of real estate and supernaturalized mythology that plagues the Middle East even today.

By every humanistic criterion, the Crusades were a horrendous exercise in futility, fueled by dualistic mythology. Beginning in 1096, with the support of the Pope, a great "people's crusade" was launched against the Muslim powers that occupied the Holy Land. Here two eschatological myths commingled, albeit unconsciously. According to the beliefs about the Jewish messiah, a scion of the House of David would reappear in Jerusalem, defeat the infidel, rebuild the temple, and from that high and holy seat rule an earthly kingdom. Christianity asserted that the messiah, Jesus, had already come. But now he was *coming again*. Thus the messianic expectancy at the heart of Judaism was perpetuated in Christianity. After all, in Jesus's own words from Matthew 24, he would be "coming in the clouds of heaven with power and great glory."

As the twelfth-century crusaders marched, sang, and cheerfully plundered and slew their way to the Holy Land, they felt they were exercising a kind of sanctified mandate. By "taking the Cross" and vowing in public to regain the Holy Land for Christendom, they also took the right to put to the sword and confiscate the possessions of any Jew, heretic, Saracen, or apostate Christian unlucky enough to be in their path. During the two hundred years following the first crusade, there were three more (or three and a half, if you count the ill-fated Children's Crusade), that were equally futile and disastrous.

While writing this chapter, I have continued my ongoing clinical work with head-injured or otherwise traumatized patients. The after-effects of either TBI or PTSD can include impaired cognition, changeable moods, anxiety and phobia, and even epilepsy and psychosis. The human brain was about the same a thousand years ago as it is now. Could it be that much of the cruel, even monstrous, behavior of the Crusades was enacted by head-injured and traumatized people? We can only speculate, but in those days people did seem to take great pride in beating each other over the head with a variety of instruments. And I have sometimes seen worse psychological problems in those who perpetrate violence than in those who are its victims. The rampant abuses of the Crusades may partly have been the result of the link between injured brains and defective mythologies.

Unfortunately, the terrible debacle of the Crusades did not seem to dissuade the Catholic Church from continuing to act out its dualistic beliefs. As the Crusades were ending, the Inquisition was beginning, this time with its projected aggressions turned within the Christian community itself. Christianity having begun as a religion of mercy and tolerance, now became an instrument of fear and terror. While from the church's perspective the Inquisition was an attempt to protect itself and its doctrines against heresies, for its victims it turned the Church itself into a many-headed, heavy-handed terrorist.

Psychoanalysts and psychohistorians alike have wondered at the vast misogyny of the witch persecutions. Was it men's resentment of the mother? Fear of male impotence in the face of female sexuality? Again we can only guess. The victim was often an older, isolated, or eccentric woman, or perhaps an herbalist, midwife, or astrologer. On the other hand, she could be a sexually attractive younger woman who caught too many male eyes. According to the film *The Burning Times*, in Europe an estimated six million women were burned as witches over a period of four centuries. The persecutor was almost invariably male and grimly enthusiastic at his profession. The mythological explanation was Eve's complicity with the serpent, which brought evil into this world and led to the expulsion from the Garden—an earlier inflection of the misogyny that continues to this day in certain fundamentalist Christian sects and in fundamentalist Islam. Women are weak-willed and men are not. Women are susceptible to their biologies, men are not. Women can't control their feelings, and men always do. Mind you, the sanction for these patently unprovable assertions was a mythological one—a story about what happened in a Garden at the beginning of time.

While Roman Catholicism avoided millennialism, it clearly did not try to free itself from dualistic and authoritarian thought patterns. Its monolithic power made all competitive or different belief systems anathema. Usually heretical movements were stamped out before they got too large, and the Roman Church held sway over most European countries until the fifteenth and sixteenth centuries, when two major events diversified Christianity's portfolio: the Protestant Reformation and the invention of the printing press.

Martin Luther's nailing of his protests to the door of Wittenberg Cathedral marked the beginning of Protestantism. Then there was the Gutenberg revolution and the translation of the Bible into vernacular languages, made available to the common man in printed form. But Protestantism soon showed that while it intended to change the way Christianity was practiced, the style, if not the content, remained much the same. As it too became a player of power, Protestantism began its own heretic-burnings and excommunications (how else, according to the *zeitgeist*, was it to achieve respectability as a religion?). Before long, each Protestant church had a traditional wing and its own reformed version, and these in turn developed splinter movements and went through their own reformations. The millennialism officially banned by the Catholic church, yet present all along in populist movements like the Crusades, now resurfaced in dozens of variants all over Europe, as people read and interpreted the Holy Bible on their own. One thing you can say about unconscious dualism: it keeps dividing!

THE BRITISH ROOTS OF
AMERICAN FUNDAMENTALISM

According to Ernest Sandeen in his *The Roots of Fundamentalism,* the French Revolution and the tumultuous 1790s paved the way for the millennialism of the 1800s in Great Britain and America. The guillotine became the symbol for the decapitation of an age and the frightening commencement of something new. Both America and France had been reborn as democratic republics of a sort never seen before. Protestantism itself was becoming stodgy and traditional. But two new opposing forces were being felt: On the one hand, the intellectual philosophies of the Enlightenment and scientific thinking were suggesting we might dispense with religion altogether. On the other, there were those who were reacting in horror to modernism and all things secular. They decided the fault lay in the Protestant churches themselves, which had become too theologically lukewarm and so needed a vigorous push in the other direction to dislodge them from complacency. Thus was born a reactionary type of millennialism that persists to this very day.

Two major players helped shape the British millennialism of the time. One was Lewis Way, a wealthy barrister turned philanthropist who became convinced that the "return of the chosen people to the promised land" must be established as a plank in the millenarian creed.[7] As an influential patron of societies, conferences, and publishing enterprises throughout Great Britain, Way joyfully spread the news of an immanent Second Coming, preceded by the return of the Jews to Palestine (a necessary feature for the prophecy literally to be fulfilled). The other figure was Edward Irving, a tall, striking Scotsman with a penchant for long-winded oratory and a great loathing of Catholicism—a common attitude among his contemporaries in the millennialist clergy. (They didn't expect to look very far for the Antichrist when a good candidate sat in holy hypocrisy in Rome—the Pope.)[8] Irving was popular and successful, an exemplar of his type of English cleric.

With Way's support, the British millenarians put together a series of meetings subsequently referred to as the Albury Conferences. At the 1829 conference, six basic principles of millennialism were enunciated, not much different from those held by today's groups. Sandeen lists them:

1. This current "dispensation," or age, was foretold.
2. It will end cataclysmically.
3. The Jews will be restored to Palestine.
4. There will be a terrible judgment, also called the Tribulation.
5. Christ will then appear.
6. A new age will begin—one thousand years under the rule of Christ—called the Millennium.

The date when these world-altering events would begin was set by the group at either 1843 or 1847—uncannily close to the date set by the Millerites across the Atlantic in America (first 1843 and, when that date failed, 1844).

Irving's fall from prominence was as sudden as his ascension. He had led his congregation in praying for the "gift of tongues." But when a loud *glossolalia* actually broke out in the church as one rather marginalized woman "received the gift," it was too much for most of the congregation. They were "a dim and weakly flock," Irving told a sympathetic listener as, en masse, they left the church in protest. The Pentecostal eruption was also too much for the Church of Scotland. Edward Irving was tried for heresy and defrocked. He died a few years later. However, Way kept on with his philanthropic and evangelical work, including establishing the Prophecy Investigation Society, which organized regular meetings along the lines of the Albury Conferences. Sandeen mentions that after 1829 there were regular millenarian meetings, including of a group called the Plymouth Brethren, at Oxford and Plymouth in England, and also in Ireland.

The most influential figure among the Plymouth Brethren was John Nelson Darby. Sandeen describes him as "an itinerant man of few domestic pleasures, a man with magnetic, electric personality qualities combined with a tyrant's will to lead and an intolerance of criticism."[9] His writing, being almost "uniformly unintelligible," was less influential than his presence. An observer described him as having "a fallen cheek, a bloodshot eye, crippled limbs resting on crutches, a seldom-shaven beard, a shabby suit of clothes and a generally neglected person."[10]

At the time of the meetings, the leader of the Irish millennialist group was the "young, attractive, widowed, but equally pious" Lady Theodosia Powerscourt. At the first two conferences, in 1831 and 1832 respectively, held at her estate in County Wicklow, Ireland, it was agreed that the Apocalypse was imminent. Questions were discussed: What were the clues for the exact date? How could they tell when the Antichrist had made his appearance? The topic was: Should we expect a personal Antichrist?

The third of these conferences the following year was dominated entirely by the Plymouth Brethren and Darby. The Irish "historicists" at the gathering decided the first fifteen chapters of Revelation had already been fulfilled and that, by 1827, "European history was hovering somewhere between the twelfth and seventeenth verses of Revelation 16." But the "futurists," including Darby, believed none of these events had happened yet— they wouldn't occur until the end of this "dispensation." Darby mounted a formidable attack upon his theological opponents, as well as on the apostasy and corruption of the organized churches. He also introduced into theological currency the concept of the "Rapture."[11] Thus it was that at this conference two key millennialist concepts—Dispensationalism and the Rapture—were introduced together. Dispensationalism is belief in divinely appointed, biblically announced epochs, or dispensations, during which specific events such as Armageddon and the Rapture happen. Which dispensations are coming when is determined by reading the prophetic books of the Bible. The Rapture, also called the Secret Rapture, is the idea that the true elect of Jesus Christ—some say they number 144,000—will be "taken into the air" to meet him at his second coming. (This was also the idea that had influenced John Calvin's "predestination" doctrine.)

People considered Darby sincere in his beliefs but extremely zealous and at times almost incomprehensible. From his standpoint, on the other hand, those who didn't agree with his interpretation of how the scripture would be fulfilled were not only wrong but were most likely in the thrall of Satan. A clergyman of the time, Thomas Croskery, described the Plymouth Brethren as prowling "unceasingly round all our churches, seeking to reap where they have not sown."[12] Darby doesn't seem to have been self-aware enough to see himself as a theological predator, trying to win converts from among the conventionally religious. He and the Brethren presumably figured that only by predicting the end of the world could they jar people into a radicalized version of what they already believed—an adrenalized approach not unlike the way Islamic fundamentalists use messianism and the idea of *jihad* to recruit from among the more conventional sects of Islam.

MILLENNIUM, MESSIAHS, AND MAYHEM

In her essay in *Millennium, Messiahs, and Mayhem,*[13] Catherine Wessinger offers a clarification of the distinction between pre-millennialism and post-millennialism.

In pre-millennialism, Wessinger says, Christ is expected to come before, during, or after the Tribulation, which will be a terrible time of war and bloodshed, usually predicted as seven years long, initiated by the arrival of the Antichrist. Christ intervenes in history and casts the Antichrist and the unbelievers into the pit, or the lake of fire. There is nothing for believers to do either to prevent or precipitate this event. Pre-millennialism, which emerged in the 1840s with Darby's influence, should properly be called "catastrophic millennialism," Wessinger says, because in its view humanity is so steeped in evil, and the world so fallen, that a catastrophe is inevitable. Only the intervention of the Savior can straighten things out. Thus any program of social betterment is regarded as anti-Christian or even of Satan, because it flies in the face of the hope that Christ will solve all problems. Pre-millennialist groups tend to be "cultic"—cults as Wessinger defines them usually being smaller groups with a negative valence that reject the principles and practices of their host culture or religion.

As cults grow larger and become denominations, they usually shift to a positive valence with respect to the culture. Thus they come more to resemble post-millennialist religions, which maintain that the Christian church is metaphorically a proxy for Christ and that the millennium either has come, or could come through effort. Post-millennialism is found among the more conventional churches, including social-mission-oriented evangelical denominations. Though they believe in the second coming of Christ, they also believe that human beings can pave the way for his coming by making the world better. This stance could also be called "progressive millennialism," since it maintains that people are capable of spiritual growth and evolution and that divine providence guides human affairs. (There is also a third position called a-millennialism, found among the mainstream churches, that says there will be no literal millennium but instead only a figurative, or inward, spiritual one.)

Wessinger tracks the typical metamorphosis of an originally pre-millennial organization as follows:

1. It begins when a visionary or founding revelator predicts the Second Coming of Christ and the End Times. The message is infectious and others join.
2. Expectation of the end of the world as they know it causes people to change their priorities. They may neglect their homes and livelihoods and give everything to the poor or to the church.
3. The predicted day comes and goes, and the world continues as usual. No one outside the group is very surprised.
4. The leaders or prophets backpedal furiously, almost always saying they weren't wrong, they were tricked by Satan, and so on. Then they set a new date.
5. The followers either quit or, because of their high level of psychological investment in the idea of "waiting for the end," accept the new explanation and start waiting again.
6. The non-event recurs and new explanations are minted, for instance: "It happened in the spiritual realm—it always happens there before it happens here! The prophecy was true after all!"
7. Someone in the sect's leadership, probably a genuine conservative who doesn't like to see so much spiritual zeal and human creative energy wasted, suggests they avoid predicting specific dates, and most of the other deacons agree.

8. They then start engaging in good works—such as constructing that hospital or school (the Adventists) or publishing house or farm (Jehovah's Witnesses).

Wessinger's analysis answered some important questions for me, pertaining to how American religions such as the Adventists and the Mormons become socially contributive and respectable while still prophesizing the imminent end of the world.

HOW AMERICAN FUNDAMENTALISM LOST ITS MILLENNIUM BUT GAINED MILLIONS

Americans make up religion anew for themselves.
—British essayist Anthony Trollope, 1862

Almost since America's discovery, Europeans who were oppressed by hidebound cultures and ecclesiastical bureaucracies projected their utopian dreams across the Atlantic, and this tendency was no less the case in the nineteenth century. "America is without parallel in universal history," is the comment in a report from a London evangelical meeting in 1846. "With all our mixtures, there is a leaven of heaven; there is goodness there. . . . I really believe that God has got America within anchorage, and that upon that arena, he intends to display his prodigies for the millennium."[14] "Brimming with optimism and hope," millennialism joined American nationalism. The Americans were a "chosen people" and their nation, "a city set upon a hill."[15]

By the middle of the nineteenth century, America was "drunk on the idea of the millennium," writes Sandeen. The proper name of the well-known Shakers of New York State and Massachusetts was The Millennial Church of the United Society of Believers in Christ's Second Appearance. The Shakers believed that their spiritual mentor, "Mother" Ann Lee, was the reappearance of Christ in feminine form, and that the highest expression of spiritual purity while awaiting the imminent millennium was to practice celibacy. For all their wondrous group dances, hymns, journals, durable furniture, and well-planned barns, that one belief eventuated in there being no more Shakers in the ensuing centuries.

All of the later influential, uniquely American millennialist religions we view here sprang from the same matrix. No less an intellectual than John Humphrey Noyes, founder of the sexually unorthodox Oneida Community in the mid-1800s, said, "I fully entered into the enthusiasm of the time . . . my heart was fixed on the millennium, and I resolved to live and die for it."[16] It was in this same climate of opinion that William Miller, a farmer, did a numerical analysis of the Bible and, through what he considered a series of incontrovertible calculations, arrived at October 1843 as the date of the Apocalypse.[17] Miller was passionate and sincere enough about his sacred detective work to be able to persuade others—usually "evangelizing" them from among the Methodists, Presbyterians, and Baptists, many of whom already believed the second coming was at hand. The movement was rural to begin with but spread to many urban areas and eventually drew from all levels of society.

As cognitive dissonance theory—developed almost a century later—would have predicted, people develop attachments to their beliefs and become extremely reluctant to give them up. The more people had sacrificed of their old lives—their previous beliefs, friends, congregations, even property—for the sake of the cause, the more passionate they became and the more they swept aside the reasonable reservations of their friends and neighbors. Some writers have melodramatized the Millerites standing on autumnal hilltops in white robes in expectation as the prophesied date and hour approached, having sold their homes, neglected their crops, and severed their ties with nonbelievers. The truth was probably more pedestrian but no less bitter in its outcome. When the autumn and winter of 1843 came and went without the trumpet sounding or the heavens opening, a new date was set for October of the following year. "But on 22 October, 1844, the sun sank as it had on every other day since creation, and Christ had not come." A believer wrote, "Our fondest hopes and expectations were blasted, and such a spirit of weeping came over us as I never experienced before. We wept and wept and wept till the day dawned."[18]

Neighbors were not necessarily kind, especially when they realized that the Millerites expected to be the raptured "elect" and were happy enough to leave everyone else behind in a miserable worldwide tribulation. "In retrospect," Paul Boyer writes, "the Millerite movement appears to have virtually destroyed pre-millennialism in America for a generation."[19]

Though Millerism was discredited, millennialism itself seems to spring back eternally. An offspring of Millerism, clearly undismayed by prophecy's failure, was the Seventh Day Adventist movement. Inspired by a young visionary, Ellen Harmon, later renamed White, the Adventist church was named and constituted by the 1860s. In 1888, White published the final form of her book, *The Great Controversy between Christ and Satan*. White was later accused of extensive plagiarism, which seemed inconsistent with her explicit moral precepts. A later medical opinion attributed this inconsistency to a rather serious head injury at nine years of age that left her in a stupor for months, unable to perform simple cognitive tasks, with a possible diagnosis of temporal lobe epilepsy. She herself, however, spoke of the thrown stone that bloodied and deformed her face as a blessing from God.

Nearly fifty years later, reflecting in the *Review and Herald* (November 25, 1884) on the effects of her accident, Ellen wrote: "I visited . . . the spot where I met with the accident that had made me a life-long invalid. This misfortune, which for a time seemed so bitter and was so hard to bear, has proved to be a blessing in disguise. The cruel blow which blighted the joys of earth, was the means of turning my eyes to heaven."[20]

Based on their founder's conversations with God, Adventists expected the Second Coming any day, but had learned from the debacle of Millerism how lethal it was actually to set a date. Over the next century the Adventists established themselves as a truly paradoxical religion: waiting for the end of the world while consuming healthful food and building socially contributive institutions at a great rate.

Though the "blue laws" and "Sunday laws" they aspired to draft into national legislation failed, the Adventists became more "denominational" and mainstream. Because of their abstention from destructive habits and commitment to a good diet, Adventists were generally healthier and longer-lived than their contemporaries.[21] Like it or not, they joined the post-millennialist types and contributed to the betterment of the world, even though because of Ellen White's eschatological ideas "they remained prone to excitement, whenever they found evidence that the return of the Lord might be near."[22]

I recall the Seventh Day Adventist booth at the 1963–64 World's Fair in Flushing Meadows, New York. Special audiovisual effects were used—brand new at the time. Thunder and lightning attended the trumpet call, and human cries rang out at the approaching end. In the splendid social-realist-style painted diorama, workers and businessmen fell to their knees as Christ and his angels appeared in the clouds. Hands were raised in prayer, symbolizing that conversion was happening everywhere, right before your eyes. Near the display, healthy-looking Adventists stood by to answer questions or, if you were convinced, to sign you up.

The Watchtower Bible and Tract Society, also known as the Jehovah's Witnesses, was started by Charles Taze Russell in 1884. In his book, *Millennial Dawn*, published in 1886, Russell predicted the end of the world in 1914 (He didn't do quite as badly as Miller, in that 1914 saw the commencement of a world war). That year also saw the birth of the Assemblies of God Church, "the leading Pentecostal denomination, still in the 1990s a mighty fortress of premillennial belief."[23] (Pentecostals do services with glossolalia and faith healings and are usually millennialists, but many millennialists, including evangelicals, do not welcome Pentecostalism.)

Another nineteenth-century millennialist church, the Church of Jesus Christ of the Latter Day Saints, also known as the Mormon church, was founded by Joseph Smith, a charismatic visionary and prophet, and, by some adverse accounts, a public liar and bigamist. He spent his early life near Elmira, New York. A prayerful youth, he said he was led by an angel to a cave where he found tablets on which a mysterious language, apparently ancient Hebrew, was inscribed. Perplexed and unable to read the inscriptions, he asked for help, and the angel returned, leading him this time to the Urim and the Thummim, magical breastplates containing jewels, which when gazed through allowed him to translate the Hebrew into a form of King James English. *The Book of Mormon* was published in 1830.

Smith converted his family first and then others. As they traveled from New York looking for Zion, the land they believed they were promised in the West, converts were gathered and others dropped away. After a hostile reception in Missouri, they moved on to Nauvoo, Illinois, which was scarcely better. Though Smith publicly denied being polygynous many times, it has been estimated that at the time of his death he had more than thirty wives. The very idea of a patriarchal male, holy or not, monopolizing so many women was apparently too much for some of the men who opposed him, and may have been one of the things that inflamed the mob that killed him when he was already in jail. His second-in-command, Brigham Young, led the Saints to their final settling place in Utah.

Mormonism has had a remarkably aggressive program of evangelism and, by some estimates, is currently the fastest-growing Christian sect in the world. However, no other branch of Christianity accepts the history or mythology of *The Book of Mormon*. Conventional evangelicals and fundamentalists are also alarmed by the practice of polygyny, which is still highly controversial and publicly denied but apparently privately practiced, particularly by conservative or fundamentalist Mormons, a schismatic subgroup. They are also alarmed by the Mormon claims that Jesus visited North America and that *The Book of Mormon* is a holy text as sacred as the Bible.

Scholars have trouble placing Mormonism on the pre/post-millennial spectrum and, in all probability, both currents run in this religion. Either way, the Mormons were convinced enough that we are all living in "the latter days" to insert the concept into the very name of the church. Whether they are all "saints" is yet to be determined.

THE FUNDAMENTALS

Despite "the Great Disappointment" of Millerism, nineteenth-century America remained clearly hungry for prophetic myths. Two influential journals of the day were *The Prophetic Times* and the *Quarterly Journal of Prophecy*. In a long series of articles titled "Israel and the Church" in the *Prophetic Times,* it was noted that "Darby's distinctive definitions informed the whole discussion" of dispensationalism and the Secret Rapture.[24] These millennialist publications, which contained the writings by or about British and Irish millennialists such as Way, Irving, and Darby, helped prepare the way for Darby's many visits to America in the later part of the century.

119

Darby was generally disgusted by the American Christians he met who believed that "works" were as important as "faith" and who seemed to value social action over pious confession.[25] When he first encountered the American evangelical thinker Dwight L. Moody, he did not like him, and called him "the active man at Chicago." Darby was on one of his many trips to America and Canada, staying in rented rooms or people's homes, thumbing his well-worn Bible, and writing lengthy biblical hermeneutics and polemics on the long train rides between destinations. Moody, who seemed fundamentalist enough to most of the people who met him, was not fundamental enough for Darby.

Within a decade or so, though, Darby decided Moody had "got on in the truth." He commented in a letter that Moody was aiding the cause of millennialist dispensationalism by "a strenuous effort of activity." These two preachers were the Isaiah and Jeremiah of the nineteenth century, deploring the established church as corrupt and urging the truly faithful to reform their ways and prepare for the End Times. While Darby converted Americans, Moody had successful preaching tours in England and Scotland. After his return to the United States he founded the well-known Moody Bible Institute around the turn of the century.

Another American influenced by Darby was Cyrus Scofield.[26] Scofield, a Tennessean, had fought as a Confederate in the Civil War, practiced law in Kansas, and then fled, leaving behind his wife and children, when accusations surfaced that he had embezzled funds from Senator John Ingalls, a former partner.[27] Scofield was arrested two years later in St. Louis on forgery charges. While he was in jail Scofield was converted, under the influence of James Brookes, a Darbyite. He became pastor of Dallas's First Congregational Church, even as his wife filed for divorce on grounds of desertion. Scofield's famous *Reference Bible* (1909), which has historical millennialist notes and commentaries appended to the text, has influenced millions of people.

Scofield believed that formal education and theological training were an absolute hindrance to understanding the truth of the scripture. He fell into the contentious paranoia that comes so easily to the fundamentalist temperament, denouncing the liberal churches and most denominations other than his own as "flocking to the banner of the Antichrist." He insisted, showing himself quite the Darbyite, that the "true believers would be Raptured out of the Tribulation."

Scholars have pointed out that, given the elemental contentiousness of the fundamentalist mentality, the various millennialist churches could achieve something like a unanimous movement only by recognizing a common enemy. Indeed, the movement, despite the many schisms within it, was growing more consolidated as a common response to the creeping secularism of the post-Enlightenment. Darwin's *Origin of Species* was published in 1859. Around the same time, Voltaire was writing sarcastic attacks on conventional religiosity. The enemy was generalized and at various times included secularism, modernization, scientism, public agnosticism, and atheism. In the second half of the twentieth century, secular humanism, religious liberalism, Communism, social permissiveness, abortion, and gay rights were added to the list.

Opportunities for millennialists to get together multiplied. In 1880, Moody convened the Northfield Conferences, which attracted many influential American clergymen of the millennialist stripe. "Perfectionists"—people who believed the Bible was an instruction manual mainly for personal spiritual growth—need not apply. The Keswick Movement among this group saw "perfectionists" (who believed in inner work) gradually becoming millennialists (in the sure expectation that Christ was coming). There were also the Niagara Conferences and the Student Volunteer Movement (SVM), a branch of the YMCA that organized volunteers for foreign missions under the motto, "The evangelization of this world in this generation."[28] The Bible Institute of Los Angeles (BIOLA), located in Orange County, quickly became a rival of the Moody Bible Institute of Chicago as a shaper of generations of evangelists. The Dallas Theological Seminary was founded in 1924 by James H. Brookes, the follower of Darby who had brought the message to Scofield in prison.[29]

In 1910, with the publication of a compendium of writings from various luminaries who had attended the conferences of the preceding decades, "fundamentalism" became a movement in its own right. A wealthy man named Lyman Stewart donated a series of grants to see *The Fundamentals*:

A Testimony of Truth published over the five years from 1910 to 1915.[30] This manifesto of fundamentalist thought was sent free to some three million Protestant leaders. Covered were major doctrines, such as biblical inerrancy and Jesus's virgin birth, resurrection, divinity, and imminent return. In the words of the influential Reuben Torrey of the BIOLA, *The Fundamentals* was intended as "the ultimate antidote for all infidelity, and the impregnable bulwark against liberalism and false cults."[31] Few of the sixty-four authors whose writings were included could be considered genuine Bible scholars. Most of them simply recapitulated the message that Christ was coming soon and spilled the rest of their ink scourging the doubters.

The World's Christian Fundamentals Association was founded in 1919. Sandeen notes that the descriptive word *fundamentalist* was apparently coined by Curtis Lee Laws in an editorial in the *Watchman-Examiner* dated July 1, 1920. Within a few years, American evangelicals, Pentecostals, and pre- and post-millennialists of all sorts identified themselves as "fundamentalists" and were identified by others as the same. A National Federation of Fundamentalists was formed, drawing from elements in the mainstream Presbyterian and Baptist churches.

BASIC PATTERNS OF
FUNDAMENTALIST THOUGHT

1. Dualistic mythology (good versus evil is continually brought forth and dramatized in the external world).
2. Literalistic thinking (spiritual and physical realities are confused); scriptural inerrancy.
3. Religious and ethnic chauvinism (our religion is the only true one; our names for God and our rituals and services are the only efficacious ones).
4. Xenophobia regarding those who are different (Catholics, communists, capitalists, homosexuals, liberals, Muslims).
5. Paranoid certainty of persecution (the world is filled with evil-

---

doers, be they communists, liberals, or intellectuals).

6. Sexism (women are to be subservient, kept in the home, and restricted mostly to childbearing and homemaking duties; God is portrayed as undeniably male, and all forms of feminism are mistrusted).

7. Historical (eschatological) literalism and urgency; belief in the End Times.

8. Fear and rejection of science and secularism (scripture is the only authority).

Almost as soon as the movement had an identity and a public presence, however, it began to fall apart into contentious factions, each trying to "out-fundamentalize" the other with claims of exclusive authority. Like Milton Rokeach's three Christs discussed in chapter 3, these guys tend not to get along. Whenever liberalism of some kind has tried to sneak in and exert its soothing, compromise-making influence, fundamentalism always managed to fall apart again due to absolutism and authoritarianism. What continued to unite them, however, was alarm about modernism, in particular Darwinism, which by this time had been around for sixty years and was accepted by most "scientifically socialized" folks as the likely truth.

The infamous Scopes trial in 1925 thus could not have been better timed. It became a lightning rod for the thunderclouds of controversy that were building throughout the nation. Pitted against the teaching of science in the public schools was the inerrancy of scripture. The battle was put forward as integral to the very soul of the nation. Also impossible to miss was the desperation of an outdated worldview fighting for its life in an unequal contest.

The witty and acerbic journalist H. L. Mencken had come to Dayton, Tennessee, to cover the trial, and his observations reached the urbane readership of the *Baltimore Sun* and its affiliates. Mencken spared no scorn about the Tennessean "throngs from the hills" who descended on Dayton, describing them as "gaping primates," "yokels," "morons," and "hillbillies." He was equally cruel about their champion, William Jennings Bryant—"his corpulence, his somber face, his anxious glaring gaze." Bryant, though personally a partisan of the common man who publicly supported female suffrage, had been hired to defend the fundamentalist position. His opponent, the urbane Clarence Darrow, retained by the ACLU—which had started the row in the first place by encouraging Scopes to teach evolution—was the unembellished hero of Mencken's stories, a master in court, and a source of terror in the town.

Scopes was found guilty. The fundamentalists cheered and felt vindicated, but the influential Mencken found rural Tennessee justice itself "guilty"—that is, hopelessly out of date—and turned the opinion of the literate country against the judgment. "The rustic judge, a candidate for reelection, has postured before the yokels like a clown in a ten-cent side show, and almost every word he has uttered has been an undisguised appeal to the prejudices. . . . It serves notice on the country that Neanderthal man is organizing in these forlorn backwaters of the land, led by a fanatic, rid of sense and devoid of conscience."[32]

Five days after the trial ended, sad old Bryant, who hadn't said much about the outcome, lay down to take a nap and died.

BILLY GRAHAM AND HIS SUCCESSORS

Billy Graham said it was a "hellfire and brimstone" preacher named Mordecai Ham who brought him to conversion on the eve of his sixteenth birthday in 1934. (He would later cavil about Ham's outspoken and paranoid beliefs about what he believed was an evil conspiracy of world Jewry.) Graham, "by his own account, was transfixed by the preacher's accusing stare, which had so unnerved him on previous evenings that he tried moving into the choir to avoid it, before finally submitting and coming forward to accept Christ."[33]

Graham's conservative religious parents had steered him away from the liberalizing University of North Carolina and urged him instead to attend Bob Jones College in Greenville, South Carolina. "To Graham, the place seemed like a reform school, with rules against speaking to girls, or dallying in hallways, and curfews that were fiercely enforced by the autocratic Jones." Graham became ill and withdrew after one term, but later he recalled Jones's Bible-based talks as "simple, almost juvenile . . . but he had the power of the Lord through him."[34]

It is a tribute to Billy Graham's humanity that he acknowledges his doubts and vacillations along the way. His best friend, Charles Templeton, who went on to Princeton Theological Seminary, went through a disillusionment with fundamentalism in the face of modern religious scholarship. It was in the late 1940s at the Taft Hotel in New York that Templeton opened up his doubts to his friend. Graham, honest and humble enough in person, despite his renowned public charisma, said, "Chuck, look, I haven't a good-enough mind to settle these questions."

Graham had to work through his own doubts before eventually reconfirming his commitment to Christ and, he says, coming to a new level in his faith. Parked squarely in the middle of American evangelism, and probably its most famous spokesperson, Graham was co-opted to come down on the side of the pre-millennialists and state his public affirmation of Armageddon and the Rapture, which he did. But as he grew spiritually and broadened his perspective, he moved "center" (toward the post-millennial position). He earned the scorn and enmity of his former colleagues on the religious right by affirming that he was "working toward world peace." Graham also refused to endorse racial segregation, another theme woven in and out of (especially Southern) conservative religious politics. He also came to the conclusion that hell "was not necessarily a bottomless pit of fire and brimstone, but the everlasting punishment of separation from God." Graham further outraged his detractors by "suggesting that devout believers of other faiths have found ways of 'saying yes to God'" and thus coming dangerously close to ecumenicism.[35]

Billy Graham is now in his eighties and in danger of being replaced by his son Franklin—an eventuality that might undo some of the sense Billy has tried to talk into American Evangelical Christianity. Franklin, reversing the stereotype that the son always veers to a more permissive and liberal style, has tried to push the movement his father founded much further to the religious right. Judaism, Islam, and all the Eastern religions, he says, are

CHAPTER FIVE

false and are distortions of the One Way: "The Bible says every knee under the earth, every knee that's in Hell, one day is going to bow [to Christ] and every tongue is going to confess Him as Lord one day."

Franklin is also not afraid to call a spade a spade when it comes to other religions: "The global war on terrorism, let's give it the name—it's Islamic. That's who we're fighting. We're not fighting the Maoists . . . the Hindus or Buddhists. It's Islamic." As this book is being concluded, Franklin Graham has come forth publicly to suggest a solution to the never-ending battle between Muslims and Jews: "They both should convert to Christianity— that would solve the problem!"

After the Grahams, two of the most influential Christian evangelists of the current time have been Pat Robertson and the late Jerry Falwell, spiritual heads of enormous bodies of opinion and political action—the 700 Club and the Moral Majority, respectively—and together founders of the Christian Coalition. Their biographies are available publicly, and the public version of their activities is available online. Both men are in favor of an armed and militant Israel and of right-wing regimes in Africa and Central and South America. Both are outspoken millennialists. As Jerry Falwell said so plainly: "I believe we are living in that generation that shall not pass away until the Lord comes and the trumpet sounds. That's why I haven't yet bought a cemetery plot. I hate to make a bad investment. I'm looking for the 'uppertaker,' not the undertaker. I'm listening for the sound of the trumpet."[36]

Fundamentalist millennialism is clearly a mischievous belief. (Sam Harris calls it faith-based nihilism.) It uproots people from common sense and established convention. It may render them fearful, hysterical, and highly unrealistic. Their brains get accustomed to thinking in cosmic and religious terms, when they could find plenty to do on the practical level of the world's many problems. True, it sometimes saves people from lives of compulsive selfishness, evil-doing, and addiction. But it leaves them little room to find the good in people different from themselves—or in themselves, for that matter. Sudden conversions based on fear and adrenaline don't seem to have much staying power; nor do they encourage true self-examination or the concept of psychological growth.

THE ROOTS OF ISLAMIC FUNDAMENTALISM

Many of the examples used thus far in this book have emerged from the dualistic religions of ancient times, Judaism and Christianity, or English and American dispensationalism. But how Islamic fundamentalism acquired its own particular and absolutist style is also of interest. I apologize in advance to serious Islamic scholars, for whom this sketch of the religion will seem cursory. My intention is to give the reader a brief introduction to Islam and then cut to the fundamentalist wing. There too I skip over details to get to my thesis, which is that all fundamentalisms have a common structure, socially, mythically, and psychologically. For an in-depth and informed study of Islam, I refer the reader to Karen Armstrong's *A History of God*, which considers Islam in the context of other religions, and *Islam: A Short History*.[1]

Islam found its start amid a seventh-century CE culture of fiercely warring clans and city-states. The Quraysh, the people of Muhammad—Islam's visionary founder and prophet—were a tough Bedouin tribe grimly struggling in their harsh land and through most of their history for mere survival. But by Muhammad's time they had managed to outwit poverty and turn the city of Mecca, Muhammad's birthplace, into a thriving commercial and finance center. As Armstrong points out, "Old tribal values had been eroded by a rampant and ruthless capitalism," and urban, mercantile values were becoming dominant.[2] Muhammad would complain that he found creeping "godlessness" among the merchants, as well as the breakdown of *muruwah*, one of the most important values of the community, according to which each cared for all. A trait associated with manliness, *muruwah* also meant courage, endurance, and dedication to "the people." A man was expected to be courageous and kind and also ready to obey his *sayyid*, or leader, at a moment's notice. Thus the "authority piece," if you will, was already culturally in place.[3]

The last phase of the pre-Islamic period was called *jahiliyah* (the time of ignorance). Pan-Arabic culture at the time had a low self-image, if you will. The Arabs admired the tenacity and even fanaticism of the Jews in a kind of love-hate relationship. But Judaism was an ethnic religion, with its "chosen people" idea and ethnically flavored laws and prescriptions. Christianity, though it started among the Jews, called itself "a light to lighten the gentiles" and reached out to "convert all nations." But it, too, wasn't quite right for the Arabs. They were too busy surviving, and they had their own pantheon of divinities—many of them former great gods of high civilizations now a little fallen, in the way that happens to what we can call god fragments. The Arabs were ripe for something—their own prophet and their own religion.

In the year 610 Muhammad was on a kind of vision quest at Mount Hira, praying and fasting, during the month of Ramadan. "Like many of the Arabs, Muhammad had come to believe that al-Lah, the high God of the ancient Arabian pantheon, whose name simply meant 'the God,' was identical to the high God worshipped by the Jews and the Christians."[4] (*El*, or *al*, simply means "divinity" in Arabic, similar to *el* in Hebrew, as in *el-ohim*, the "shining ones," or angels.) But the merchant was not prepared for a firsthand encounter with one of the holy angels of al-Lah.

Muhammad's vision was terrifying and numinous. He felt himself enveloped by a "devastating divine presence." An angel had suddenly appeared and commanded, "Recite!" The merchant protested that he did not know how to recite; he was no *kahin*, or soothsayer, possessed by *djinn*, spirits.[5]

Later the angel Gabriel appeared to him "in the form of a man with feet astride the horizon." Muhammad apparently described this figure, saying, "Whatever region of the sky I looked, I saw him as before."[6] Overwhelmed, Muhammad crawled into the lap of his wife, Khadija, and said, "Cover me." Khadija not only comforted Muhammad, she praised his moral qualities. They consulted her cousin Waraqa ibn Nawfal, a recently converted Christian and a man learned in the scriptures. Waraqa, after hearing a recital of the vision and the events surrounding it, "had no doubts at all. Muhammad had received a revelation from the God of Moses and the prophets, and had become the divine envoy to the Arabs."[7]

Muhammad's revelations were cruel, rather than gentle. "They tore my soul away from me," he said. He would enter trancelike states, go into cold sweats, and lower his head in grief—a posture, Armstrong mentions, not unknown to great Jewish rabbis when they go into deep prayer. The *surahs*, or verses, of the Qur'an were revealed, it is said, to Muhammad bit by bit over about twenty years. Some say its verses were engraved on the hearts and minds of his listeners, but other traditions say the prophet had them written down. As with the Bible, an authoritative text was only assembled after the prophet's death, by the caliph Uthman, and is called the "Uthmanic recension."

Muhammad was gifted not only with visions but with a certain genius. Armstrong comments that "when he died in 632, he had managed to bring nearly all the tribes of Arabia into a new united community or *ummah*. He had introduced to the Arabs a spirituality that was uniquely suited to their own culture, and which unlocked such reserves of power that within a hundred years they had established their own great empire, which stretched from the Himalayas to the Pyrenees, and founded a unique civilization."[8]

As the religion developed, a *Muslim* became one who was totally surrendered to the Creator. We mentioned Quraysh resistance to the full prostration called for at daily times of prayer. (Who was this crazed prophet, they wondered, who prescribed the same ritual for commoners as lords?) Yet they could not resist the poetry of the recital of the holy book, the Qur'an being extremely beautiful when spoken by native Arabs. The visionary had done as the angel had asked him to do. His "recital" became his holy book. "By approaching the Koran in the right way, Muslims claim that they experience a sense of transcendence, of an ultimate reality and power that lie behind the transient and fleeting phenomena of the mundane world."[9] The very sound of the Qur'an apparently had convincing power. When the young Umar ibn al-Khattab, a virulent opponent of Muhammad, discovered his sister, who had secretly become a convert, listening to the recital of the Qur'an, he knocked her, bleeding, to the ground. In a state of remorse, he picked up the manuscript, and began reading— and was converted on the spot.

Some thought it was a political mistake for the prophet to denounce the worship of an entire pantheon of useful goddesses of childbirth, wisdom, and old age in favor of faith in the one true God, al-Lah. He lost a lot of followers on that one and triggered civil wars. His opponents accused him of atheism. The issue involved a triune Great Goddess figure, the Banat al-Lah, also called "the Daughters of Fate," who resembled the Norns of ancient Greece.

When the nomadic Ionians and Dorians brought their wolf gods and sky gods into the settled goddess-worshipping areas of the Greek Peloponnesus, a similar dilemma ensued. Robert Graves and other scholars have suggested that the "marriages" among gods and goddesses, even the conflict-filled ones, had a compromise-making function. In an alternative mythology, the Babylonian sky god Marduk dismembers the giant goddess Tiamat and uses her parts to make the world. The new religion of Muhammad would become exclusively patriarchal and monotheistic, but at a certain cost. The following is the Islamic statement of faith in the Qur'an:

He is the One God;
God, the Eternal, the Uncaused Cause of all being.
He begets not, and neither is he begotten
and there is nothing that could be compared to him.[10]

The first of the Pillars of Islam, sung from minarets and in mosques all over Islamdom, states: "I bear witness that there is no god but al-Lah and that Muhammad is his Messenger."

Compare the preceding with the opening words of Christianity's Nicene Creed:

I believe in one God, the Father Almighty, Maker of heaven and earth, and of all things visible and invisible.

And in one Lord Jesus Christ, the only-begotten Son of God, begotten of the Father before all worlds; God of God, Light of Light, very God of very God; begotten, not made, being of one substance with the Father, by whom all things were made.

Of course, many of the Christian creeds were accessible at the time of Muhammad, so in terms of resounding affirmations of faith about the unknowable God, they are senior.

There are themes of religious sanity and tolerance in Muhammad's religion that are probably surprising to most Westerners who hear only about Muslim fundamentalism and extremism. Islamic texts do state repeatedly something that Judaic and Christian ones do not—or at least do not seem to state often enough—"that the God they worship cannot be contained by human categories and refuses simplistic definition."[11] Regarding tolerance across religious and cultural boundaries, Armstrong stresses that "Muhammad never asked Jews or Christians to convert to his religion of al-Lah unless they particularly wished to do so, because as *Dhimmis*, Abrahamic people, they had received authentic revelations of their own."

Unfortunately, Muhammad's fair-minded and ecumenical attitude—at least for other People of the Book—was returned to him badly. The Jews became antagonistic. They used to assemble in the mosque "to listen to the stories of the Muslims and laugh and scoff at their religion." They claimed the authentic scriptural knowledge of the stories from the Old Testament, whereas they dismissed the Muslim versions as inaccurate. Armstrong says that "Muhammad's rejection by the Jews was probably the greatest disappointment in his life."[12] In 624, the prophet commanded the Muslims to pray facing Mecca (called the *qibla*), rather than Jerusalem.

The *hejira*, the emigration of Muhammad and his followers to the city of Medina in 622, became the date from which Muslims reckon the religious calendar. Every fit and healthy Muslim has a duty to make a *hajj*, a comparable sacred journey to Mecca, at least once in his lifetime.

After a brief illness, Muhammad died in 632. Almost immediately there were disputes about the succession. Those who chose to follow his close friend Abu Bakr became the Sunnah, or Sunnis. Sunnah means "practice," as in imitating the prophet's wisdom and gentleness, his kindness to women and to animals. Those who chose to follow Ali ibn Abi Talib, Muhammad's cousin and son-in-law, formed the sect of Shi'a Islam. In 680, Muhammad's grandson was killed by the Ummayad Caliph Yazid in a massacre that is still mourned in Islam. In Shi'a, Ali is named as the first Imam, or leader, of the *ummah*, the community of believers.

The *hadith* are traditions related to the words or deeds of the prophet from various sources, and differing versions of it are venerated by different groups, along with the Qur'an. Twelver Shi'ites, as they are called, venerate the twelve descendants of Ali through Husayn, until the last Imam went into hiding in 939. (Another group, called the Seveners, believed the seventh Imam was the last.) For the Twelvers, the twelfth Imam will resurface in time as a messiah, the Mahdi, and inaugurate a golden age. Millennialist Islamics, like their Christian counterparts, can be divided into pre- and post-millennialists, based on the role of the Mahdi. (With Iran recently under threat of conflict with the United States, millennialism has broken out again in that country, and there is talk of the Mahdi.)

At times during its historical trajectory, Islam was clearly an evangelical religion. At other times, evangelism was forbidden. Nonetheless, spread it did, along with Arab hegemony, throughout the Middle East and up into Persia (modern Iran), north and west into Turkey, and westward across North Africa. By the year 750, under the Ummayad Caliphate, Islam and Arab culture stretched westward into Spain and eastward as far as Afghanistan. In the early days especially, Christians and Jews were granted liberty and considered *dhimmis*, protected minorities.

Shi'ites have been regarded as the fundamentalist wing of Islam, but they were not always so, having contributed many influential philosophers and rationalists to the history of the religion. At the present time, Shi'a Islam is found largely in Iran, with a minority in Iraq, and Sunni forms predominate in Egypt, Iraq, and Saudi Arabia. The modern theocracy in Iran started in the late 1970s, after the deposing of the Shah and the grand coup of the ayatollahs. The Iran-Iraq war could be considered a Shi'a versus Sunni war, in which the infamous Saddam Hussein was a "good guy" for America, representing liberalism and modernism among Muslims, fighting against the far more fundamentalist regime in Iran.

The ayatollahs, having instituted a repressive type of *shari'a* (Islamic religious law) in Iran, deplored the promiscuous lifestyle and loose values found in "modern" countries and outspokenly called America and Israel "the Great Satan." The writings of the modern Ayatollah Khomeini recall the thirteen-hundred-year-old slight by the Jews and Muhammad's decision to shift his fledgling faith's holy city from Jerusalem to Mecca. "Since the Jews of Bani Qurayzza were a troublesome group," he says, "causing corruption in Muslim society and damaging Islam and the Islamic state, the Most Noble Messenger (Muhammad) eliminated them."[13] The Ayatollah apparently relied on this ancient event to determine the Shiite posture in regard to Israel and the Jewish cause.

According to strict Shi'a Islam, the ideal form of government is a theocracy, which can only be brought about by careful adherence to the laws revealed to Muhammad by al-Lah. A woman's natural role is as wife, housekeeper, and mother. Women are to be separated where possible from men because of female sexuality's powerful effect on men. In *Pious Passion*, Martin Riesebrodt comments that Shi'a maintains an essentially similar posture to New England Puritanism.

ISLAM'S NEGLECTED DUTY

Muhammad ibn Abd al-Wahhab founded the Wahhabi movement in the mid eighteenth century. Even though it is a Sunni form, it insisted on a Shi'a-like "return" to tradition—although according to some scholars of Islam, the doctrine he promoted was new. Wahhab successfully converted the illiterate Bedouins living in the desert of Nejd, including Muhammad Ibn Sa'ud, the leader of a gang of raiders, to his version of Islam. Wahhab and Sa'ud agreed to cooperate: Sa'ud would be the *emir*, the political leader, while Wahhab would be the *sheikh*, the religious leader. Wahhab issued a religious decree, a *fatwa*, that all non-Wahhabis were infidels. Critics say this gave Ibn Sa'ud the cloak of religious legitimacy he needed to persecute innocent people.[14]

For the first time, writes Jessica Stern, *jihad*, holy war, was proclaimed against other Muslims. Their goal was nothing less than to replace orthodox Islam with their puritanical doctrine. For Wahhabis as for conservative Shi'as, *shari'a*, Islamic law, is the proper governance of the state.[15] However, they reject the tradition said to come from the prophet himself, that war is a *lesser* form of *jihad*.

The intellectual architect of modern extremist fundamentalism, however, was Sayyid Qutb. An Egyptian schoolteacher of puritanical temperament, Qutb came to the United States in 1948 to study. During his visit the state of Israel was founded, and he observed, unfortunately, what he felt was international indifference to the fate of thousands of Palestinians, as the Americans and British put their "Zionism project" in place. He also saw what he described as "evil and fanatic racial discrimination" in the United States—not to mention what he judged licentiousness among American women.

In 1951, Qutb returned to Egypt, where he became known, particularly through his writings, for religious social criticism. Not surprisingly, his considered opinion of life in the United States was that it was culturally shallow, promiscuous, and hypocritical. Qutb was also critical of Arab leaders, whom he described as "arrogant, and corrupt."[16] He said it would be legitimate to wage a *jihad* against them—which led to many murders in subsequent decades. Qutb was imprisoned in Egypt, tortured, and, in 1966, executed. In revenge for his death, however, an offshoot of the Muslim Brotherhood, to which he belonged, murdered Egyptian president Anwar Sadat.

In Qutb's view, *jihad* is a duty of every Muslim, which unfortunately has been neglected throughout much of Islam's history. That is, *you are not really Islamic if you leave holy war out of your life.* The Islamic terrorist associations Hamas, Hezbollah, and al-Qaeda, among others, owe ideological inspiration to Qutb. And his death in Egypt strengthened the resolve of the Muslim Brotherhood.

Muhammad had brought a measure of order to a disorganized world, uniting clans and culture groups. Because of his influence, most Muslims are clean, sober, socially productive folk. The Sunni group spread far wider than Shi'a did. Saudi Arabia is Sunni, but Wahhabist, but the radical Sunni form endeavors to "out-fundamentalize" the Shiites.

The question we are leading to is: How do some sectors of Islam not only turn fundamentalist but embrace the virulent forms that foster extremism and terrorism? While not dismissing the social and economic factors that contribute to the problems of religious fanaticism, for the sake of this narrative I would say it happens when groups try to "out-fundamentalize" each other. When a concretized sacred narrative is the measuring stick you have for reality, some things qualify as clearly holy, others not. When fundamentalists, whether Islamic or Christian, fight among themselves, it is usually over interpretations of the holy text. Since the text itself is infallible, the power struggle—for that it surely is—is over who conforms best to their own conservative interpretation of the scripture and does not deviate from the divinely-decreed rules of behavior.

The Wahhabists, the Shiites, the Muslim Brotherhood—all of them claim the others have gone soft. This is an extremely useful strategy, along with the outright declaration that the other is Satan, because whoever uses it now has a premium on the truth. Among the babble of the voices of the believers, theirs is closest to the source of power. For them, the chosen people, the elect, there are no more errors. This is an extremely important issue, because the fundamentalist's trick—a sleight of mind, if you will—is to point with disgust to the many shortcomings of the world and compare it to the perfection that is God's alone. In the monolithically mythologized point of view, the creation is flawed, but the Creator is not.

As fundamentalists thus try to out-fundamentalize each other, the inevitable path seems to be social violence. In chapter 3, we saw this principle enacted in the case of the Branch Davidians. Any act, however abhorrent by general human standards or universal ethical principles, may be justified by appealing to the all-powerful God. And if I stay loyal to my vision of the perfect, God's perfection leeches into me, despite my flawed humanity. This idea of the infallible holiness of your own cause is combined with xenophobia and paranoia and made a mental habit, first by practicing it on your own people. Then, when there is a chance to project it on a larger scale—for instance, across an ocean and onto another people with a different language, religion, and culture—the result can be genocidal. We have not just what Samuel Huntington called a "clash of civilizations" but something more resembling a nuclear reactor—a bomb, only one in slow motion. Social imperfections, economic frustrations, and the daily grind of living all fuel the smoldering rage into an inflammation that incites people to radical actions.

Many Muslims do not agree with the extremist approaches of their coreligionists and prefer to hold their religion in a live-and-let-live fashion.[17] Up until the disastrous American and British intervention in Iraq, liberal voices within Islam seemed to be winning out in the global picture. Now many who were previously moderates are agreeing with the jihadists. Given the turbulence and privation in their own world, Islamic fundamentalists clearly have social causes to which they can point to justify extremism. Now added to that is the reckless violence enacted on them by an imperialist power.

THE SATANIC VERSES

The title of Salman Rushdie's internationally acclaimed 1988 novel, *The Satanic Verses*, comes from an incident in the life of Muhammad that is significant for our discussion.[18] The pagan goddesses he had been preaching against, al-Lat, al-Uzza, and Manat, triple goddesses of the harvest, fertility, and childbirth, had women followers. Many of these women—not to mention their children and families—were attracted to the prophet's teachings but could not bring themselves to part from their original religion.

Muhammad had been meditating on this quandary, and then he thought it was God who put into his mind these words: "These are the high-flying cranes; verily their intercession is accepted with approval."[19] When that verdict, which meant the goddess religions were no longer interdicted, reached the ears of the Quraysh, there was great rejoicing. The account, documented in the work of the Muslim historian and interpreter of the Qur'an al-Tabari (d. 923), then says that the angel Gabriel came to Muhammad and rebuked him: "Muhammad, what have you done?" It seems that the words had not been from God but were delivered by the slithery, interposed voice of Satan. Then God, it is said, "removed the words which Satan had cast on his tongue," and the conflict between the pre-Islamic goddesses and al-Lah resumed, as did the persecution on both sides.

Thus the prophet withdrew from the Qur'an those verses "prompted by Satan" that would basically have allowed a religion of the women to coexist alongside, or even within, Islam. Sadik al-Azm mentions that the three goddesses, the "high flying cranes" (or angels) were also called daughters of al-Lah and addressed in sacred chants that the prophet probably knew by heart from childhood. It is quite clear, also, that though the voices heard were ostensibly those of a demon and then an angel, the conflict was also within the bosom of the prophet. In one fell swoop, Islam was pushed in a firmly male-oriented direction; and goddess worship and any role for females, even as demi-goddesses or angels, in the community of the holy was swept from the table, as was the art of pragmatic compromise. A subtext was that Satan is powerful and his influence found everywhere, so much so that he could confuse even the prophet himself. Thus the issues contained in the original incident of the Satanic Verses are loaded ones culturally and mythologically.

Thus we are led to the present time and the *fatwa* placed on a writer of modern fiction, and a good one at that, who dared to use a subject from his own religion as an inspiration for his art. The book is actually remarkably free of condemnations of Islam or other direct assaults on the religion. The Ayatollah's problem seems to be that Rushdie drew material from an "inviolable" sacred source for a manifestly secular narrative. Khomeini's death sentence of Rushdie reads:

67/11/25 (Feb. 14, 1989) Announcement on the publication of the apostasian book: *Satanic Verses*: In the name of God Almighty; there is only one God, to whom we shall all return; I would like to inform all the intrepid Muslims in the world that the author of the book entitled *The Satanic Verses* which has been compiled, printed and published against Islam, the Prophet and the Koran, as well as those publishers who were aware of its contents, have been sentenced to death. I call on all zealous Muslims to execute them quickly wherever they find them, so that no one will dare to insult the Islamic sanctions. Whoever is killed on this path will be regarded as a martyr, God willing. In addition anyone who has access to the author of the book, but does not possess the power to execute him, should refer him to the people so that he may be punished for his actions. May God's blessing be on you all (Ruhollah Al-Musavi Al-Khomeini).[20]

The Western world woke up a little that year to the reality of fundamentalist Islam and the very idea of such things as *fatwas*.[21] Rushdie, in 1990, agreed to a kind of public apology. He said he embraced the fundamental tenets of Islam, almost apologized for the misunderstanding, and agreed to cancel the paperback edition. Rushdie's murderous critics, though, did nothing to withdraw or modify the death sentence, and continued their efforts, while he continued to stay in hiding.

Finally, in December of 1991, he recanted his recantation at Columbia University, saying that though reconciliation had long been proffered, the other side would not budge. A moving letter by Rushdie to Taslima Nasreen, the Bangladeshi physician, author, and feminist also under a death sentence by Islamic fundamentalists, reveals how Rushdie felt about his own plight:

> How sad it must be to believe in a God of blood! What an Islam they have made, these apostles of death, and how important it is to have the courage to dissent from it. . . . Perhaps in your darkest moments you will feel you did something wrong—that those demanding your death may have a point. This, of all your goblins, you must exorcise first. You have done nothing wrong. The wrong is committed by others against you. You have done nothing wrong, and I am sure that one day you will be free.[22]

The fear and hatred of Islam by non-Islamics reached a zenith after the *fatwa*. People wondered why Khomeini would be so bloodthirsty and judgmental. But it is true that just eight months earlier, Khomeini had had to agree to a humiliating cease-fire in the eight-year war with Iraq, in which Sunni fought Shiite in a bloody mutual immolation. It was August of 1990 that Hussein marched his formidable armies into Kuwait, precipitating the First Gulf War.

"Rushdie," writes Sadik al-Azm, an apologist, "did no more in his novel than take Tabari's entire story [from the *hadith*] and use it in the manner typical of modernist novelists, satirists and artists in general, [It was] first class raw material for dramatization, personification, fictionalization, and so on. [He just tried to make it] . . . relevant to the drift of his times, and in the end contribute to the formation of a new and more appropriate kind of sensibility, spirituality and even religiosity."[23] It is doubtful that Khomeini and others who supported the *fatwa* really bothered to work out the details from the original story and compare it to Rushdie's handling of the plot. The author had simply used a sacred story relating to the life of the prophet, something the Islamic conservatives thought was off-limits to literature—especially modern literature of the type Rushdie was trying to create.

There was an analogous—but not so lethal—response in Anglican England to D. H. Lawrence's short story "The Man Who Died," a fictional narrative of Jesus surviving the crucifixion and finding an earthy, sensual love in the arms of Mary Magdalene. Similar fundamentalist responses greeted Nikos Kazantzakis's *The Last Temptation of Christ,* which first appeared as a novel and then was made into a film—both of which were highly controversial. The film was banned in Rutland, Vermont, as well as other places.

Critics of the *Satanic Verses* affair have speculated that while the Ayatollah's death sentence did more to promote sales of the book than any favorable literary review, the Islamic world could have used the occasion in a very different way: as an opportunity to celebrate an Islamic writer of world-class talent and make the religion itself more accessible and palatable to Westerners. More and more people might have read the Qur'an or searched there for the original story. A studied tolerance could have promoted the idea that Islam was not only a religious player on the world stage but also a source of well-wrought and sophisticated art.

Instead, the response indicates the toxic state to which patriarchal absolutism can descend after a few centuries, if not mediated by a spirit of compromise. Perhaps the ayatollahs did not want the visionary nature of Muhammad's choice exposed, or the idea that the prophet could be "fooled" or could change his mind to get too much press. It may be left to posterity to determine whether Islamic theology could use some "high-flying cranes"—feminine faces of the divine—to mitigate its potent masculine god-image.

In February 1989, over one hundred intellectuals from Arab and Muslim countries demonstrated against the *fatwa* in the Human Rights Square in Paris, stating that no blasphemy could do the damage to Islam that Khomeini's decree had done—in effect, before the eyes of the world, portraying that most Muslims were potential assassins. It would be appropriate here to say that most Sunnis are not Wahhabists, nor are most Shi'ites fundamentalists. In fact, it is among the Shi'ites that the Ismaelian Gnosis is found. It is one of the most liberal, humanitarian, and devotional branches of Islam, engaged with the *ta'wil*, called in Western philosophy the *Mundus Imaginalis*—the bright world of mythic forms and divine beings that hovers just a veil or so away.[24] And the Shi'ite Sufis, along with the Sunnis and non-Islamic civilizations, have all been inspired by the great thirteenth-century mystical poet, Jalalludin Rumi, who has given world spiritual culture some of its most sublime insights.[25]

Contrarily to the mystic vision, the fundamentalist mind thinks Satan is whispering everywhere. Its considerable zeal and creativity feed its paranoia, and the world becomes sibilant with intrigues and malign plots. And there is a rather amazing symmetry between Islamic fundamentalists and our dispensationalist friends in America when it comes to intolerance, extreme judgmentalism, and the projection of evil. You could say they deserve each other. Is there poetic justice in two bands of patriarchal fanatics facing off, unconsciously mirroring each other's worst flaws? We could be amused, but for the fear of what may happen to the rest of us while the blind patriarchal giants "duke it out" on the world stage.

This kind of inflated conflict has empowered the world's atheistic partisans to seek stage time and counsel us to avoid any and all dangerous thinking about God, since it seems to get humanity into so much trouble. Responding to the accusation that religion has started more wars than any other force in history, professor of religion Huston Smith has countered that, while religion has been implicated in wars, there are many other causes as well, economics and politics being two major cofactors. Some of recent history's most horrendous genocides and social persecutions have been carried out by secularists and atheists, namely, the purges of the Stalin era, China's genocide of religious Tibet, and the excesses of the Pol Pot regime in Cambodia.[26]

The next chapter notes that fundamentalism is not limited to theologies but can work its mischief in the secular realm as well. Thus it is not simply the volatile and intoxicating idea of God that is the culprit, but a certain psychological condition of trying to know and label everything, whatever the philosophy or cosmology, and getting stuck in and limited by our own categories of thought.

SECULAR FUNDAMENTALISM

Modern society has merely replaced one orthodoxy (religion) with another one (secular scientism).

—George Marsden, *Fundamentalism and American Culture*

T he question has probably already occurred to the thoughtful reader: Does the fundamentalist habit of mind ever occur separately from religion? In this chapter, I respond with an unequivocal yes.

It's true that religion and fundamentalism are old friends; they may have been together since the beginning of human conceptualizing, when the gods gave their decrees and humans obeyed, or (unthinkably) disobeyed. We know that in shamanic and preliterate societies there were penalties, even death or exile, for breaking taboos concerning sacred places or objects, eating certain animals, coming in contact with a menstruating woman, touching a corpse, and so on. These ritual prohibitions and observances, together with the myths that explain them, later became the basic patterns of formal religions: the sacredness or forbiddenness of certain foods, the holiness or "uncleanness" of certain objects, animals, or people.

Such associations are viscerally as well as cognitively instilled into the participants. We have looked at how the human nervous system collaborates in our religious ideas and attitudes, loading them with powerful emotional charge. The specifics of a cultural or religious conditioning fit into neurological patterns that are nonspecific in nature. This is why we find certain *generic attitudes*—veneration, aversion, submission to authority, and hierarchy—accompanying all religious systems, regardless of particulars.

These same generic attitudes are operative when *any* kind of belief or reality system, regardless of content, enlarges to encompass "everything" and thus moves into a kind of "sacred modality." At its extreme as seen in an individual, this tendency is called "megalomania," and its psychological presence is found in adolescents and academics alike, as well as in televangelists and heads of state. I have also touched on the neurobiology of certitude. Especially when the dopamine neurotransmitter system is involved, along with certain limbic circuits, the person is convinced that he not only knows everything worth knowing, he is also completely right in his perceptions—an attitude sometimes called "righteousness" that is by no means the exclusive privilege of Old Testament prophets.

In this way, virtually any system of thought can become fundamentalist. Modern political and economic theories become sacred just as readily as religious beliefs. Consider all the "isms" of modern thought: Marxism, social Darwinism, and movements within science such as logical positivism and behaviorism. We find in them the same simplistic absolutisms, dualistic thought patterns, authority structures, hierarchies, and even persecutions of heretics as in religion. As historian George Marsden states in the quote that begins this chapter, modern society, for all its claims to secularism, has merely replaced the orthodoxy of religion with the orthodoxy of scientific secularism.[1]

Like theology, secularist science pretends to be a total account of what is real. Like theology, it postulates laws and has rules and procedures (that function like rituals) administered by synods of (often male) dignitaries. We find orthodoxies in politics, in scientific and professional associations, and in universities. Bitter struggles and excommunications take place in these organizations over which school of thought shall prevail, and careers are made or broken on the grinding wheels of these orthodoxies.

The intensity of these conflicts, present everywhere, shows that the mythic template, with its built-in dogmas and polarities, is universal. The power of myth revealed by Campbell thus extends far beyond those things normally recognized as mythic. It is interwoven into the very reality systems through which we perceive and learn about the world.

We build our reality systems systematically as a series of logical models that Piaget called "schemata." An accumulation of schemata, say David Feinstein and Stanley Krippner, is on its way to becoming a *personal myth*, a more comprehensive psychological style of thinking and behavior.[2] In science, what Thomas Kuhn calls "paradigms" work similarly. Paradigms are practical theories that inform thought and shape research—hypothetical constructs about how to think and solve problems in a given field of science.

Science as a method—what we might call pure science—has no pretense of being a belief system or asking for any kind of faith other than in the empirical process itself. Science works by formulating hypotheses and putting them to experimental proof. Hypotheses are usually limited to a specific area; they are not sweeping generalizations about reality. But paradigms held by individuals work unconsciously as well as consciously. In fact, in the dark, fertile unconscious, both myths and paradigms shapeshift. The larger the paradigm's explanatory reach, and the more unconsciously it is held, the more likely it is to become inflated. In this way, scientific beliefs morph into a simulacrum of religious ones.

The "religious" version of science, called *scientism*, puts itself forth as a type of myth: an explanation of everything. In religion, the supreme realities are spiritual. In scientism, they are material; in fact, anything not directly observable may be dismissed. Scientism mocks anything that hasn't been validated by its rituals or approved by its prelates and publications, thus setting up its own kind of dualism.

Once we understand that any system of thought can become fundamentalist—and aren't threatened by it—we can look at myth-like dynamics at work in all sorts of nonreligious places. This chapter begins with a generic essay on science in some of its more fundamentalist manifestations. Thereafter it explores the fundamentalist mentality as it shows up in medicine, psychotherapy, New Age thought, and even skepticism.

SCIENTIFIC FUNDAMENTALISM

Institutions are ambiguous. They bring out the bad in people along with the good; I don't know any institution, religious or otherwise, that is pretty, through and through.

—Huston Smith, *The Way Things Are*

If both science and religion are reality-determining systems, the question arises: Which reality is true? A 2006 *Time* magazine article, "God vs. Science," called the war between science and religion "a caged death match"—strong language in a rather moderate publication.[3] The current "atheist literary wave" is at the forefront of secularism's reaction, not only to strident religious fundamentalism but also to its complacent cousin, conventional religiosity. The moderate position is still the major religious form in America. But the critics say the whole religious mindset, with its tacit acceptance of supernatural authority, has paved the way for the fanatics. Even the titles are outspoken: *The God Delusion* by Oxford biologist Richard Dawkins, *The End of Faith* by graduate student Sam Harris, and *Breaking the Spell* by Daniel Dennett are three best-seller examples. *God: A Failed Hypothesis*, by physicist/astronomer Victor Stenger, as well as a new condensation of unpublished lectures by spiritually skeptical astrophysicist Carl Sagan, titled *The Varieties of Scientific Experience*, have been released even as this book is in production.

Procrustes was a legendary Greek hotel keeper who had only one bed for guests. If they were too short to fit the bed, he stretched them out; if they were too long, he would cut off whatever didn't fit. Scientism is a Procrustean epistemology that wants to make everything fit its own template. The problem lies in the psychological attitude, both rigid and grandiose, that wants answers. When an answer isn't available, this mindset is willing to fill one in based on knowledge at hand and declare it true, rather than stand with open curiosity before what remains a mystery—as Einstein seemed to do until the end of his days. In my experience, most scientistic thinkers rely on primitive versions of Cartesian and Newtonian thinking and have yet to appreciate the astonishing emptiness and paradoxicality of the universe revealed by post-quantum physics. They also seem to have missed the *observer effect*, a concept according to which the presence and position of the observer must be taken into account in any observation of a process.

Sadly, much of mainstream Western thinking has come to align itself with scientism. Huston Smith, author and former professor of religion at MIT, explains how this happened: "We simply slid into assuming that the most reliable viewfinder available to our human lot is the scientistic one that edits out spiritual truths, in the way X-ray films omit the beauty of faces."[4] The temples of scientism are the universities, for the most part, where knowledge is compartmentalized into disciplines and departments and subjected to rigorous scrutiny for agreement with the current canon. By their "dry as dust" analysis, says Smith, they are killing the spirit.

For the secular scientistic thinker, it's clear that God didn't create man, man created God. This being the case, humanity is making itself crazy trying to please something it made up. Yet the angriest secularists also seem to be the most fundamentalistic materialists, convinced that matter, blundering around in random or mechanical (Newtonian) movements, is about all there is. Their new secular religion, unconsciously held, has now replaced all previous forms. But therein lies the hubris. It is not always wise to reject the ideas of your ancestors, even if they seem absolute or limited to us now.

In scientism we find all the telltale signs of fundamentalism: simplistic ideas held with strong emotional conviction and offered as the only way to see the universe. And such is the penchant for dualism in the fundamentalist way of thinking that the position immediately invokes its opposite, resulting in ferociously constellated points of view. (The anger on both sides tells us the limbic system is involved.) When Senator Ted Kennedy, a suitable exponent of secularism and modern thinking, publicly debated televangelist Jerry Falwell, a suitable spokesman for the conservative religious right, the debate was referred to as "mutual diatribe" to the point of exhaustion, with no resolution in sight. This debate can be considered the elemental conflict of our time.

In his compelling book *Alternate Science*, Richard Milton offers fine examples of scientific fundamentalism at work through the centuries since the European Enlightenment. One, strangely enough, concerns meteors. For generations, meteors had been collected for their sometimes unusual characteristics, distinct from those of earth rocks. The story was passed down since medieval times that these objects had "fallen out of the sky." In the post-Enlightenment atmosphere of the late eighteenth century, which prided itself on its scientific outlook, the idea was laughed at. Such is the power of scientific skepticism that all over Europe many fine meteors were thrown onto rubbish heaps like any old stones. (Thus in most European museums there are no meteors collected earlier than 1790.) No less a person than Antoine Lavoisier, regarded as the father of modern chemistry, said to his fellow academicians: "Stones cannot fall from the sky, because there are no stones in the sky!"[5] But the scientific fundamentalism of his statement was disproved by a small meteor shower in L'Aigle, France that dropped more than two thousand rocks out of the empty sky onto the village and surrounding area.

The reaction to the discovery of electricity gives us another example of scientific fundamentalism. Milton writes: "When the nineteenth century's greatest experimental physicist, Michael Faraday, announced that he had found a new source of energy simply by moving a magnet in a coil of wire, many educated people found the claim impossible to believe and looked on the young man as a charlatan. Magnetism was invisible; how could the invisible generate electricity, as in the generator, or move matter, as in the electric motor? Faraday responded with perhaps the most memorable words ever uttered by a scientist: 'Nothing is too wonderful to be true, if it be consistent with the laws of nature.'"[6]

And here's another example: The Wright brothers struggled from 1903 to 1908 to get the public to accept that they were flying heavier-than-air craft. Even though they had demonstrated their machines before witnesses many times, their claims were dismissed by the *New York Herald*, *Scientific American*, and U. S. Army. Simon Newcomb, professor of mathematics and astronomy at Johns Hopkins, published an article showing scientifically that powered human flight is impossible. It wasn't until Theodore Roosevelt gave the Wright brothers a chance—and was rewarded by the sight of Orville circling his craft over Huffman Field near Dayton, Ohio—that the scientific community came around. Within a decade, the Army was using aircraft for espionage and combat in World War I.

The inventory of scientistic dogmas at work ranges from popular derision at Edison's electric light—people claimed it was impossible even as Edison was lighting up several blocks of a New Jersey town—to learned scientists declaring Joseph Niepce's first photograph a fraud. They also dismissed the value of Marconi's first wireless transmissions (some said that, being invisible, the phenomenon didn't exist; others said that even if it did exist, it had no practical application). About these revolutionary scientific contributions Milton comments: "All were threshold phenomena initially. Equally these embryonic phenomena are feeble and vulnerable to early extinction, just as living embryos are precarious and defenseless. The nailed boot of scientific derision alone may be enough to trample the life out of such delicate seedlings."[7]

I add two personal stories here. At Columbia University in the 1960s, the psychology department was dominated by B. F. Skinner's school of behaviorism, which tried to encompass the entire complex and chaotic subject of human behavior in a model based on operant conditioning. Students were not only given a fresh experimental rat or pigeon each semester, they ate and slept concepts like contingent reinforcement, extinction, generalization, and discrimination. Skinner's *Verbal Behavior* was the accepted scripture. As a maverick scholar I was doing a private study on psycholinguistics and had been reading Noam Chomsky and his concept of generative grammar in language acquisition. Children learn language not just through "reinforcement history" but also through a correspondence between social signals and an internal, changing set of rules innate to them. Put on the behaviorist hat and you could see one set of principles at work; put on the cognitive, Chomskian hat, and another set came into play. My well-researched and, in retrospect, rather thoughtful paper on the topic earned a C, whereas much simpler Skinnerian party-line papers got A's.

The other event occurred many years later, after I had moved to the Hudson Valley and begun teaching psychology. A respected local astronomer had built a large reflector telescope and had a hilltop observatory to which he would invite small groups. I had enjoyed an evening of star-watching with him and, a month or two later, mentioned it to astrologer Eleanor Bach. Eleanor, working with a Princeton astronomer, had set up an ephemeris of the asteroid belt and regarded the asteroids as a key to the "fragmented feminine image" of our time. I was so impressed by her technical knowledge of the planets that I invited her to come to the observatory at the next opportunity for stargazing. But when the two star lovers met, the astronomer pulled himself up to his full height (he was fairly short) and his eyes crackled like the Grand Inquisitor's. He launched into a complete denunciation of anyone foolish enough to believe in astrology, while the astrologer continued to smile beatifically, and the other guests snickered at the scientific fundamentalism of their astronomer friend.

MEDICAL FUNDAMENTALISM

Medicine is supposed to be a handmaiden of science, and over the centuries the two have often traveled together. Yet in some ways the history of medicine shows it to be closer kin to myth than to science. In prehistoric times, illness was understood to be caused by evil spirits, or the introjection of magical objects that had been sent by sorcerers and that the shaman-healer would then "suck out" as part of the cure. In ancient Greece, even at the time of the Iliad (1100 BCE) it was believed that merely praying to the "divine physician" Aesclepius or sleeping in his temple could bring a cure in the form of a healing dream.

It was the fifth-century BCE philosopher Empedocles who ultimately set the course of Western medicine for the next thousand years. His theory that the entire world could be resolved to four elements—earth, water, air, and fire—led early physicians to identify and base medical theory on four "humors" in the human body: *sanguine, phlegmatic, choleric,* and *melancholic.* For Hippocrates, a contemporary of Empedocles and famous as the "father of modern medicine," medicine was largely removed from the realm of magic and the supernatural, becoming a "science" based on the humoral theory and other theories of the time that spanned physics and biology. Hippocrates also believed in systematic diagnosis and the importance of ethics in medical practice, but his successors held to the simplicity of the humoral theory. (An exception was Asclepiades of Bithynia, who rejected the humoral theory and urged Asclepian-style cures such as diet, hygiene, and massage.)

Galen, a Greek physician who came to Rome in 164 CE, is regarded as the founder of experimental physiology, based on his dissections of apes and pigs. (Human dissection was taboo and would remain so until the High Renaissance, when Andreas Vesalius of Padua published the first accurate anatomies, which showed where Galen was wrong.) Though he was empirical in the matter of dissection, Galen was also a "humoral fundamentalist." As one author wrote, "A voluminous writer who stated his views forcibly and with confidence, Galen remained for centuries the undisputed authority from whom no one dared to differ."[8] Described by another author as "Hippocrates' great, systematizing heir," Galen's words "were regarded as beyond dispute or question, like church dogma. So blinding was the light of Galen's authority that medieval anatomists were unable to see the contours of the organs that lay before them. The liver, they asserted, against all the evidences of their senses, did indeed have the five lobes that Galen attributed to it"—whereas in fact the liver has four.[9] Thus, medical authority occluded physicians' direct perception of the structure of organs they were examining.

It was the sixteenth-century physician Paracelsus, born Theophrastus Bombastus von Hohenheim, who finally broke the grip of Galen's authority. One of the most famous and flamboyant men of his time, he publicly burned the works of Galen. This of course infuriated the medical establishment, for whom Galen was scarcely less holy than the Bible. Paracelsus spoke out against the widespread practice of "bleeding" patients to relieve toxic humors. It would take medicine several more generations to recognize how truly dangerous this practice was, since often the leeches used to bleed one patient had just been used on another infected person (and bacteria don't need official recognition to work their many kinds of mischief).

Though proclaiming himself a religious man, Paracelsus disagreed with the long-standing Christian view of illness as a punishment for sin. In his cosmology, God's providence permeated nature and had seeded nature with healing secrets—remedies—as recompense for the many maladies humans had to endure. Following a principle called the *doctrine of signatures*, physicians could detect the *signature* of a providential God in all manner of natural objects—for instance, a plant remedy for kidney problems might have kidney-shaped leaves. A few centuries later, a similar philosophy would be the basis for Samuel Hahnemann's homeopathy theory. Modern medicine would reject Paracelsus's philosophy of signatures, while accepting his use of synthesized chemicals as medicines.

It was a contemporary of Paracelsus, Girolamo Frascatoro, who first proposed the infectious theory of disease. His great work, *De Contagione*, was published in 1546. In particular, Frascatoro was convinced that the ravages of syphilis were due not to problems of the humors but to a kind of "seed" transmitted between people. The medical academies, however, could not countenance the idea of invisible little agents of disease spread by contact. As happens with many fundamentalisms, people stuck with what they knew. Though over the next few centuries a number of physicians, among them Kirschner, Virel, and Pedi, advanced the same idea, it was still rejected by the academies of medicine because it went against dogma.[10] Thus when Louis Pasteur first proposed his microbe theory of disease in the nineteenth century, he too was laughed at—until, through experiment after experiment, he showed the world how fermentation, particularly in dairy products, was due to bacterial cultures. Pasteur eventually developed the homeopathic "like cures like" idea into the principle of immunization. He discovered the vaccine for the deadly disease anthrax, paving the way for the entire modern science of vaccination. The microbe theory has of course now become the standard for Western medicine, against which all alternative theories are measured and deemed acceptable or "heresies."

Less famous but equally influential in understanding infection was the nineteenth-century Hungarian physician Ignaz Philipp Semmelweis, called "the savior of mothers." Women who gave birth in hospitals attended by doctors, rather than at home under the care of midwives, had mortality rates as high as 25 and 30 percent, often dying of horrible infections. This is because the doctors were going from treating infectious wounds, amputating gangrenous limbs, or performing autopsies right to the birthing room— *without washing their hands.*[11]

The death of a physician friend of Semmelweis's from a puerperal infection, following his examination of a woman who subsequently died of the same infection, gave support to the innovative physician's reasoning. "He concluded that the medical students who came directly from the dissecting room to the maternity ward carried the infection from mothers who had died of the disease to healthy mothers. He ordered the students to wash their hands in a solution of chlorinated lime before each examination."[12] The idea was not popular, and Semmelweis's professional colleagues scoffed at him. In 1849, he was dropped from his post at the clinic and threatened with professional disgrace. However, when Semmelweis's procedures were followed and the results were tracked in true scientific style, mortality rates dropped from 18 percent to less than 2 percent.

In 1861 Semmelweis published his principal medical work, on etiology, stressing the need for antiseptic procedures among physicians, surgeons, and nurses to prevent disease. But the weight of authority still stood against his teachings. A conference of German physicians and natural scientists, including the famous pathologist Rudolf Virchow, rejected his doctrine. (Virchow, one of the proponents of modern cell theory, was clearly an advanced and innovative thinker in other areas.) The years of controversy gradually undermined Semmelweis's spirit. In 1865 he suffered a breakdown and was taken to a mental hospital, where he died shortly after.[13]

In Semmelweis's case, hidebound medical orthodoxy and the "hobnailed boots of derision" brought the life of a brilliant contributor to a tragic end. Just a few years after his death, his ideas were universally accepted. Joseph Lister, the father of modern antisepsis, hailed Semmelweis publicly for his work: "I think with great admiration of him and his achievement."[14] Unfortunately, the great reversal of stubborn medical opinion came too late for Semmelweis to enjoy. No wonder he went crazy—he had a simple solution to a lethal problem, and he couldn't get a bunch of medical fundamentalists, committed to the accepted view despite the evidence, just to wash their hands.

By the early 1900s, Pasteur, Semmelweis, and Lister had prevailed. Hygiene was becoming ritualized and routine, and microbe theory had become the new orthodoxy. In a classic instance of scientism, the microbe theory was then applied to everything. If there was a syphilis spirochete, then there must be a microbe causing schizophrenia. Likewise, pellagra, with similar mental symptoms of derangement but also a characteristic rough skin, swelling of the joints, and devastating fatigue, must be caused by a pellagra "bug." Therefore, when Joseph Goldberger, a physician in the U. S. government's Hygienic Laboratory (predecessor of the National Institutes of Health) said the real cause lay in a nutritional deficiency, he was laughed off the block by the "microbe fundamentalists."

But Goldberger had done his homework. He had noticed that pellagra was epidemic in certain poor areas of the South where cane sugar, corn syrup, and other concentrated sugars, as well as bleached wheat and corn flours, had recently been introduced. "The work of Italian investigators, as well as Goldberger's own observations in mental hospitals, orphanages, and cotton mill towns, convinced him that germs did not cause the disease."[15] In such institutions, inmates contracted the disease, but staff never did. Some early pilot studies supported his theories—he enriched the diet of some children suffering from pellagra and the illness disappeared. In 1915, the Mississippi prison system provided some volunteers who agreed to eat only a nutritionally depleted, corn-based diet—and they developed pellagra rashes after five months. The missing nutrient was the B vitamin *niacin*, now routinely included in enriched flours and other B-complex vitamins.

Goldberger became so frustrated with the disbelief and criticism he received from microbe fundamentalists in the medical establishment that in 1916 he publicly performed a potentially lethal experiment on himself. He shot a pellagrin's blood into his own arm and that of his assistant, Dr. George Wheeler. He took swabbings from a pellagrin's nose and throat and put it on their own. Neither of them contracted pellagra. Even then, a few doctors continued to staunchly oppose his theory.

It was the German physician Paul Ehrlich who coined the term "magic bullet," an unwitting mythogem of modern medicine. He applied this term to Salvarsan, the preparation that killed the syphilis spirochete. The appealingly simplistic idea of the single-remedy medication permeated modern medicine and was indeed encouraged by the discovery of insulin, sulfa drugs, penicillin, and antibiotics. Even today, the "magic bullet" psychology persists, and the idea of side effects is unwelcome to many physicians who are looking for simple solutions to complex problems. Since only medical professionals are licensed to prescribe medications, and since their choices are influenced not only by their allopathic medical educations but by the pharmaceutical companies who present every new offering as a wonder drug, this orthodoxy has significant health consequences.

Another area where cognitive medical fundamentalism occurs is in the diagnosis. In the late nineteenth and early twentieth centuries, doctors were inclined to give illnesses impressive sounding Latinate names—*dementia praecox, myasthenia gravis,* and so on—as if the very act of naming settled the issue for once and for all. Between the Latin diagnosis and the "magic bullet" mythogem, people often find themselves treated not as biochemically and genetically unique individuals, but as members of diagnostic categories. If you fail to respond to the prescribed treatment, you are "medically refractory" and may get kicked out of treatment.

In the area of mental health, psychology fought back against the (more medical) psychiatric model by demonstrating that diagnosis is an extremely subjective process and not statistically reliable. That is, different doctors give different diagnoses based on their unique perceptual filters. Even so, the tendency remains for both medical and mental health professionals to presume an all-knowing authority. In worst-scenario cases, they will treat the diagnosis rather than the person and stick to their diagnosis and its standard treatment despite evidence to the contrary. Such medical fundamentalism can induce enormous frustration, not to speak of continued discomfort, for the beleaguered patient.

In the early twentieth century, supported by the Carnegie Endowment for Education, the Flexner Commission was constituted to survey all existing health disciplines to develop standards of practice. While it was a laudable intent, in practice the commission was largely shaped by the agendas of the American Medical Association and the burgeoning pharmaceutical companies. Not surprisingly, the study came out in favor of these interests and declared that all energy medicine, for example, was unscientific "quackery." The AMA then not only engaged in a disinformation campaign but actually helped to draft legislation prohibiting use of these methods. The chiropractic and osteopathy guilds, realizing they were being excommunicated as legitimate healing disciplines, fought back with some success and achieved legitimacy as professions in their own right. Half a century later, Chinese acupuncture (clearly an energy medicine) gained a footing in American alternative medicine. The medical profession generally looked down its nose at acupuncture, but the populace embraced it, and now millions of patients visit thousands of licensed practitioners in America as well as in the rest of the world.

Time and again, I have seen conventional doctors' eyes glaze over and their jaw clamp when acupuncture, qi gong, or herbal medicine is mentioned. They are heresies, outside the medical "box." It is galling for the priests of medical orthodoxy when their patients defect to another belief system, and sometimes they just write them off. This is especially sad because, from their privileged position, physicians who are also knowledgeable in alternative methodologies could easily choreograph multiphasic healing programs that combine both approaches for the benefit of their patients. But this approach would require giving the "heresies" their due. If good introductory courses in alternative medicine or the once-discredited energy medicines (which have made an amazing comeback in recent decades) were included in medical school curricula, doctors could operate from a broader knowledge base. Some doctors and medical schools in fact seem to be moving in this direction.

It can be a great education to travel to India or Indonesia and then get sick. People may steer you to an *ang-ma* practitioner for stiff joints, an *ayurvedic* practitioner for immune weakness, the Chinese acupuncturist for liver or spleen problems, or a shaman or *balian* if your problem seems to be psychic or spiritual. Contrarily, if you have a virulent bacterial infection, bring out the tetracycline. It is available in the funky pharmacy right down the street that also specializes in rare homeopathic remedies and Tibetan medicine. Westerners may pause and wonder about the likelihood of abuse, but in those societies abuse does not seem endemic; people just want to feel better, as we all do everywhere, and they will use what it takes to do so.

In other countries, a pluralistic or "ecumenical" approach to treatment seems to be standard. Many European pharmacies offer herbal, nutritional, and homeopathic remedies right alongside the allopathic drugs. Russia and Japan are outdistancing the United States in energy medicine approaches, including noninvasive techniques such as biofeedback. In America, however, Ciba-Geigy, Merck, and Pfizer maintain the holy altar and banish the heretics. The form of medicine practiced in America today remarkably resembles our penchant for simplistic theology.

PSYCHOTHERAPEUTIC FUNDAMENTALISM

Sigmund Freud was an original thinker and great innovator. But once his system of psychoanalysis became internationally accepted, he decided it provided the only genuine way to think about the psyche. In a letter to his student Carl Jung, who would eventually break away, he insisted that psychoanalysis should become "a dogma, an unshakable bulwark." Central to the new orthodoxy was the so-called psychosexual theory: Every male child secretly desires his mother and wants to kill his father—the Oedipus complex. All girls have "penis envy" and want to have sex with their father—the Electra complex.[16] Freud was never able to prove any of his psychosexual ideas scientifically, nor demonstrate the existence of the *id, ego*, and *superego* (his Nobel prize was for *literature*, as if implying that these parts of the personality are elegantly constructed fictional characters). This is not to say that psychoanalysis has not helped people. It does, however, contain a psychodynamic fundamentalism.

Jung was anathematized by Freud for his belief in a spiritual guiding force in the human unconscious. Jung called it the "anagogic principle," or the Self. As he wrote in his autobiography, he knew that publishing *Symbols of Transformation*, his first major book espousing that theory, would cost him his friendship with Freud. (It did.) Some time later, Jung, confronting the new orthodoxy that had begun to form around his own theories, groaned, "Thank God I am Jung and not a Jungian." It is a quaint truism by now that Freudian patients have "Freudian" dreams; Jungian patients have juicy Jungian "archetypal" dreams; and Adlerian therapists, schooled in Adler's "will to power," experience thinly disguised power urges. The famous scientific studies by Jerome Frank, during the fifties and sixties, on the efficacy of psychotherapy showed that most psychotherapy indeed benefits patients, especially in the beginning. When questioned, the therapists attributed their client's improvement *to the method they themselves were using*, while the patients attributed it to the therapist's warmth, magnetism, and attentiveness. In other words, therapists tend to be fundamentalists of their own method, while clients get better because of who their therapist *is*, rather than what he or she says or thinks.

Here is a disturbing convolution of the fundamentalist tendency in psychotherapy. Fairly early on in his career, Freud was confronted with evidence that many of his female patients had been sexually molested. Freud responded with the "seduction theory," which said it was all in the women's minds. Because they wanted their prestigious, phallus-bearing fathers, brothers, and stepfathers to desire them sexually, they *imagined* that the abuse happened, but it didn't really. In this piece of psychoanalytic fundamentalism, the weight of the analyst's authority wins out against the patient's memory.

It took the work of Freud librarian Jeffrey Masson to bring to public light that Freud probably knew all along that many of the reports were true, yet he still suppressed them in order to put forward his theory. Moreover, the early forms of this particular orthodoxy obviously favored patriarchy and patronized women. It wasn't until the last two or three decades of the twentieth century that psychiatry, psychology, and social work finally woke up to the pervasiveness of familial sexual abuse—generally by teenage or adult males on younger girls, though sometimes also on younger boys. Courageous work by therapists and self-disclosing clients brought the problem before the public eye, with the result that, in most states, mental health professionals are now legally mandated to report suspected sexual abuse. Yes, that's progress—but trust the fundamentalizing human mind to mess things up still more.

Some therapists dogmatically maintain that if someone is neurotic or has serious problems, they *must* have been sexually abused. Therefore, they will probe until they find sexual abuse, assuming that otherwise the client has no chance of healing. This has led to the widespread scandal called "false-memory syndrome," by means of which well-meaning therapists have left families fractured for decades, or forever. The accusations and defenses that flow on both sides can be enormously emotionally destructive.

As a mental health professional, I have seen both kinds of fundamentalisms just described. The first case was a young woman, a bank teller, who came to me reporting daily panic attacks, terrible anxiety, and migraine headaches. I was able to elicit Eva's story in enough detail to leave little room for doubt: she had been serially molested by a sociopathic uncle.

Unfortunately, Eva's first therapist, repeating Freud's own fundamentalisms, had told her in the very first session that this was surely a screen memory, covering up the fact that she really wanted to have sex with her uncle because she knew the uncle was secretly having an affair with her mother. Infuriated, Eva stalked out of the session. After that, she mistrusted the entire profession and only came to see me, with trepidation, two years later. It took three years of intensive therapy to elicit all the details of the abuse and work through the tumultuous emotional explosions—especially when she confronted her suspicion that her mother knew she was being molested all along and didn't protect her. The uncle had already passed to his eternal reward, and we spent a lot of therapeutic time weighing the pros and cons of confronting the mother, who was still around. Eva decided not to, and years later told me she was happy with that decision. Eventually the story has a fairly happy ending. The panic attacks and daily migraines went away. Eva was able to get out of a destructive relationship with an alcoholic husband, remarry, bear two children, and raise them normally. Because she didn't wrench the family dynamics with confrontation, in addition Eva now has a passable relationship with her mother and, best of all, a grandma for her children.

The second example did not end so well. Judy also suffered from anxiety and panic, as well as obsessive-compulsive disorder. Her therapist felt stymied and increasingly began to rely on the old default assumption that Judy must have been sexually molested. The patient said she enjoyed a close, warm relationship with her father, with lots of snuggling and warm physical contact, but she couldn't remember any incident. The therapist probed further and further, finally leading the patient to a confused jumble of events that the therapist, but no one else, was certain must have happened. Exceeding her mandate even further, the therapist then convinced the patient to confront her father about the abuse. The patient did so, and soon even police and lawyers were involved for incidents in the dim past that Judy couldn't really remember but according to the therapist must have been repressed. The therapist was so certain and dogmatic that Judy finally left therapy—her health not improved but her father's life, and her relationship with him, now in a shambles.

Now in therapy with me, she faced what seemed an even more horrible truth—that she might have ruined the life of, and her relationship with, the parent who really loved her the most. It was sheer agony, and not easy to fix because the situation had gotten so out of hand. In this sense, therapeutic fundamentalism may be the worst kind of all, because it can go to the core of the person's self-concept, into their very soul. James Hillman has deplored the psychotherapeutic fundamentalisms in which many therapists are unconsciously mired as *soul destroying*, because they substitute an alien narrative for the person's own soul quest for authentic selfhood.[17]

There are many fundamentalisms in psychotherapy. One is the "abreaction" model I believed in for years—that therapy for a repressed or traumatic event in your past consists of reliving the event, with emotional recall. In some situations this can be quite effective. In others, the emotional recall seems to retraumatize the person. A recent study shows that asking people with post-traumatic stress disorder (PTSD), such as that brought on by the events at the World Trade Center, to remember the traumatic occasion may do more harm than good.[18] As a therapist of forty years' experience, it seems to me that each client deserves an approach unique to their biological and social history. The key is for the therapist to check in frequently with the client before continuing to impose his or her "good ideas." Ask: "Is this working? Does this approach seem to be helpful?"

SKEPTICAL FUNDAMENTALISM

It is hard to resist pointing out that skeptics, who like to deconstruct everybody else's fundamentalisms, are often quite fundamentalist themselves. And, in true form, they fail to discern this thread in their own thinking. Over the years I have frequently come across a magazine called *The Skeptical Inquirer*, the explicit mission of which is to debunk the mythmaking tendency of the human mind. To be sure, sometimes the magazine's job of unmasking is quite compelling, but after a while skeptical journalism becomes boring. And why? It's because the *modal personality* of the skeptic is so predictable and so, well, fundamentalistic about its beliefs and its point of view .

Let's sketch this modal personality, drawn from a variety of articles and op-ed pieces in the magazine: *What you see is what you get in this world, and nothing slips around the boundaries of the known. We humans already know most of what there is to be known. Our best guesses about things involve the scientific laws of the universe that we have already discovered. However, qualified skeptics aside, most of the world is filled with credulous buffoons who will believe anything.*

Among the favorite topics critiqued by skeptics are ESP, astrology, extraterrestrials, energy medicine, thought-field therapy, chiropractic, homeopathy, acupuncture, and the benefits of prayer. For the fundamentalist skeptic these diverse fields are all of a kind. Each deserves derision, not inquiry—judgment and dismissal, not understanding or rapprochement.

For instance, regarding prayer, the skeptic presumes the studies that show positive results are either accidental ephemera or outright frauds: "All the studies that indicated intercessory prayer actually helps people in some way are flawed. But why should it take a $2.4 million Study of the Therapeutic Effects of Prayer (or STEP) to prove what any sensible person knows already? Prayer is self-hypnosis!"[19]

Of homeopathy, the *Skeptical Inquirer* says: "I have my tongue firmly planted in my cheek on that one—the true believers in homeopathy will always come up with some ad hoc hypothesis to rationalize the failure of their beloved dogma." The magazine cites a woman named Wendy Kaminer, self-described as "a critic of various irrational behaviors," who says that nonetheless she was helped by homeopathy and encourages the thoughtful reader to "try it herself." The article comments, "If I go to a homeopath and think it's helped me, then I'd be irrational not to continue seeing the homeopath. But what does *help* or *helps* mean? Those are weasel words; they have no cognitive content though they are full of emotive meaning." In other words, poor Wendy has succumbed to delusion.

For some people, a near-death experience (NDE) is the most profound experience of their lives. Survivors report an unmistakable quality of spiritual renewal, not unlike many religious conversion experiences. Because of almost losing their lives, they newly experience life as an exquisitely precious gift. The subjective experiences that often accompany the NDE—the journey down the tunnel, the life review, and being met by a "being of light"—are now well-known, thanks to authors like Elizabeth Kubler-Ross, Raymond Moody, and Kenneth Ring.

One time I attended a lecture by Dr. Raymond Moody, author of *Life after Life*. He shared with us that once, in a similar setting, he was publicly challenged by a surgeon who said that in his years of practice he had never heard the kind of nonsense Dr. Moody was spouting. Moody, a rather mild-mannered man, just went on lecturing. At one point he asked if anyone in the audience had experienced the kind of NDE he was describing. Included among the dozen or so people who raised their hands was a well-dressed middle-aged woman sitting next to the doctor. The surgeon turned and stared at her in astonishment. "You never told me such a thing!" he accused. "You never asked," she replied, "and I knew you would just think I was crazy." The doctor's skeptical fundamentalism had foreclosed the sharing of a deep and meaningful experience between himself and his wife.

Such a foreclosure is perfectly congruent with the *Skeptical Inquirer*'s attitude. Reviewing a thirteen-year Dutch study of NDEs, the *Inquirer* reported, "Nor can we be sure, of course, that those who report having had an NDE actually had one. Two of the participants first reported having an NDE two years after their close call with death. It is possible they constructed a false memory."

The skeptical fundamentalist constructs an orthodoxy of *disbelief*, certain that any anomalous experiences human beings report must be frauds. "People are such suckers that you can find dupes anywhere—but you can be sure that *I won't be taken in . . . not me!*" But skeptics *are* taken in—by the scientistic myth that there is nothing in the world that has not already been described and understood. The skeptical posture is as rigid and unyielding as any other fundamentalism.

NEW AGE FUNDAMENTALISM

When do New Age beliefs turn fundamentalist? Perhaps when someone decides it is "bad karma" rather than social inequity that keeps minorities oppressed. Perhaps when people think aliens are controlling Congress, so why bother to vote. Perhaps when someone uses aromatherapy or massage to deal with a life-threatening illness instead of going to a physician. Perhaps when a person turns to their horoscope instead of psychotherapy to understand why they make the same mistakes over and over. Once again, it is attitude, not content, that makes a belief fundamentalistic. Are practical details ignored while indulging in idealistic fantasies? Do magical solutions replace real ones? The following story shows a darker side of New Age fundamentalism.

A friend, a marvelous professional dancer, fell while doing an acrobatic trick and within an hour was mortally ill. He almost died several times in the hospital waiting room. The doctors made several incorrect diagnoses—muscle spasm, spinal fracture, seizure disorder. (We can imagine the consequences of inaccurate yet dogmatic thinking in the field of emergency medicine.) In the nick of time, a young trauma doctor recognized the symptoms of a ruptured spleen, and an immediate operation saved my friend's life.

When I visited my friend once he was home from the hospital, he seemed grim and depressed. "What's up?" I asked.

He had just been visited by mutual friends of a New Age bent. They told him the accident was the inevitable outcome of his lifestyle, and that *nothing happens without one's own wishing it to happen.* "They said I brought it on myself," my friend shared. "And this is the kind of *karma* I have and will have, if I don't change my attitude."

"How are you supposed to do that?" I asked.

"I think I'm supposed to start a daily yoga practice and meet their guru next summer."

"Oh," I said. "And that'll do the trick?"

"Yes." We both laughed.

"I'm just glad you're a survivor. You're pretty amazing, you know." I gave him a hug and reminded him that bad things do happen to good people. The nonjudgmental approach worked, and he had brightened considerably before I left.

We are inclined to try to extract meaning from a sudden tragedy or other trauma. But that kind of insight is best left to the suffering person to come up with, in good time and after much thoughtful reflection. It is people's haste and incaution that makes them leap to "spiritual" explanations for something that goes wrong. My friend had not only to process his own pain and recovery but also deal with other people's interpretations of his situation, based on their own limited view and their own mythology, that is, based on what would make *them* feel better.

Clearly, there are many kinds of fundamentalisms. The issue, again, is not the *type* of thinking but its *style*. Is it closed to modification? Are its tenets advanced with a covert agenda of wholesale agreement, coercion, or conversion? Does it deal in absolutisms? Does it denounce opposing points of view or seem paranoid? Does it avoid critical thinking?

New Age fundamentalisms often miss out on the philosophical rule called "Occam's razor": Don't use a more complex—in this case, metaphysical—explanation when a simpler, more practical one will do. I can remember a friend in the sixties bewailing her "car karma" as the mischievous thing broke down once again, leaving her stranded. I observed to her that she also had a way of trying to save money by buying old beat-up cars. When she upgraded to "good used" and then finally to new, guess what? Her car karma changed. The New Age search for answers in the nonordinary is not much different from the prophetic millennialist's adding up the verse numbers of certain Old Testament prophecies to determine when the End of the World will come.

I am not suggesting the human race should or could give up trying to fathom the ways of the divine. I just think, as the great Irish poet William Butler Yeats said in his mediumistic book, *A Vision*, that we must be "extremely cautious" when interpreting what comes from the spirit realm because the "spirits like to fool you!"

At its best, science is an enormously powerful, impartial mode of thinking that extends our knowledge of the universe. It also proposes a kind of pragmatic, practical way of living that is not belief based. We cannot eliminate our beliefs entirely—that would be counterproductive. However, the next chapter discusses how to keep them limited, and more humble.

THE FIVE-MINUTE
FUNDAMENTALIST

It is not any one brainwave state or condition that makes for optimal brain health; it is the ability to move flexibly between states as different life-tasks or challenges arise. . . . Openness to surprise has helped many who were condemned to a hopeless life.

—Len Ochs, developer of the LENS

If fundamentalist habits of thought plague the human species, how, then, can we trust ourselves to think clearly and not get mired in our own delusions? Can we identify and then deal with a deeply embedded tendency that comes automatically, with conviction, and determines so much that we think and feel?

The situation may look bad, but in fact it is far from hopeless. This chapter considers various ways of awakening to the perennial human tendency toward fundamentalist thinking, in ourselves as well as in our religions and philosophies of life. We do it by mindfulness techniques that include questioning and reflecting, thereby discovering a new perspective on our old ideologies that reveals the fundamentalisms in them. Since it is an example I know well, I begin with my own story of traversing multiple belief systems until I found a perspective from which I saw the fundamentalist dialectic I'd been passing through. I tell the story of a room full of psychologists discovering that we are all fundamentalists some of the time— in moments of high anxiety or low despondency, we all seem to engage in fundamentalist thinking—but we can keep it brief and proportionate, limiting it to five minutes at a time. The chapter concludes with a discussion of three self-reflective techniques that can help us be aware of our internal processes and maintain inner flexibility, followed by an exercise to help the reader analyze his or her own exposure to fundamentalist thinking.

A DIALECTIC OF SPIRITUAL GROWTH

We live in a time of such deconstruction and reorganization of beliefs that psychologically and spiritually potent learning materials are available everywhere. Many modern people during the course of their lives have moved through several belief systems, and I place myself among them.

Growing up as the son of a pastor, first in the Presbyterian Church and then in the Swedenborgian "New Church," I attended religious summer camps and often associated with the "born-again" variety of Christians. But whenever someone asked if I had been "saved," the question prompted a complicated and uncomfortable inner response. I couldn't get my mind around what "saved" meant. Was it a single decisive event that either happened or didn't? I loved and admired what I knew of Jesus, but what did it mean to give my whole self, body and soul, as it seemed I was being asked to do? I knew that, in those circles, a complex answer was definitely the *wrong* answer. Nevertheless, I went to church every Sunday until I went to college, and stories and passages from the Bible, along with the singing of hymns and formulaic recitations of faith, were deeply ingrained into my personality.

Coming of age, though, initiated a long and sometimes painful process of loss of faith. After reading Freud's *Future of an Illusion* and taking intellectually rich and challenging contemporary civilization courses at Columbia, doubts that had begun to surface during my teenage years matured into full-fledged contradictions, accompanied by existential angst. Without knowing it, I was caught on the horns of my first serious philosophical dilemma. If a religion is supposed to be completely *true* and you discover fallacies in it, then presumably it is completely *false*. By my sophomore year I had decided that, like most of my friends, the only honest position was agnosticism, maybe even atheism.

Soon I became filled with a deconstructionist's zeal toward all sheeplike believers (as I decided I had been), and I'm sure I was patronizing to the few friends who were still faithful to their religions. At that time, nothing seemed more absurd than the supernaturalist concoction served to churchgoers like baby food. Many of my professors were of the same persuasion. Skepticism and an almost automatic deconstructionism and analysis followed any new experience, so that I soon lost the primordial sense of wonder and sense of the sacred I had enjoyed in my earlier life. Whatever appeared on my personal horizon was greeted by a sardonic and worldly cynicism. This phenomenon peaked for me around the age of twenty-one. But such a posture exacted its toll—a wary hypervigilance, and ultimately a pervasive depression, emerged as the fruits of my atheistic fundamentalism.

At Columbia, people with existential angst hung out in the West End Bar (later famous because Paul Simon and Art Garfunkel were habitués). The place was full of mildly or seriously intoxicated intellectuals, including a group of fiercely subversive atheists, more seasoned and outspoken than I, to whom I naturally deferred. During my junior year, however, I renewed my friendship with Jack Kerouac, whom I had known in high school and who also hung out at the West End. Kerouac had a Dionysian, enigmatic spirituality about him that was life affirming, while absolutely scornful of institutionalized religion. *On the Road* and *Dharma Bums* both contain enticing portrayals of the spiritual quest. Kerouac romanticized the magical powers he attributed to his character Japhy Ryder, drawn from Taoism, Zen, and the secrets of Tantric yoga—irresistible to the ladies who swarmed around Japhy. What most transformed me in this friendship was Kerouac's deep, loving quality and uncompromising honesty. For a while I became a (non-card-carrying) member of the Beat Generation. Such immortal hipsters we seemed that Kerouac's death a few years later was simply astonishing to me. Beat religiosity introduced me to Eastern religions and was definitely an emotional step up from atheism. But the tendency to be literalistic persisted.

Then I read Hermann Hesse, and within a few months *Siddhartha* and *Demian* became my bibles. In fact, assuming a stance of Hesseian fundamentalism, I decided that anyone who hadn't read Hesse or understood that life is a spiritual journey must be pretty out of it. On the positive side, I began to think of life as an intelligible adventure, rather than as a bad joke for which annihilation is the only sure outcome. Whatever else one may feel about Hesse, his fiction awakens a thirst for spiritual initiation and a quest for transcendence.

This phase was soon followed by immersion in the works of Ouspensky and Gurdjieff, beside whose penetrating insights all previous knowledge now paled. My eyes scintillated with a knowing light as I met with Gurdjieffian friends, certain that we were *awake* while others were *asleep*. This was great incentive to do "the work" that is central to Gurdjieffian practice. I did meet some apparently self-actualized people, and I learned a kind of mindfulness designed to keep one self-aware in the coping and struggling with life—a technique called "self-remembering" that I still find valuable.

As my friends and I demonstrated, though, Gurdjieffian fundamentalism also consists of an inflated superiority about one's own awareness, in comparison to the unconsciousness of the rest of the world. The principle of *conscious is good and unconscious is bad*, along with a new kind of hypervigilance, replaces one's previous way of being. My young wife, Robin, then a graduate student at NYU, pointed out that, in its quest for a kind of superconsciousness, "the work" was a terrible Apollonian prejudice that left out instinct, the fertile intuition, and the darkness where we rest and dream. She also observed that some of my "awakened" friends were also brilliant sociopaths who actually accomplished very little while lording it over others.

I soon came to see that Robin was "right on." Within the first year of our marriage we each entered Jungian analysis. Play, imagination, dream, and creativity had been neglected in a Gurdjieffian fundamentalism that glorified consciousness alone. After that, I began to use Robin as a BS detector, particularly about gurus and belief systems that were one sided, or that looked fair but smelled otherwise.

At one point we encountered Hindu fundamentalism in the person of a handsome and charismatic kundalini yoga teacher with whom we both studied for about a year. The daily practices and observances were strict and time-consuming. Then one eye-opening day, the guru criticized Robin's manner of dress (too attractive) and told us to "stay far away from people with lower-chakra vibrations." As we drove home from our *darshan*, she said, "He sounds like one of my Southern aunts." The aspiring Hindu fundamentalist in me was shocked at such impiety toward a "perfected" being, but I was learning to trust her perceptions. We followers had been instructed

to observe a strictly vegetarian diet, drink only water, and be pure in everything—even married people should only have sex once a month, on the
night of the full moon. But not long afterward came the revelation that our
teacher himself ate meat freely, smoked cigarettes, drank brandy, and, though
married, often had beautiful devotees in his bed. When his freaked-out followers confronted him about his double standard, he said he was spiritually evolved enough not to be defiled by his actions. An unconscious defer-
ence to authority in the students seems to have led to a grandiose fundamentalism (a holy invulnerability) in the teacher.

Zen seems to float above most illusory entanglements, but it has its
own style of fundamentalisms. On one intensive meditation retreat at a
large and beautiful zendo in the Catskills, I participated in (mindful) fire-
wood stacking and (equally mindful) washing of the monastery from end
to end on my hands and knees. I then meditated for the remainder of the
time I was awake, maybe ten hours a day. The incessant yammering of the
mind gradually stilled as the days passed, and a pervasive quiet seemed to
fill the monastery and the grounds. But whenever it came time to eat, I was
asked to repeat a prayer that said: "I take this food *only for medicinal purposes.*" I knew how much time and love had gone into the (organic vegetarian) food, for the previous day I had cut the carrots and potatoes for the
delicious soup we were all eating. But I could not in all honesty say that one
little phrase, because I knew I also ate the food for enjoyment. It reminded
me of reciting the Nicene Creed in Sunday school and finding myself silent
or lip-synching the words, but not connecting to them. Then I started to
listen to the rest of the affirmations and credos I was saying aloud with
others in unison. Proclaimed with deep monkish voices at each gathering,
these precepts were impressive and hypnotic, but I was not sure I could
abandon previous conflicting beliefs and say these other ones, praisewor-
thy though they be, with conviction. It was not the practices that seemed
fundamentalistic to me in this setting, but the things I was asked to believe.
A number of times I came close to taking Buddhist vows. But when I meditated on the nature of the vows and the specific meanings of what I would
have to say, I realized that at that stage of my life, as a "householder" with a
family and a profession, I could not, in honesty, fulfill them.

Not long afterward, one of the most esteemed *roshis* in the lineage was accused of sexual improprieties. In the ensuing brouhaha, it became clear that, beneath the elaborately decorous surface, the tradition was riddled with petty rivalries and jealousies. Other scandals began surfacing in Hindu and Buddhist traditions around America about the deeds of various "perfected beings," and I began to wonder why we so easily project our own potential perfection onto others.

COMING HOME SPIRITUALLY

I was finishing my degree at Columbia, and thoroughly confused, when I first met Joseph Campbell at the C. G. Jung Foundation in New York. After one of his lectures he invited me to sit down and talk. He listened attentively to my recitation of spiritual affiliations and disillusionments, chuckling at times—something I didn't understand fully until writing his biography years later. (It turns out Campbell had been through quite a journey of his own to get where he was when I met him—at the top of his game.) He looked at me kindly and offered the interpretation that is now one of my permanent beliefs.

To paraphrase his words during a complex conversation: "Each of those systems, intensely encountered, probably taught you something appropriate to your stage of spiritual development at the time. Together they make you who you are now, which is far from a finished piece of work, and will participate in creating who you will become." Then, in a memorable phrase, he said, *God is not found in the become and set-fast, but in the becoming and the changing.* I wasn't well-read enough then to place this statement, but the metaphysic was Goethe's and an important piece of Campbell's own evolution. He continued: "Don't let your theology become static, because the living God is the opposite of fixed and frozen. The moment you think you've got him, you've lost him. Look at how susceptible you've been to other people's ideas. You've treated each source, from yoga to Jung, as if it were the Bible."

I sat thunderstruck. He had my essential "life myth" better than my analyst. And his response was offered with such warmth and lack of judgment that I could accept it—and afterward move into a new phase of accepting myself as a *becoming* person, not a finished product.

Campbell himself, who was extraordinarily accomplished in so many fields, seemed like a "finished product," but he always freely acknowledged that he still had much work to do on himself. Besides, when I introduced Robin (she with the BS detector) to him, her response was unlike her reactions to any of my previous charismatic teachers. She was enthralled by Campbell and asked me to take her to every lecture he gave in New York. She was the most impressed by hearing him tell us, despite all his learning and eloquent storytelling, "Don't just listen to me, go to the myths." We found ourselves returning often to drink at "St. Joseph's well."

Time and again, Campbell took us past egotism and the cult of authoritative personalities into the realm of spiritual and creative revelation for all of humankind. I have heard spiritual leaders praise religious egalitarianism while still owning a special loyalty to their own tradition. But Campbell was the true exemplar of spiritual democracy. In his hands, every myth could move you, and every symbol was a cipher from the creative source-realm, trembling with implication. Though he was a one-man show, Campbell spoke in the thousand-tongued language of the soul.

In retrospect, those audiences of a few dozen people in the sixties and seventies were receiving a concentrated foretaste of the magic with which Campbell would later magnetize millions of Americans in the *Power of Myth* series with Bill Moyers. His simple message was nevertheless profound and far reaching: The vast display of world mythology, from the most primitive to the most refined, inflects one "shapeshifting yet marvelously constant story" of humanity's quest for an authentic experience of living. The sacred was not available in merely one place (the authoritarian model); to the contrary, it could be found everywhere. It revealed itself even more splendidly to those who quested with integrity—as in the mature hero's journey. But having made a journey and glimpsed enlightenment was no excuse to claim privileged knowledge. In fact, for Campbell, whoever so claimed privileged knowledge had already lost it.

My encounter with my own fundamentalist thinking was a dialectical process—and one that was a mix of suffering and mini-enlightenments, as

I have tried to chronicle. The meeting with Campbell somehow quieted the discordant friction of the inner fundamentalisms and freed me to see through, not only the symbolic forms of myth, but the kaleidoscope of my own belief systems. I lightened up, got more flexible, and, I'm told, easier to live with.

DISCOVERING THE FIVE-MINUTE FUNDAMENTALIST

In moments of high stress or threat, we all seem to become fundamentalists. A neighbor's dog bites someone, and they stop taking daily morning walks down the street and start a communal campaign against the neighbor. A woman betrayed by her husband says, "All men are betrayers. I'll never marry again!" Then she lives the rest of her life in the grip of that personal mythogem. In more grim circumstances, Israeli Rangers on a patrol in Gaza shoot and kill a Palestinian teenager's best friend, and he instantly resolves to become a suicide bomber. At such moments, decisive neurological events are happening. The primitive centers in the brain overwhelm the more complex thinking and control areas in the frontal lobes, and we engage in black-and-white thinking. "You are with me or against me!" we say. "You're going to apologize or else!" When the limbic system is engaged, we become simpler, more fundamental creatures.

Crisis, trauma, and strong emotions trigger individuals into equally strong—but not very well-examined—positions. Collective threats do the same thing to groups and cultures. We have seen how personal immaturity and confusion leave us open to collective influences and simple solutions. It is also true that people who have grown beyond simplistic thinking are less vulnerable to mass movements and destructive ideologies. Personal development, flexibility, and toleration for paradox can free people from stereotyped collective thinking. In effect, to live in a world tolerant of its own complexities and paradoxes, we have to grow people who are immune to fundamentalisms.

The insight came around 1995, at a conference of the International Transpersonal Association in Santa Clara, California. I was co-leading an introductory program on shamanism for psychologists with Dr. Bradford Keeney, probably one of the most significant and best-published "white shamans" of our time.[1] The room was full of mental health professionals from many countries eager to explore ancient wisdom with us. But the ones from the American Midwest had begun complaining. They had been going through what they felt was "religious persecution" because of their beliefs— right here in America.

Their vexed outpouring became the centerpiece of the program, and Keeney and I spent a lot of time helping people in genuine anguish process a version of what has been called "paradigm shift," or alternately, "culture wars." One woman therapist had owned a successful New Age shop in Kansas, with everything from dream catchers to oracle cards, but her premises had been systematically vandalized. "Get out, witches" was scrawled on the building in paint. One night the building, including her therapy office, burned down—"due to unknown causes," the fire department said. The woman hastily left town for California, where her style of spirituality might be more acceptable. There had been public denunciations against yoga studios and Vedantist study groups, and Klan attention to Kabbalist and Wiccan societies. One healer's massage practice was boycotted because he had Buddha statues and incense in the massage studio. Another psychologist, part Native American, was forbidden to go to the old Indian grounds to pray— the land was now privately owned.

The stories went on and on, making it clear to all that Christian fundamentalism had departed not only from the American founding fathers' religious tolerance but also from its preceptor's philosophy of love and forgiveness. The fertile discussion on what to do even included how to use Christian ethics—*turn the other cheek*—to deal with Christian intolerance. The issue was so large, and the resentment so voluble, that our workshop was in danger of turning into a "fundamentalist-bashing" session, and that seemed unproductive.

So Brad and I took a new tack that was enormously successful. I came in after lunch one afternoon acting as if I were at an Alcoholics Anonymous meeting. I went around the group shaking hands and saying, "Hi, I'm Steve, and I'm a fundamentalist." Then I told something "fundamentalistic"

I had thought or done in my earlier life, and something I'd done in the last couple of days. I added, "Yes, I'm a fundamentalist, I admit it. But I'm trying to keep it to five minutes for a given belief system. Still, I can't always see it myself, so please help me out."

The group laughed but got the principle. We started the afternoon session with an exercise in identifying our inner fundamentalist, noting how many times he or she had come out in our lifetimes and how we constantly battle the tendency to be judgmental or jump to conclusions. The exercise shifted the group from a fundamentalist-critiquing "it's us against them" psychology to a "we are they" mentality as we brought forth and viewed together our own tendencies to think and act in fundamentalist ways. The group agreed this was also a *relationship* matter. We could help each other out with nipping these tendencies in the bud.

The process was a marvelous leveler, and a larger issue became evident: We were collectively caught between worldviews at a pivotal point in history. An almost palpable compassion for "stuck fundamentalists"—ones who really can't think otherwise—emerged. When it came time to beat the spirit drum and do a shamanic ceremony, the group was primed. There were tears, emotional catharses, and insights.

The following day, the members of our workshop group, their own inner work accomplished, followed the time-honored pattern of the "wounded healer." As Brad led the ceremony with a much larger group of about four hundred, we invited people to process what it felt like to be living in a society going through its own death and rebirth. A lot of emotional processing boiled to the surface. Our workshop members instantly spread throughout the room and organized people into small healing groups. Participants were processing the results of this large group ceremony—in a good way—for days to come.

I have since used some of the same exercises with workshop participants and individual therapy clients who have been disillusioned or traumatized in their encounter with organized religion. The same exercises work for anyone experiencing a loss of orientation and meaning in a fragmenting society. A selection of these exercises, designed to help a person identify their own five-minute fundamentalist, can be found at the end of this chapter.

George Lakoff's *Don't Think of an Elephant* does a nice job of teaching us how to talk with people whose minds are politically just the opposite of our own.[2] In a related way, this book is intended to help you think both psychologically and mythologically about beliefs—other people's and also your own. It is one thing to notice and find yourself reacting to the fundamentalisms in someone else's religion, and quite another to recognize them in your own and then go through the painful yet courageous process of questioning, considering, and perhaps choosing to change or expand your religious outlook.

RELIGION'S OWN EXAMINATION OF CONSCIENCE

Why shouldn't we analyze the religion in which we were raised the way anthropologists analyze the religions of the societies they study? What is its structure? How does it endorse society's values? Is it patriarchal? Legalistic? Cooperative with or antithetical to nature? How did this religion come up with its definition of what is "good" and what is "bad"? Does it support the social structure of the community? Which values does it affirm and which does it negate? On the darker side, consider the tradition over the years. Has it disempowered minorities or women, or fomented holy wars or inquisitions? Does it justify colonialism or exploitation? Does it tend to support or disapprove of violent solutions to conflicts? Does it look down on other religions? Does it overlook the crimes of its clergy? A religion itself should be able to do the same kind of examination of conscience it asks of its participants.

A durable and truly spirit-infused religion has probably already addressed these questions in some measure. Social scientific studies have shown that one difference between the more thoughtful wings even of evangelical religions and their fundamentalist counterparts is willingness to enter a dialogue with those of differing beliefs. Religious groups unwilling to allow for mutual accommodation in these ways meet Kimball's requirements for "becoming evil." Thoughtful evangelicals like Jimmy Carter have made this precise point, as Carter has in *Our Endangered Faith*. I have thought of making up a bumper sticker that says, "Zero tolerance for intolerance!" Would anyone understand it? Would people honk?

A decade and a half ago, psychologist-writer Dan Goleman, commenting on the abuse of spiritual privilege, suggested that the task for spiritual seekers in the current age is to look at the practical side of any group or movement with which we seek affiliation.[3] Using the Internet, we can now research the politics and social policies of any religion in which we are interested. Recently my adult son, who runs a theater company, was offered some work by a high-profile church organization in California. Before he accepted the contract, he looked carefully on the Internet at the church's position on the Iraq war, abortion, and gays. Fortunately, the church passed with flying colors, and he was able to do a creative and mutually beneficial project for them without regrets. The church indeed "walked its talk" on the level of social responsibility.

A long-time friend who is part Native American but living in Hawaii found that her family was helped when they joined the Jehovah's Witnesses. In an area of the islands where pot smoking and alcoholism were rampant, here was an entire sober and law-abiding community interested in community support, education, and child care. Church and social life helped her feel that she was "belonging to something" larger than herself and mitigated the sense of loneliness and alienation so many people suffer from in modern society. Her children attended both the church school and Sunday school.

As time went on, though, my college-educated and quite resourceful friend wanted to contribute to the active governance and administration of the church. She was blocked, politely but firmly, time and again. When persistent, she was finally told that "governance" was the business of male elders and that women had other duties. She tried to conform to the rules as they were explained to her, but her doubts and misgivings kept surfacing, and she and I discussed them during telephone counseling sessions.

There were native Hawaiians in the church, and my friend bonded with them, discovering that they had many things in common. Sensitive to the Hawaiians' cultural disenfranchisement at many levels in Christian and white-dominated society, my friend proposed that the parish sponsor some

Hawaiian cultural days so the Hawaiian members would feel more included. Again she was met with a polite but firm refusal. Reminding the native Hawaiians of their original culture, she was told, would only confuse them in their Christianity.

As the Iraq war came up, my friend learned that a large bloc of the church—in fact, many of the male elders—were pro-war, and some believed the war would hasten the End of Days prophesied in the scriptures. She began reading between the lines of the literature and listening beneath the words of the sermons and homilies; and, as she did, she became increasingly malcontent. When it came to certain serious social issues, church members simply submitted to the authority of the elders. The whole congregation was never asked for a consensus on how they felt.

She had invested so much of herself in the church that it was with sadness that my friend began a gradual process of detachment. These days she practices religion eclectically, mingling Christian Pentecostalism with Hawaiian Huna and an earth-centered spirituality.

In our eclectic and melting-pot world, there are thousands of such stories to be told. Religion is at its best as an aid to living, but where it inverts the relationship and places its own needs and values counter to practical living and common sense, it works pathologically.

THE SELF-LIBERATING POWER OF THE INTROVERTED MIND

I would be remiss if, at this point in the discussion, I did not offer some practical skills to help keep the mind flexible and free from the dualistic, obsessive, and authoritarian tendencies we have discussed. The sections that follow contain hints about how to do that. But they are just hints. I think the authentic new age will be brought about by individuals who are both self-reflective and creative. It is said that Carl Jung, who used the phrase "self-liberating power of the introverted mind," took a different route to work every day so that his mind would not become habituated or stale. Jung intended his approach to self-healing, which he called "individuation," to be a never-ending process of growth and spiritual development. He also believed that the age-old tradition of alchemy was not just primitive chemistry but a psychological practice of "cooking oneself" for spiritual development—a precursor to psychotherapy, with a lot of useful metaphors contributing to self-transformation.

Self-liberation? "Cooking ourselves"? These concepts are not just New Age fluff but are emerging as increasingly essential to the human enterprise. They provide part of the tool kit for living in a world where fundamentalism is sabotaging our adaptability as a species. The principle is better understood in traditional Eastern cultures, and in monasteries or cloisters, than in today's distracted and extraverted society, but its essence is simple: Human consciousness carries a highly intelligent and analytical ability. Turn it back on itself, and unexpected transformative things begin to happen. The Native American goes to a solitary hill to "cry out for a vision" and does not eat or drink until one comes; the yogi seeks *samadhi* by isolating himself in a cave; the novelist secludes herself in a cabin in the woods to write. The mind liberates itself in psychotherapy through processing its contents in the presence of an attentive and sympathetic therapist. The same principle can work when drawing or painting or modeling clay and then interpreting it, or when a child builds a private world in the sheltered space of a sandbox. Millions of people have found such practices powerfully self-revelatory.

Two of the following processes can be done individually or in a group. The third involves a transaction between a person and a "little robot," as I call it—a biofeedback machine.

Psychological Journal Keeping

The practice of keeping journals and spiritual diaries was popular in the nineteenth-century Swedenborgian, Transcendentalist, Quaker, and Shaker communities of America. Carl Jung kept journals of his dreams and active imagination exercises. American psychologist Ira Progoff, inspired by Jung, developed a comprehensive technique of journal keeping, with many sections. I studied Progoff's technique over several years with him and instituted the practice in my psychology classes.

The structure of the psychological journal is a matter of personal preference, but the sections can include: (1) a daily or periodic diary; (2) dreams and associations/interpretations; (3) waking dreams and active imagination; (4) intersections (serendipities that have arisen in your life); (5) stepping stones (evaluations of stages in your developmental process); (6) creative projects, poetry, and/or writing tasks; and (7) spiritual/religious questing—even "conversations with God." You can also create sections for your subpersonalities, such as, "romancing my inner lover," or "dealing with my critical judge." There are no psychological journal orthodoxies!

The advantage of having sections is that it structures your way of thinking—which is useful, but not obligatory. Most important is simply keeping the journal and *periodically reading over it*. I emphasize the latter because without it there is no feedback. Texas psychologist James Pennebaker's experiments in the 1980s and 1990s showed that keeping a psychological journal and later reading it has measurable psychological benefit. And the principle seems to work regardless of gender, age, or education.

If you doubt the power of this technique, keep a journal for a month or more, then gather with three or four friends and read your journals together. I guarantee that you will not only be moved; you will experience surprising mutual understanding, bonding, and emotional support.

Dream Sharing and Analysis

Jung said that dreams have a compensatory function to waking consciousness; that is, they fill in the blanks. If we missed something obvious in a situation, our dreams might point it out to us. Therefore, if a dream interpretation comes too easily, it's good to look again. Both Jung and Italian psychiatrist Roberto Assagioli felt that dreams could also help with psychosynthesis—Assagioli's term for integrating dissociated parts of the self. Their contemporary, Herbert Silberer, a German analyst, insisted that dreams have an *anagogic* function—they can lead you somewhere new that you need to go, or offer creative insights—an idea also shared by Jung.

My own background in dream work includes years of personal analysis with the Jungian analyst Edward C. Whitmont, followed by more years of clinical supervision from him as I worked with the dreams of my own psychotherapy clients. Whitmont earned every bit of his reputation as a "wizard" who could take a raw dream and a few psychodynamic details and open out the secret workings of the dreamer's psyche. He was particularly gifted at confronting people with secret fundamentalisms they had repressed or denied.

Dreams seem to flower best in community settings. In *The Shaman's Doorway*, published in 1976, I was looking for ways to help modern people create "dream societies" such as traditional people had. Among the North American Iroquois and the Malaysian Senoi, for example, entire communities participated in dream rituals that enriched their mythological landscape and deepened their shamanic lore.[4] My wife, Robin, and I have led therapeutic dream groups for about fifteen years. If a dream is simply presented to an attentive group of kindred spirits, extraordinarily rich insights and creative ideas can flow. The same dream viewed from different people's perspectives reveals different elements or facets, so that, in the group setting, dream fundamentalism of the "single meaning" type doesn't fare so well. There is always another angle to consider. The richness of the group's interpretations reveals the richness of the creative psyche.

Dream interpreter Jeremy Taylor has group participants agree to rules of safety and confidentiality—because dreams can be intimate and personal—and an interpretation of another's dream in a group setting always starts with: "If this were my dream...." This, too, helps to derail fundamentalism in dream interpretation—as we have seen, the worst fundamentalisms are the ones that reduce a person's inner experience and soul life to a pre-set formula, or stereotyped idea.[5]

A recent dream of my own exemplifies how imagery can point the way to something overlooked. As I was working on the last two chapters of this book, I awoke one morning with an amusing image, whether from a dream or simply hypnagogic (coming out of sleep) I could not tell. The image was of a dwarfish, blue, hunchbacked Mel Brooks saying, as he does many times in the movie *Spaceballs* (a very funny *Star Wars* spoof), "May the Schwartz be with you." "The Schwartz" is Brooks's comic equivalent of something mystical: "the Force" that Luke Skywalker must master in the *Star Wars* trilogy. In his own film, Brooks himself plays the dwarfish figure of "Yogurt," the equivalent of Yoda in *Star Wars*. I told Robin the dream. We both laughed, and during the day, whenever I met her (or the dog) I would say, with a thick Yiddish accent, "May the Schwartz be with you."

The little vignette seemed silly enough until the next day, when I had a sudden "aha." Next to my bed was a book a client had loaned me: *What Really Matters: Searching for Wisdom in America* by Tony Schwartz.[6] I had been busy alternately running a conference and writing and hadn't really looked at it yet. I now sat down with it more seriously and found it amazingly relevant to my thoughts and the task at hand. Schwartz, a successful ghost writer for Donald Trump on his bestselling *Making the Deal*, settled into a depression after the project was over. The depression occasioned his exhaustive search for wisdom, as he describes in the book, through the human potential movement, yoga, and meditative disciplines for "what really matters."

Insights from reading Tony's book helped me undertake the biographical part of this chapter—I so appreciated the integrity with which he describes his spiritual search—his initial obtuseness, fumbling, and gradual awakening. I return to some of Schwartz's ideas in the next and final chapter because I believe his quest for "what really matters" was also a search for a "natural religion." I couldn't thank my imaginal "Yogurt" enough! The Schwartz, indeed, was with me.

Biofeedback and Self-Regulation

A third method that may assist the mind is biofeedback. In brief, biofeedback places a person in contact with his or her own somatic signals through some kind of feedback device. A simple example: Place a stethoscope on a person's stomach so she can hear her bowels gurgling—as in irritable bowel syndrome. With the information loop closed, the gurgling—hence, the unwanted spasming—automatically decreases. Hook a person up to surface electromyography, which measures muscle tension, and he or she can learn to lower the tension by lowering a tone, or a bar on a graph. The same principle works with blood pressure and even hand temperature, where learning to warms one's hands can lead to some control over migraine headaches or help Raynaud's syndrome, in which extremities are perennially cold.

Over about twenty-five years of running a college biofeedback laboratory, I observed students reduce muscle spasticity, lower blood pressure, and even overcome performance anxiety in sports or music using biofeedback. The main attractions in the lab, though, were the EEG, or brainwave, devices. Even though we allegedly "live inside our heads," most people are still mystified by the "darkness" inside their skull (indeed, the brain has no sense receptors), such that we usually know *what* we are thinking, but not so much *how* (the mood or energy behind our thoughts). Almost from the beginning, there were students hooked up and meditating, or seeing how brainwave training would affect their consciousness. The most interesting part was reading the students' journals at the end of the semester. Many reported they felt more "self-aware." Some who had always labored under attention-deficit problems said they felt "less ADD." Students who perennially daydreamed were more alert to when their minds were wandering. One woman told me five years after taking the class that not only had her grades gone up but she was less emotionally reactive in situations that would previously have "triggered" her.

We call this process of getting a handle on the internal energies that drive or co-opt our thoughts "metacognition" or "mindfulness" training. The success stories provide us with an illustration of the "self-liberating power of the introverted mind." But until I encountered the neurofeedback of Dr. Len Ochs in 1996, I could not understand why simply doing brainwave training in the lab should help people become more aware, and less reactive emotionally, in circumstances *other than* the ones in which they were training. My problem was that I was stuck in an old paradigm. You could call it a scientific fundamentalism of a sort. I had been trained in operant conditioning, where behavior is strengthened by rewards or "reinforcements." In conventional neurofeedback (the brainwave-based subdiscipline of biofeedback), this is the model. You are asked to change a brainwave (without quite knowing how you do it) to get what is presented as a "reward"—a bar graph rises, or Pac-man eats little pellets, robots march across the screen, rocket ships or balloons fly, or a beautiful mandala changes color.

Ochs's method is based on an entirely different principle that hadn't even been articulated until his impressive results made a theory necessary to explain them. The early software harnessed a light flashing at an offset frequency (in Hertz, or cycles per second) to avoid a seizure, which might be triggered if the light flashed at the same dominant frequency as the brainwaves. When neurologically sensitive people (with traumatic brain injuries, for instance) felt overstimulated by the lights, Ochs dimmed them to the point of finally masking the LEDs. The effect still took place even with the layers of masking. *What, then, was the healing mechanism?* When a private grant made possible a careful analysis of the system by Lawrence Livermore National Laboratories, extremely weak radio waves turned out to be the only possible agency of treatment.

As Ochs himself says in my 2006 book *The Healing Power of Neuro-feedback*,[7] the entire thing was a series of felicitous blunders, because according to the old paradigm these radio waves shouldn't have any effect at all. But new evidence always forces science to revise its theories. In this case, both clinical and experimental evidence from humans and animals verifies the new paradigm. Ochs's method, now called the LENS, or "low-energy neurofeedback system," is based on a brain-changing principle: human beings seem to be living energy fields that can be affected electromagnetically—with astonishing benefits, as the book and a subsequent volume of research studies show. And it happens almost instantaneously, *without conscious intention.* This is a benefit, since leading biofeedback clinicians have often said that the biggest impediment to success in biofeedback is the person's own will, working dysfunctionally. The LENS method has already helped not only the brain-injured and the traumatized, but also people with anxiety disorders, depression, obsessive-compulsive disorders, and ADD, as well as autistic spectrum disorders. My own ongoing research with the method is in brain flexibility, optimal performance, and the self-actualizing potential of the human being with a healthy brain (see figure 2.6, page 30).

During my work as a clinician, I have watched people's neuroses, blocks, and rigidities gradually morph into talents, capabilities, and flexibility with the help of the LENS. A more formal list of the benefits, as presented in a paper at a recent conference, includes ease of functioning, improved self-esteem, multiprocessing, clarity of dreaming, enhanced sensory awareness, and better problem solving. Moreover, this method of treatment seems to improve intuition, facilitate spiritual disciplines such as meditation and yoga, empower self-actualization, and enhance a sense of "natural spirituality."[8] This modest neurological process offers a way of re-membering split-off parts of the self and finding inner balance.

One additional biofeedback method bears mentioning, because its basic roots are available to everyone in that it involves breathing—which is one of the few human functions that can be done totally unconsciously or totally consciously. The method is called alternately HeartMath® and Coherent Breathing. The goal is to breathe slowly (about five or six breaths per minute) and deeply, from the abdomen. This activity sets up what is called "resonant" or "coherent" breathing, using diaphragmatic motions to regulate the heart and other rhythm systems throughout the body. HeartMath claims that when a person is in this state, the incoming afferents (as mentioned in chapter 2) pass through the ascending thalamic nuclei and avoid the amygdala—and hence the fight-or-flight response. Thus, as spiritual disciplines from the East have long intimated, breathing slowly and deeply allows you to think more clearly and "cleanse the doors of perception." One becomes less vulnerable to being emotionally overwhelmed and "steadier" in one's perceptions.[9]

In national conferences dedicated to biofeedback and neurofeedback, HRV, or "heart-rate variability," is increasingly recognized as an indicator of health; the heart, like the brain, needs to be flexible and, in fact, considered as part of "the emotional brain," an organ intimately tied in to our well-being. The healthy heart and brain are naturally flexible and move easily between states without prejudging, that is, without prejudice. When emotion flows easily and naturally, people are warm, colorful, and creative. They keep their fundamentalisms brief; they don't cling to unworkable strategies with a death grip.

Recognize your inner fundamentalist, give him or her honor, but no more than five minutes before at least considering the opposite truth, and then another truth, and then another. Treat life as something becoming and changing rather than fixed and set fast—or sitting before the baleful eyes of a cosmic judge. Cut yourself some slack for being susceptible to religions and intellectual fads. Learn to tolerate the same proclivities in others. Write letters to yourself (in journal form) and heed your dreams. The mind that minds itself grows and flourishes.

FIVE-MINUTE FUNDAMENTALIST EXERCISE

The following questions are meant to help you get to know your inner fundamentalist. They are centered on the religion to which you have been exposed (or its counterpart, a secular orthodoxy) and your relationship to authority, since fundamentalist thinking shows up in these areas for most people. Some readers will just want to read through the questions and give a little thought to each. Others might want to grapple with the questions more seriously, perhaps answering them in a psychological journal or a small essay. They can also be used to stimulate discussions in a group, or to share with others.

I. Religious History (if not applicable, go on to II)

1) As if you were a social scientist, review the religion in which you were brought up. Did the religion:
   a) make absolute truth claims?
   b) make supernatural assertions that are impossible to verify outside scripture?
   c) emphasize supernatural rewards or punishments (heaven or hell)?
   d) emphasize a literal devil and point to real people or institutions supposed to represent him?
   e) discount the discoveries of science or evolution?
   f) say or imply that women should be subservient?
2) In what way was the religion presented to you? (Pick one and explain why or how.)
   a) as an ultimate authority to be accepted blindly

b) thoughtfully, with explanations

c) critically (i.e., you should know about this, but form your own opinion)

3) In regard to other religions, were they presented as:

a) false, bad, or blasphemous?

b) simply wrong (not enough of the "right ideas")

c) alternative windows on the truth?

4) Did your parents, guardians, or parochial authorities adapt their presentation of religious truth to your growing intellectual level? If so, in what ways? If not, how might such an approach have been helpful for you?

II. Secular/Scientific Orthodoxy

1) If your parents were something other than religious (atheist, agnostic, socialist, ethical culture, etc.), did they present their view as if it were:

a) ultimate truth?

b) their personal preference, but you could choose as you would?

c) inconsistent, and different from time to time?

d) part of their own evolution as thinkers?

2) Were people who believed differently:

a) tolerated?

b) dismissed or made fun of?

c) invited into dialogue?

3) Was science presented as:

a) a practical discipline for examining reality?

b) a world view?

c) the only road to truth?

d) a flawed system to be suspicious of?

III. Communal Beliefs

1) In your religious upbringing, what questions could you or couldn't you ask in your family/community?

2) If you asked probing questions, what was the response?

3) Have there been times when you chose a group or community because you felt understood?

4) If yes to 3, chart and list the beliefs of communities or groups to which
you have been drawn.

5) Have these groups changed over time, and if so, what is the trajectory
of change? Do you feel finished or open to new affiliations?

IV. Relation to Authority

A. With Others

1) In dealing with others, what is your style?

   a) authoritarian (coercive)

   b) leadership-oriented (noncoercive)

   c) democratic

   d) laissez-faire or anarchistic

2) Does your style of authority change with changing social groups? Identify the style of authority you use with:

   a) peers

   b) subordinates

   c) children

3) Does your style change as emotion gets involved?

B. With Yourself (both as an authority and a follower)

4) What style of authority do you use with yourself?

   a) self-coercive (forcing or scolding)

   b) self-exhortation (cheerleading)

   c) self-rewarding (giving yourself incentives for good behavior)

   d) intrinsic motivation (i.e., the activity itself is inherently
      rewarding)

   How does this style relate to the way you treat others? (Look for similarities and differences.)

5) Which style of authority that you use with others or yourself corresponds to which emotion (anger, frustration, curiosity, love)?

6) Which style works better for you, and under what circumstances?

IV. Healing

1) Regulate your breathing to a steady rate of about six breaths per minute of abdominal breathing (known to be ideal for certain kinds of inner processing) and do shorter or longer periods of mindfulness training in which you watch yourself change from belief to belief, from impulse to impulse (or to self-restraint). The breathing will help remind you and bring you back to the task. Write about these things in your journal.

2) Find a friend or friends whom you trust and with whom you can share this kind of self-examination.

   a) Confess the most outrageous fundamentalistic thing you have thought or done, in a distractible moment.

   b) Talk or write about all the *sinful* things you have done. Immediately afterward:

   c) Talk or write about all the excellent things you have done (including creative, whimsical, and loving) to head your inner self-reproacher off at the pass.

3) Form a five-minute fundamentalist support group (recovering Catholics, Witnesses, Hassidim) that does all of the above in a group setting. This is especially useful if you think you have work to do in the areas discussed here. Establish ground rules. (For instance, avoid judging or one-upping any group member's experience. Instead, you might say: *If that were my experience, I would feel . . . horrible, wonderful, chagrined,* etc.)

4) If you don't want to take the chance of alienating your friends, you could do this exercise just as an imaginative one on your own. But if you want to be a risk-taking social scientist, try this: Find two friends who have almost totally different belief systems. Invite them to have a dialogue in which you act as the moderator and recorder. Pledge each person to fairness, set a goal of mutual understanding if not agreement, and establish basic rules of civility: no name-calling, provocation, or outright derision.

   a) Record the session and take notes as you moderate. Sum up their positions at the end and *ensure an amicable parting.*

b) Go over the notes and recordings and invite speculation as to why each person inhabits the universe the way they do. Look for further interesting nuances in the conversation and communication.

c) Reflect upon whether your own perspectives were affected by the dialogue. Write about your insights in a journal.

d) Notice how this exercise affects your relationship with each of the friends.[10]

− 9 −

NATURAL RELIGION

Free thinker! Do you think you are the only thinker on this
earth in which life blazes inside all things?

> —Gerard de Nerval, "Golden Lines"

For many, many years religion and science had gone hand
in hand like lovers. . . . But science has faithlessly torn itself away from religion with the results that we see in pol-
luted rivers, destroyed environments, and poisoned human
bodies. I think it's high time that science was brought back
into the realm of the spiritual so that it would wear the
blanket and feel the caress of spirituality and have a reverence for the world and all that dwell in it.

> —Vusamazulu Credo Mutwa, *Song of the Stars*

This chapter moves toward synthesis and some hope for our wayward
species. Underneath the flawed neurology and psychology, the bad
ideas, and the egregious theology, I believe a kind of *natural religion* awaits
humanity. As we have seen, the capacity to respond to the splendor of the
universe and the sacredness of life is built into our nervous systems. It seems
clear that the healthier the nervous system, the more open the mind. And
the more open the mind, the healthier the religion.

"Minds are like parachutes: they work best when they are open," said a
well-known bumper sticker. I suspect that, in today's religious free fall into
the future and compared to fundamentalists, moderates are in for a softer
landing. There are many more adherents among the mainstream Christian
denominations, as well as other faiths, who understand the conditional nature of our belief systems. There are also the "scientifically socialized" who
nevertheless long for spiritual meaning in what is otherwise a universe of
randomly hurrying matter. It is from these populations that Campbell drew
the enthusiastic millions who watched his *Power of Myth* series and read his

books. I believe these are the open minds who could lead the way to a renewed and more natural religion for us all—people who are already as respectful of other traditions as they are devoted to their own, who can take off hats in a mosque, a temple, or a church, or stand in a sacred grove of trees or by a holy mountain and feel a thrill of awe.

We have a genuine chance, in this twenty-first century, as never before, to achieve the flowering of the diverse and spiritually informed society only dimly seen but wisely provided for by the framers of the American Constitution. At the time of the American Revolution, membership choice was pretty much limited to a narrow range of Christian denominations. Now, two and a quarter centuries later, we have mosques and temples and *iglesias* and Christian Science reading rooms and Societies of Friends, and yes, *sanghas*—brotherhoods of all sorts—including the atheistic Ethical Culture society. It is a religious and philosophical bouquet, far more varicolored than could ever have been envisioned when the seeds of religious freedom were first planted.

In 1976, my wife Robin and I were in India, where she was gathering material for her Ph.D. thesis. It took us a month to get over our initial culture shock at the poverty and overcrowding. Finally, we found a haven in the Theosophical Society World Headquarters in Adyar, near Madras, which has one of the finest philosophical and religious libraries in Asia, with hundreds of thousands of volumes and palm-leaf manuscripts. After her daily researches in the library, during the cool of the early evenings we would walk along a sheltered cove off the Bay of Bengal, and every couple of hundred feet we came upon a beautiful small shrine dedicated to one of the world's religions. The native Vaishnavite and Shaivite ones we expected, but there were also Buddhist, Christian, and Islamic shrines, the last with passages from the Qur'an in beautiful Arabic script. Further on stood a Jewish temple. None was greater than the others, and all were equally well maintained. Each invited a contemplative visit. If you opened your mind and heart, suddenly you stood with the millions of human souls through the ages who had embraced that tradition. This, I thought, is the spiritual model for the next century. Reading the writings of the Theosophical founders, especially Annie Besant, deepened the conviction.

Theosophists had taken the lead in finding the wisdom in all the world traditions.

I have met many formerly disillusioned Christians and Jews who swore that Joseph Campbell's way of presenting mythology saved their own religion for them by showing them its universality, meanwhile introducing them to the wisdom present in other traditions. Campbell paved the way for what I am calling natural religion by leveling the mythological playing field; that is to say, he showed how the *sacred* is a viable category of human experience without being the exclusive property of any one religion. To speak plainly, the "ours is better" approach to religion is history; it belongs in the refuse heap with other chauvinisms and ethnocentricities. At this time in human history to claim exclusive ownership of the conduit to God is not only dangerous and foolhardy, it is patently absurd.

I believe the majority of Americans are already inclined in the way I am suggesting; they just lack a coherent voice, which is why the fundamentalists *seem* at times to be winning out. Concretized beliefs produce unanimity of intention; liberal and open-ended beliefs, though more creative, are diverse and harder to bring into focus. Each constituency seems to keep pretty much to itself, and its members mostly talk to others who understand the same language. What would happen if they met in respect and mutual spiritual support and agreed that the one intolerable thing, for any tradition, is intolerance?

Campbell kept saying that we need new religious forms that reflect the knowledge and science of the time. He felt that religion and science need to go "hand in hand," as the Zulu wise man says in the epigraph to this chapter, "like lovers." The new tools and instruments, the telescopes and microscopes and radars and MRIs, increase the depth and subtlety of our investigations, until we realize that, in the words of Lakota visionary Black Elk, "There is no end to the new worlds for our vision." The same parts of the brain that get stuck in dualistic, hierarchical, and obsessive thinking can, when set free, allow us to perceive the complexity of the world around us and to see paradoxically, layer upon layer, dimension upon dimension. (Wouldn't that have to be, metaphorically speaking, "how God sees," too?) I think the theology of natural religion would emerge more as a never-ending process, rather than a fixed account. It would call for all the tools we have at our disposal, including the psychological ones discussed in the last chapter. Naive religionists of the fundamentalist sort continually shoot themselves in the foot by imagining that the mind of a cosmic divinity is fully revealed in a single holy book, and it is a mind, well, not unlike their own. We need instead religions that have a penchant for open inquiry, the tolerance of ambiguity, intellectual freedom, and the realization that, whatever the state of our knowledge and accomplishment, the outlines of the great and living divine presence always recedes, just beyond our gaze.

A SEARCH FOR THE GENUINE NEW JERUSALEM

In chapter 5 we examined forms of Christianity that by their literalism took the spiritual quality out of religion and placed it in history—in the (miraculous) past and some anticipated millennial event at the end of time. But there have been in America, since its beginning, other, wiser, and more sustainable forms of Christianity. The mainline Protestant denominations—the Methodists, Presbyterians, Episcopalians, and Congregationalists—following the lead of Roman Catholicism, have generally held themselves back from millennialism. They have also by and large supported humanitarian causes like the abolition of slavery, voting rights for women, and aid to the poor and the downtrodden. Among the more liberal branches, the Quakers solved the problem of religious authority by having religious meetings without clergy. The Friends were also outspokenly for peace and for peaceful settlements to disputes. The Unitarians and Universalists, who eventually joined to form Unitarian Universalism, tended to be well-read intellectuals and promoted a more inclusive, ecumenical Christianity.

Among these other Christian forms was the uniquely American quasi-religious tradition called New England transcendentalism, an intellectually subtle, socially responsible, nature-friendly tradition established in the nineteenth century. It was right there alongside the literalist, millennialist Millerites, Mormons, and Seventh Day Adventists, who prided themselves on anti-intellectualism, refusing to read any sources, theological or otherwise, beyond a few familiar writers with ideas similar to their own. The guiding spirit of the transcendentalists was the essayist and poet Ralph Waldo Emerson. Educated at Harvard, which he entered at fourteen years of age, he was ordained into the Unitarian ministry in 1829, the year he also married Ellen Louisa Tucker. Her death a mere two years later occasioned a profound emotional and spiritual crisis for Emerson, and he resigned from his ordination—but not his spiritual questing.

Emerson's spirituality was complex and inclusive, ready to embrace the natural world and reconcile with the science of his time. Consider the following passage: "As the air I breathe is drawn from the great repositories of nature, as the light on my book is yielded by a star a hundred millions of miles distant, as the poise of my body depends on the equilibrium of centrifugal and centripetal forces. . . . [In this way] of the universal mind each individual man is one more incarnation, all its properties consist in him."[1]

Emerson's transcendentalism was largely inspired by the writings of Emanuel Swedenborg, the eighteenth-century Swedish natural scientist turned visionary whose books were popular in intellectual circles throughout nineteenth-century England and America. Swedenborg, too, looked for ways to reconcile biblical truths with the unfolding revelations of science. He felt the Bible was the inspired word of God, but its mysteries were best understood spiritually rather than literally. If you really love the Bible, Swedenborg said, meditate on it and let each passage open out like a symbolic flower speaking to your psychospiritual evolution.

Swedenborg was an exemplary scientist of his day, interested in chemistry and mineralogy, but also in astronomy, physics, and biology. He gained access to the forbidden dissecting rooms of Paris and published his anatomical speculations in liberal Amsterdam. At about fifty-five years of age he went through a "spiritual crisis," which he describes in his *Journal of Dreams* and multivolume *Spiritual Diary*. Unlike the dramatic conversion stories popular among evangelicals, he was not a scoundrel, nor was he saved from drink or a life of sociopathy. He confesses that his main spiritual problems were intellectual pride and trusting too much in his "natural mind." After an inner experience of meeting Christ directly, Swedenborg believed, his "spiritual eyes were opened" and the Lord instructed him in how to extract "spiritual sense" from the literal words (which he called "the natural sense") of the Bible.[2]

Already a prolific scientific writer, after his conversion Swedenborg completed dozens of more volumes of biblical exegesis. Throughout his commentaries he interspersed statements that would raise eyebrows now, let alone in his own time: that he talked with angels on an almost daily basis, that he had visited heaven and hell, and that all of his biblical hermeneutics were guided by "the Lord himself."

Probably the main reason Swedenborg was not tried for heresy was that he was a Swedish nobleman, a baron who sat on the prestigious Swedish Board of Mines, and that he led a scholarly and socially responsible life. Nor did his writings contain anything politically inflammatory—though his works had to be published in Amsterdam, not Sweden. Swedenborg corresponded with Sir Isaac Newton and caught the attention of Immanuel Kant, who sent a trusted emissary, a merchant named Joseph Green, to see if the old Swede was crazy. Green reported that the baron seemed quite sane, sociable, and urbane, even though he matter-of-factly affirmed that everything he had written about conversations with angels and visits to supernatural places was true.

Though Swedenborg said he only wanted to reinvigorate Christianity and "never wanted to found a church," after his death, one was begun in his name, in England. The movement—called "the Church of the New Jerusalem" after the special attention Swedenborg gave to the image of the Heavenly City "descending from heaven" in the Book of Revelation—gradually spread to Germany, America, Australia, Africa, and southern India. Though the denomination remains numerically small worldwide, Swedenborg's influence as a "cultural creative" is significant.

In Swedenborg's view, nature is not evil; it is just different—"lower" in the sense of congealed into matter—than the spiritual realm. Everything in nature hints, through a precise symbolism he called *correspondences*, at something spiritual. Likewise, though the Bible appears to be a history of a people, it actually portrays the soul's journey. The human soul has "natural," "spiritual," and "celestial" levels that are inextricably interwoven. When you die, you shed the "natural" level like a suit of clothing and dwell entirely in the spiritual and celestial realms.

In one fell swoop Swedenborg avoided all waiting for the Second Coming of Christ by saying he had seen it take place "in the spiritual world" in the year 1757.[3] He wrote: "By the Lord's advent is not meant His appearance in the clouds, but the acknowledgement of him in Hearts by Love and Faith"—a psychospiritual rather than a historical event.[4] Since the Second Coming had already happened, Swedenborg thought we could now expect, and joyfully participate in, accelerated spiritual evolution—sorry, no great bloodbath on the plains of Megiddo or hurling of sinners into the lake of fire.

In Swedenborgianism, regeneration of the soul is a lifelong process of maturation; salvation is not accomplished by a single capitulation of belief. God is presented as wanting us to grow spiritually, that is, to grow in complexity and discernment and come to do good in the world spontaneously, not because of fear of divine wrath.

Here is the Swedish visionary's psychological antidote to fundamentalism: "No one should be instantly persuaded about the truth—that is, the truth should not be instantly so confirmed that there is no doubt left. . . . [That would be] second-hand truth."[5] He goes on to say something astonishing to most modern people, though not to those in traditional or shamanic cultures—that our minds are constantly in the presence of spirits. When we think good thoughts, good spirits flow into us; when we think bad thoughts, bad spirits flow in. Habitual good thinking inclines us toward the state called "heaven," and habitual bad thinking toward "hell"— which, like heaven, *is not a place but a state of mind or spirit*. Swedenborg's idea of evil thus guards against it being projected out onto others. If you really want to take on the problem of evil, *address it in your own psyche.*

Since Swedenborg was a naturalist, it's not surprising that lore drawn from biology and even paleontology permeates his spiritual writings. Though he lived a century before Darwin, on his own he reconciled the apparent age of fossil specimens with biblical accounts of, say, the Flood by concluding that the biblical authors simply didn't have enough knowledge. He took the story of the Garden of Eden as a parable.

By the mid-1800s, Swedenborg's thought had spread throughout America and Europe. Sampson Reed's famous Swedenborg-influenced *Growth of the Mind,* which in turn influenced Emerson, was circulated throughout the eastern states of the burgeoning American nation, as were Emerson's own essays with Swedenborgian subtexts. John Chapman, "Johnny Appleseed," the nineteenth-century American cultural hero, was a convinced Swedenborgian. He handed out pages of "The Writings," along with apple seeds and seedlings, to people in frontier communities. He called his pages from Swedenborg "Good News right straight from Heaven." Because of his rustic pilgrim lifestyle, he was befriended by the Native Americans, who regarded him as a type of medicine man. He was even initiated into the Iroquois medicine societies and given lore not usually shared with white men. Chapman thought the Iroquoian theology was just fine—it matched what he had read in Swedenborg: that the natural world parallels the world of the spirit, that dreams are messages of the soul, and that truth-telling and respect for all are the foundations of a well-lived life.[6]

Swedenborgian and transcendentalist ideas have had wide influence. There is good evidence that Swedenborg's ideas of the spiritual equality of women and men, and the innate worth and spirituality of the African people, empowered both the women's suffrage and the Emancipation movements of the nineteenth century. Transcendentalism gave a wisdom and a texture to American culture that it simply would not otherwise have had. Besides inspiring American artists such as those in the Hudson River school of painters, who saw nature filled with divine splendor, the philosophy gave support to naturalists such as John Burrows and John Muir, for whom the natural world was not fallen and corrupt but a tangible revelation of the Lord's bounty and endless creativity.

Without intending to endorse any church or philosophical school, it seems worthwhile to point out that the foundational values of Swedenborg and Emerson's thought head in the direction of what I am calling natural religion. They do not lead to inner dualism or fear of reward and punishment or End Times scenarios presided over by a cosmic judge. Rather, they portray religion as something inextricable from everyday life, to be worked out psychologically through conscious practices. Their intellectual landscape includes thoughtful places for nature, science, other philosophies, and other religions. There is no place for a projected evil because there is no inflated devil figure. People's worst characteristics are exaggerations of natural appetites and instincts over which they have lost control. Spiritual growth starts with the utilization and understanding of the nature within us. These kinds of religious values do not fashion for themselves a historical dead end, but rather leave space for a living and growing edge to their worldview.

MATERIALISTIC RELIGION VERSUS NATURAL RELIGION

We might wish we could have said to the nineteenth-century preachers of an imminent Armageddon: "Why couldn't you have relaxed your anti-intellectualism and read a little more widely and deeply (including a close reading of Darwin himself)? Why couldn't you too have seen all around you the tangible evidence of a nature that is not fallen and corrupt, and thus is not to be downtrodden, used up, soiled with our debris, and ultimately poisoned?" (There are consequences to the biblical interpretation that we have *dominion over* rather than *stewardship of* nature. It is the ultimate anthropomorphic conceit, which goes with an image of an anthropomorphic God for whom one may speak, and whose ways can be known thoroughly by men.)

The spirituality of the fundamentalists is ultimately materialistic. God is all about laws and obedience rather than subtle spiritual hints and insights—actions, rather than engaged perceptions or self-aware psychological processes. God's presence within the creation is conceived only as gross divine interventions. Because they occur in linear, historical time, every event in history is important, and every bit has to be anthropomorphic high drama because the mythologized dramatic action inclines toward that splendid and terrible apocalypse at the end of time.

Fundamentalist rhetoric portrays the Lord of the Universe intervening in time and space repeatedly. But the accumulated evidence of both history and prehistory (including the revelations of archaeology and geology) reveal that God is *noninterventionist*, rather than *interventionist*, in this organically unfolding creation we inhabit together. Catastrophes such as the flooding of New Orleans may be called "punishments of God" (by Robertson and Falwell) for licentiousness and liberalism, but these events also have perfectly sensible natural explanations, such as global climate change and the "greenhouse effect." (One is likely to miss the significance of the latter by focusing too much on the former.) Compared to the authoritarian, dominionist God of the fundamentalists, I would counter that the God of our perennial experience seems more like a liberal, letting his children do what they want and suffering their own consequences.

Moreover, if we put aside the anthropocentric notion of history as linear and eschatological and simply look at the operation of the universe itself, we see that it more closely resembles the circular, "eternal return" conceptions of the Hindus and various pagans. The years go around, as do the days and weeks and months, and the planets in their orbits return every so many years. "Everything the Power of the world does is done in a circle," says Black Elk. "The sky is round and I have heard that the Earth is round like a ball, and so are all the stars. Even birds build their nests in a circle, for theirs is the same religion as ours."[7]

As a young man, Albert Einstein was a patent clerk who held no academic position. He did, however, have a unique way of imagining himself riding alongside a beam of light and seeing what things were like at 186,000 miles per second. He also had an unusual ability to render what he saw into the universal language of mathematics. This is how he found $E = MC^2$ and saw that matter is resolvable into energy. Einstein moved our understanding beyond the mechanistic Newtonian physics that had ruled science for a couple of centuries and into the realm of quantum physics, where everything is dependent upon everything else—as in relativity. It is the relational aspect of his theory I want emphasize here.

In the fundamentalist's creation, God, the prime mover, acts with the overwhelming intentionality he is credited with in the book of Genesis. He says it, and the universe has no choice but to obey and make heaven and earth, gardens (presumably with their serpents already in place), man and woman, and so on. It is a mythological account of creation based on psychologically primitive ideas about willpower and magic—blown out of all proportion.

Einstein's God, by contrast, moves through the subtle but powerful energies bound in the atom and the stupendous cosmic displays that pulse through the visible universe. His God has no quarrel with evolution; in fact, it is clearly his *modus operandi*. The living God works in the becoming and the changing of everything *in relation to everything else*. People cannot act without affecting the universe, and God must be as affected by us as we are by him, or her. Relativity, or relationship, as a cosmic principle was thus established early in the twentieth century. It could not but put an end to the old one-way authority-trip gloss on God.

In 1929, a rabbi sent Einstein a telegram: "Do you believe in God? Stop. Answer paid. 50 words." Einstein responded first that "God does not play dice with the universe"—most likely a rebuke to the probabilistic quantum physicists with whom he was feuding at the time. Then he added that he believed "in Spinoza's God, who reveals himself in the lawful harmony of all that exists, but not in a God who concerns himself with the fate and the doings of mankind."[8]

The seventeenth-century Dutch Jewish philosopher Benedict Spinoza was the first to propose a "universal religion," *religio catholica* (having little to do with organized religion or the Catholic Church). For Spinoza, God is in and thoroughly *of* nature. Thus we can learn more about God from studying the universe than from reading a holy book.

It is worth analyzing some of the fundamental differences between the natural form of religion being proposed and the old orthodox form.

In the view presented in the scriptures of the Abrahamic traditions, God makes the creation magically and *separate from himself*. Creation thus abandoned, as it were, falls lower and lower into its intrinsically sinful nature. Much of the Old Testament, from the expulsion from the Garden onward, is made up of sinning creatures and divine displeasure in response—manifested through world-destroying floods, forty-year exiles into the wilderness, and God allowing evil and godless people to run roughshod over his chosen ones to teach them a lesson because they keep giving in to their sinful natures and forgetting about God. Creation thus devolves from bad to worse until Jesus, a more gentle pedagogue than Yahweh, comes to redeem hopelessly fallen humankind.

Thus compounding error upon error, this story, being mythological, goes deep into the psyche and operates there unconsciously, affecting everything else the theology touches: God's wrath, humanity's perpetual error and sin, and the need for redemption through a savior. This pathologized psychology persists through Paul's gloss of Jesus not as just a gentle wisdom teacher but as a cosmic sacrifice of appeasement to a God who sits apart in judgment on his own creation. It ends up in the fundamentalist fairy tale of the Millennium, a future return to the paradise from which we were expelled so long ago, with Christ as a just but irresistible ruler.

The answer from natural religion is as simple as it is profound. In words attributed to Jesus by the Coptic Gospel according to Thomas: "The Kingdom of the Father is spread upon the Earth and men do not see it" (Logion 113:170). "Cleave a piece of wood, I am there; lift up the stone and you will find me there" (Logion 77:26–27).[9] God's nature is our nature, and ours is his. Thinking symbolically, each of us is a "son" or "daughter" of God, made "in his likeness" and carrying the germ, the energy hologram, of the divine in our flesh and spirit.

Natural religion is based on the idea that there is goodness in the self and the universe and intelligence and consciousness in all things, though inflected differently in each. A poem by Gérard de Nerval, written a half-century before Einstein, captures this well:

GOLDEN LINES

Astonishing! Everything is intelligent.
—Pythagoras

Free thinker! Do you think you are the only thinker
on this earth in which life blazes inside all things?
Your liberty does what it wishes with the power it controls,
but when you gather to plan, the universe is not there.

Look carefully in an animal at a spirit alive;

Every flower is a soul opening out into nature;
a mystery touching love is asleep inside metal.
"Everything is intelligent!" And everything moves you.

In that blind wall, look out for the eyes that pierce you.
The substance of creation cannot be separated from a word. . . .
Do not force it to labor in some low phrase!

Often a Holy Thing is living hidden in a dark creature;
and like an eye which is born covered by its lids,
a pure spirit is growing strong under the bark of stones.[10]

NATURAL SPIRITUALITY: WHAT DOES IT LOOK LIKE?

I do not belong to any one religion. Thus they all belong
to me.

—Swami Agnivesh

As I was writing this book, my wife and I attended a peace conference in Bangalore, India, sponsored by the Art of Living (AOL), an international movement established by the Indian guru Sri Sri Ravi Shankar. AOL began as small groups meeting in people's living rooms. The movement is organized around practice more than belief, and no effort is made to detach the participant from his or her own religion. Having grown exponentially to become the world's largest nongovernmental organization, AOL and its sister organization, the International Association for Human Values (IAHV), also started by Shankar, has an exemplary program of charitable activities. They have been first responders in major planetary disasters, including 9/11, Hurricane Katrina, the tsunami in 2004, and earthquakes in Pakistan and Kashmir. Sri Sri says he "wished to form an organization based on inspiration, not indoctrination." Judging from the committed practitioners we met, he succeeded. Inspiration was everywhere, and dogmatism inconspicuous.

The conference in Bangalore, marking AOL's Silver Anniversary, was the largest peace conference ever organized, with 2.5 million people gathered on the Jakur Airfield. Representatives from 144 countries attended, and most were presidents or prime ministers. Sadly, the only major country not to send an official government representative was the United States. Nor did the event, covered all over the rest of the world, receive any noteworthy press or media coverage in America.

One of the luminaries at the conference was Swami Agnivesh, an old friend and associate of Sri Sri, a member of the Indian Parliament, and a champion of the downtrodden. Gurdjieff titled one of his books, which was then made into a film, *Meetings with Remarkable Men*. This sums up the sense of my first meeting with the Swami. Dark of skin and classically handsome, with a sparkling direct gaze, he was dressed in the orange of the Hindu renunciate, with an orange turban. Everywhere he went, people bowed deeply or fell to the ground in front of him. Invariably he would lift them up sweetly and embrace them, saying they didn't need to make such a fuss.

He spoke before a plenary group in a spacious auditorium on the AOL grounds, addressing the distinguished international audience in English with great clarity and directness. "We must join together," he said, "to free religion from those who would hijack it, and bend it to their will. Heretics of the world, unite; all you can lose are the chains of your own dogmas!" With those words, he had my full attention. This book was in its early, conceptual stages, but he seemed to be talking directly to the preoccupations of my own mind.

Agnivesh began with some autobiographical reminiscences. As a curious, lively, and intelligent lad growing up in an orthodox Hindu family, he had many questions about the representations of gods that surrounded him. "Daddy, when Vishnu goes to sleep, does he need a different pillow for each of his (several) heads, or can he just use one big pillow?" "What does Shiva do with all his extra arms—can he play different musical instruments with them? Is he a one-god orchestra?" He told us his childhood image of God was of a giant who walked on the roof and sometimes looked down in a terrifying way. These and other wonderfully imaginative speculations of an eight-year-old prompted scoldings from the adults around him—Hindu fundamentalism being no different than any other kind. He said he learned to shut up around his parents and the Brahmin priests, but he couldn't stop asking questions in his mind. Then he heard a different message from a senior swami called Swami Hari Das, contradicting the images of Vishnu and Shiva everywhere: "I don't think God has legs," the holy man asserted. "He doesn't walk around on the roof." Young Agnivesh was now thoroughly confused.

At age seventeen, Agnivesh encountered the radical Arya Samaj movement, founded by Swami Dayananda, which actually encouraged doubt and dissent—a welcome attitude, he said, that empowered his lifelong journey in both religious and political arenas. Dayananda, too, as a boy, had doubts about orthodox religion. Forced by his father to fast during the annual celebration of Maha-Shivaratri, he wondered why lots of delicious food was nevertheless placed before the image of the god. Usually, the food was all gone by the next morning. One year he resolved to stay awake during Maha-Shivaratri, and see where the offering of holy food went. He found that it went into the bellies of a multitude of mice. After that he refused to "worship idols" and dedicated himself to finding the true nature of God.

The following is constructed from my notes on Agnivesh's public lectures and later personal conversations with him:

There is a yearning in the human mind for freedom. The divine potential is there in all of us. *Sometimes the ability to question is far more important than having all the answers.* Man always tries to create God in his own image. I am most uncomfortable with the people who try to hijack God—some of them have become immensely wealthy and powerful, especially in America, but Indian gurus often follow the pattern too. When religion becomes institutionalized, you get authoritarian leaders and blind followers. It's not really God they're manipulating; it's people's minds, which are part of *samsara* (the illusion).

Why should we not question the religion into which we were born? After all, we had nothing to say about it. We were born into a certain family in a certain society, and were too young to question yet. But as we grow up there is no excuse for not questioning. This is how we get second-rate religions, even if they are basically good to start with. You can't enter into a business contract till you are eighteen. You shouldn't get married until you are mature enough to choose your spouse. Religion is more important than either of these, yet we are supposed to accept it as a spiritual infant.

Religious stories are mythological, beautiful, as long as you don't mistake them for historical facts. Jesus was born of a virgin. A star guided the wise men to him and stood over the stable of his birth. These are wonderful stories, but when you make them literal and unquestionable, build them into billion-dollar industries, and tell everybody they are sinners and there is only one way to redemption, then I think there are serious problems. The Hindu religion with its guru ideal is scarcely better. You remain a psychological child by turning all responsibility over to the guru. East or West, in conventional religion you are surrounded by people who are all saying they believe the same thing. They are truly a herd of sheep—Christianity got that right.

Why would you want to think that somebody died for your sins? And before you even have a chance to commit them! Isn't it in Kazantzakis's *Last Temptation of Christ* that Jesus comes up in disguise in the crowd just as St. Paul or some evangelist is preaching that "Jesus died for your sins"? He is upset and says, "Why are you saying all that about me? That's not my message!" Jesus is told to shut up and go away. "We'll handle this our way, from now on." "They won't believe you, they'll believe us," say the preachers who have hijacked his story.

Spiritual values have to be lived. My own meditation is probably closest to *vipassana*. I work on mindfulness. When I breathe, I notice that I am not the one who is breathing. Who, then, is breathing for me? I experience God in my breathing; I experience God in my own compassion. The way to God is to practice compassion. I urge people to go back to a proper concept of God. God is inside, outside, everywhere. You can't escape God. God doesn't require special food, special practices, or special sycophancy. Ask yourself, "What is the most creative presence in my life?" Be honest, be true to yourself. You might meet God that way.

We are standing at a crossroads. Maybe *we can be the change* we want to bring about. To reclaim God, become a spiritual activist. Ask yourself when it is important to stand up to untruth, to injustice. How can you bring down the false walls some people try to build around God? For me, as I went along, keeping my vow of poverty, I would feel the presence of invisible hands guiding me. There would be some new path.

Both Sri Sri Ravi Shankar and Swami Agnivesh convinced me that social responsibility is not only a part of natural religion, it is a core piece of any new movement that wishes to really "walk its talk" in this world, where we can now fully understand the magnitude of poverty and human suffering.

Moving now from India to Africa, I turn to my friend and mentor, the Zulu *sangoma* Credo Mutwa, whom some call "the wisest man in Africa." His words opened this chapter, so it seems fitting for him to serve as the African contributor to the search for natural religion:

> We in Africa believe that the soul goes through a number of incarnations in its development—toward reaching the goal of maturity. We believe that our present human stage is but one of several stages through which the soul must pass, and we use the symbolism of the butterfly's development from egg to caterpillar, to pupa, and then to adult, as a symbol for the upward movement of the soul through various incarnations.[11]
>
> I think God could be the Source from which all living things come. There is a Source of all order and logic in creation. When one looks at a tree, for example, one can see the artistry and the logic behind each leaf, each branch, and each layer of bark upon the tree. A tree is a highly advanced sort of living machine, and that living machine could only have been created by something that was just as alive and just as wonderful. That is God, I think.[12]

Though I am not sure the "intelligent design" Christians would feel comfortable finding their position supported by a Zulu shaman, this seems to me a wonderful example of natural religion. Indeed, if there is an authentic underlying spiritual truth, it should show up in many places. Baba Mutwa's spirituality is not unlike Hinduism in seeing the soul go through many "incarnations" on its long-term growth trajectory, and not so dissimilar to transcendentalism in finding a radiance and a symbolism in natural processes. Mutwa says his way of teaching spirituality is storytelling. Storytelling, he says, unites us with the minds of our ancestors and with all of humankind at once. The great Zulu storytelling cycles begin with one word: *Indaba*. Then the storyteller says, "I am a story, and you are too, my friends. We move now into the timeless web of stories." Mutwa sometimes adds: Don't try to turn them into historical facts. They are stories. Their role is to inspire and instruct the soul.

I conclude this little world tour in search of fragments of natural religion with an extraordinary story told by an authentic Christian mystic. In 1923, Jesuit paleontologist Pierre Teilhard de Chardin was somewhere in the Central Asian desert studying geological and human artifacts he knew were far older than the Bible—yet the scientific contradiction only deepened his Christianity. It was the Feast of the Transfiguration, and he was far from any church. Taking the sky as his cathedral, Teilhard made an impromptu altar and said a mass, which he later wrote about as "A Mass Said upon the World." It is a moving outpouring from the lonely soul of the priest-archaeologist to the God he loved:

> Once upon a time men took into your temple the first fruits of their harvests, the flower of their flocks. But the offering you really want, the offering you mysteriously need every day to appease your hunger, to slake your thirst is nothing less than the growth of the world borne ever onwards in the stream of universal becoming.
>
> Receive, O Lord, this all-embracing host which your whole creation, moved by your magnetism, offers you at this dawn of a new day. . . .
>
> Yet in the very depths . . . I sense it—a desire, irresistible, hallowing, which makes us cry out, believer and unbeliever alike: "Lord make us *one*."[13]

As he consecrated the host and the wine, the body and blood of his Lord, Teilhard felt rays of spiritual blessing flash from his impromptu altar to the furthest reaches of the universe. Teilhard allowed the contradictions and paradoxes he faced as a believing scientist to make his vision transparent and luminous.

WHAT REALLY MATTERS

Austrian psychiatrist Edward C. Whitmont, who was director of clinical training at the C. G. Jung Institute in New York for many years, collected dreams from his patients that seemed to re-envision spirituality in our time—particularly incorporating the exiled, repressed feminine element and the Dionysian principle of ecstatic union. His earlier books, *The Symbolic Quest* and *The Return of the Goddess*, are now classics of clinical archetypal psychology. Later he focused on what he felt was the essence of soul transformation in *The Alchemy of Healing* and *Dreams: A Portal to the Source*. Having trained for years under Whitmont, I, too, began to analyze patients' dreams, and as mentioned in the last chapter, lead regular dream groups with my wife, Robin. Our dreamers were people of both genders and all ages and walks of life, yet a great number of them had dreams of searching for what could be called "the chapel at the heart of the world." That is to say, in a dozen different disguises, personal imagery that had profound transpersonal significance was erupting into their dreams. The following sketch captures the major elements of what they shared. It is told in the first person singular, as this is how dreamers usually tell their dreams.

I am struggling through what seems a labyrinth, leaving the secular city. I am lost; there are elevators and stairways and hallways that lead nowhere. Sometimes the corridors lead into an underworld, or subway. Sometimes there are dark and terrible places, and sometimes there is a feeling of death or abandonment. But then a mysterious and unexpected Guide shows me where to go, or a dog may help sniff out the way.

At last the Chapel is attained. It is made of natural materials and beautiful glass, so that the sky and nature seem to be both inside and outside it. The people are gathered or are gathering; sunlight or starlight streams through the fragrant, foliage-filled space. I see ladders, and angels, or athletes in colorful garments are ascending and descending on them. Outside or nearby are animals, patiently watching.

A ceremony of exquisite delicacy and attunement is performed on an altar; the celebrant is a woman or a man with knowing eyes or an expression of poignant compassion. Sometimes there is a divine child in a manger, and sometimes an animal is revealed as a divinity. Sometimes there is inspiring music, and sometimes there is a sudden eruption of play, as clowns and acrobats emerge from nowhere and parade through the scene. It is both solemn and playful.

I awaken with my heart beating, tears welling up, and a memory of radiant light permeating the dream.

People having had some variant of this dream feel they have visited a sacred place where a new spirituality is being born. The dream seems to say we are now to find spirituality in the labyrinth of our lives in a way that can only be called "playful" because it is spontaneous, not forced. There are also frustrations and limitations, which must be integrated, but there are also guides and helpers along the way. In this new state, we realize *we belong in this universe.* Our billion-celled brains echo the intricate complexities of the outer world. A light in nature shines through and shows us our own natures. When we see it and let it in, we are home.

In his book *What Really Matters* (1995), Tony Schwartz describes his own journey home to a new spirituality. The epigraph to the opening chapter, titled "A Longing in the Heart," is a quotation from Jung that I couldn't get out of my mind after I saw it: "One does not become enlightened by imagining figures of light, but by making the darkness conscious." It is a gradual enlightenment, not a blinding realization, that Schwartz models— which is what Jung also put forward and Campbell imagined in his hero's journey. Schwartz puts himself on the existential line, trying various spiritual and artistic disciplines, workshops, *vipassana* meditations, and writing about both the successes and, wonderfully, the failures. I find this kind of autobiography, a descent into the darkness of unknowing that yet leads to personal or transpersonal illumination, the core religious literature of our time.

Schwartz tries brainwave biofeedback with neurofeedback pioneer Joe Kamiya, analyzes his dreams with researchers Montague Ullman and Jeremy Taylor, and spends long hours discussing matters of consciousness with Ken Wilber. His own longing in the heart empowers a spiritual search that gradually "makes the darkness conscious." This is a path of integrity, or, in the words of one of his interviewees, meditation teacher Jack Kornfield, "a path with heart." "Transformation does not often occur in a flash," Schwartz writes, "nor in the course of a weekend workshop. Real discovery and change . . . require sustained and committed practices. Nor does any single practice I encountered address the full spectrum of what it means to be a human being—perhaps least of all those practices that claim to provide absolute answers."[14]

Fundamentalists do imagine "figures of light"—with blinding powers and chastening light-swords such as they wield in Timothy LaHaye's and Hal Lindsey's novels. These figures not only glow with what Freud identified as wish fulfillment; they tell us a lot about the inner fantasy lives of the imaginers, reared on comic book superheroes, television, and movies. The problem of evil need not be worked out psychologically in the *tribulations* of our own souls; Jesus and the archangels take care of it, and it is vanquished forever.

Real spiritual transformation, however, is a lifelong process in which you're never done. Dark and light alternate in us and around us daily. Why should we demonize the dark? It is where our rest is consummated and our best dreams are born. Darkness around the roots of trees is as important as the sunlight that ignites the chemistry labs in their leafy tops. Because we live in the presence of energy congealed into matter, we face matter's inertia, opacity, and ability to obscure and conceal. We have those very qualities in ourselves, our own flesh, and our "fundament"—"fundament" usually meaning bowels and other earthy parts. It is silly as well as ungrateful to repudiate matter and our own embeddedness in biological processes. Nature is simply the prerequisite for life as we know it.

In his visionary book *The Biology of Belief*, medical school professor Bruce Lipton describes his own autobiographical journey into the heart of darkness—this time of a scientific as well as personal nature. He has to challenge the dominant Newtonian paradigm of his colleagues with risky, untried ideas based on the post-Einsteinian quantum paradigm. At the same time, his personal and professional life falls apart, and he experiences financial disaster and becomes deeply depressed. Abandoning familiar landmarks, he finds himself, like other visionary explorers, on a sea of unknowing.

As a cellular biologist, Lipton studies the humblest creatures possible: the cells themselves. Getting past his indoctrinated presuppositions from mechanistic science about how cells work, he discovers that the cells, of which all life is made, begin, in a sense, to talk to him. They reveal themselves as exquisitely responsive living entities who reflect the universal energy in which they are swimming. This was more than a simple insight. Lipton writes: "I saw something that was so profound it immediately transformed my life . . . the mechanics of the new science revealed the existence of our spiritual essence and our immortality. For me the conclusions were so unambiguous I instantly went from non-believer to believer."[15] Lipton came to believe that we are made in the image of the universe. One of life's basic principles is the cooperation of the cells, which allowed evolution from single-celled organisms to many-celled creatures like ourselves. "I learned from the cells that we are a part of a whole," Lipton says, "and that we forget this at our peril."[16]

I believe the ability for love, compassion, and mutuality, which Lipton tells us is the very nature of our cells, will ultimately win out over the specter of violent competition and "survival of the fittest," which has been passed along as a kind of biological fundamentalism. We are not just desperately alienated intelligent creatures trying to make the best of a stupid, indifferent, and cruel world. We are the gifted, loved, and privileged children of a billion-year-old mother sometimes called Gaia. The conversation with nature—the world around us—has to be opened and kept open, and honored in such initiatives as global warming treaties and antinuclear proliferation efforts. Men and women need to learn to work together, study differences and commonalities, learn each other's language. When we look for the glint of the spiritual in nature—in animals, in other people, even in experience as it unfolds before us—we begin to find inspiration everywhere. It rises from all things to find us. God talked to the biblical writers through visions and inspired texts, the burning bush and the whirlwind. He talks to us now in particle clouds of electrons and zero-point fields—and the encounters of our daily lives. All around us, millions of creatures are working out their destinies even as we humans work out ours. We know now what works best: flexibility, humility, and learning to talk to each other and to other living things.

Slow down, look, and listen more carefully. Dilate the heart with compassion. Under the light of consciousness, judgment and anger vanish, leading to a dawning awareness, or perhaps a chuckle. This is natural religion. And when we get over all the *sturm und drang* of one age and its archetypes dying and another coming along, maybe our religions will find their way to normalcy and adulthood, stop the death struggles with each other, and be more humble about their mistakes—and, ultimately, less afraid.

The following prayer is dedicated to that glorious day.

INCANTATIONS TO THE HIDDEN GOD

How you drove a chariot in battle,
How you walked as a pilgrim,
one-eyed and with a broad flopped hat,
How one day you went naked
black and female and wore
a terrible necklace of skulls
to wake us up.
How you danced wearing
a bear mask.
How you went down into the
Underworld, to sit as a judge of men.
How, hawk-winged,
you carried the sun to its zenith.
How as a beautiful youth you died again and again,
how many times have we wept for you,
sung holy dirges, and made sweet things
for your birth.
You were the voice from the whirlwind,
You were the golden calf,
and He who threw down the calf.
You were Mother of us all,
and how many times you wept

for all your children.
The fire from your terrible waking eye
ignited the God of Love
to holy ash.
When you dance your Rapture
the universe becomes a burning ground.
Let those who feel that day is upon us
Learn to find patience and compassion for
All that live in our fragile, beautiful world.
Let us use your terrible sword to slay our egos,
not our brothers.

NOTES

CHAPTER ONE: THE PHANTOM RULERS OF HUMANITY

1. Bastian (1826–1905) was often cited by Campbell as Jung's predecessor in an archetypal theory. Joseph Campbell, *Primitive Mythology*, vol. 1 of *The Masks of God* (New York: Viking, 1959), 32.

2. This is my simplification of Campbell's more detailed "Four Functions of Mythology." See Stephen Larsen, *The Shaman's Doorway* (1976; repr., Rochester, VT.: Inner Traditions, 1988).

3. Personal conversation with Jerome Bruner. See also Jerome Bruner, *Actual Minds, Possible Worlds: The Jerusalem-Harvard Lectures* (Cambridge: Harvard University Press, 1986).

4. Sigmund Freud, *Beyond the Pleasure Principle*, ed. and trans. by James Strachey, introd. by Gregory Zilborg (New York: W. W. Norton, 1961).

5. Sigmund Freud, *Early Psychoanalytic Writings*, introd. by Philip Rieff, *The Collected Papers of Sigmund Freud* (New York: Collier, 1963); Otto Rank, *The Myth of the Birth of the Hero and Other Writings*, ed. Philip Freund (New York: Vintage, 1959); Anna Freud, *Psychoanalysis: For Teachers and Parents*, trans. by Barbara Low (Boston: Beacon, 1960); Melanie Klein, *Love, Guilt and Reparation and Other Works 1921–1945*, in *The Complete Works of Melanie Klein*, introd. by R. E. Money-Kyrle (New York: Dell, Delta, 1975); Wilhelm Reich, *Character Analysis*, 3d ed., trans. by Vincent R. Carfagno (New York: Pocket, 1976).

6. C. G. Jung, *Symbols of Transformation: An Analysis of the Prelude to a Case of Schizophrenia*, 5th ed., trans. by R. F. C. Hull, Bollingen Series 20: Vol. 5, *The Collected Works of C. G. Jung* (1956; repr., Princeton: Princeton University Press, 1967), foreword, xxv. Jung also discusses his search for his own life-myth in his autobiography, *Memories, Dreams, Reflections*, recorded and ed. by Aniela Jaffé, trans. by Richard Winston and Clara Winston, 1961. (New York: Random House/Vintage, 1963).

7. Stanley Milgram, *Obedience to Authority* (New York: Harper, 1974); Hannah Arendt, *The Portable Hannah Arendt* (New York: Viking, 2000); Erich Fromm, *Escape from Freedom*, in *The Holt Collected Works of Erich Fromm* (New York: Holt, Rinehart, and Winston, 1976); Eric Hoffer, *The True Believer: Thoughts on the Nature of Mass Movements* (New York: Harper Torchbooks, 1951).

8. Joseph Campbell, *The Hero with a Thousand Faces*, Bollingen Series 17 (1949; repr., Princeton: Princeton University Press, 1973). Joseph Campbell, *The Masks of God: Primitive Mythology* (New York: Viking, 1962). Joseph Campbell, *Myths to Live By* (New York: Viking, 1972).

9. David Feinstein and Stanley Krippner, *Personal Mythology: The Psychology of Your Evolving Self; Using Ritual, Dreams, and Imagination to Discover Your Inner Story*

(Los Angeles: Tarcher, 1988); Rollo May, *The Cry for Myth* (New York and London: W. W. Norton, 1991); Sam Keen and Anne Valley-Fox, *Your Mythic Journey: Finding Meaning in Your Life through Writing and Storytelling* (Los Angeles: Tarcher, 1973); Jean Houston, *A Mythic Life: Learning to Live Our Greater Story* (San Francisco: HarperSanFrancisco, 1996); Stephen Larsen, *The Mythic Imagination: Your Quest for Meaning through Personal Mythology* (New York: Bantam, 1990); Joseph Campbell, with Bill Moyers, *The Power of Myth*, ed. by Betty Sue Flowers (New York: Doubleday Anchor, 1988); *Joseph Campbell and the Power of Myth*, with Bill Moyers, 6 videocassettes (New York: Mystic Fire Video, 1988).

10. Joseph Campbell, *The Inner Reaches of Outer Space: Metaphor as Myth and as Religion* (New York: Harper & Row, 1986), 13.

11. Ibid., 22.

12. Ibid., 15. I have taken the quote directly from Campbell; my Bible has slightly different wording but contains the same passages in Deuteronomy.

CHAPTER TWO: THE NEUROBIOLOGY OF BELIEF

1. Andrew Newberg, Eugene D'Aquili, and Vince Rause, *Why God Won't Go Away: Brain Science and the Biology of Belief* (New York: Ballantine, 2001); James Austin, *Zen and the Brain: Toward an Understanding of Meditation and Consciousness* (Cambridge, MA: MIT Press, 1998).

2. The work of Donald Hebb, Edward Tolman, and N. McLaren all point to the fact that our perception is really made of "cognitive maps," those cascades of stereotyped information called "engrams," "memes," or "mythogems."

3. Al Gore, *The Assault on Reason* (New York: Penguin, 2007).

4. Daniel C. Dennett, *Kinds of Minds: Toward an Understanding of Consciousness* (New York: Basic Books, 1996).

5. Strong and Elwyn (1943) quoted in Robert Ornstein, *The Psychology of Consciousness* (New York: Harcourt Brace, 1977), 101.

6. Michael Gazzaniga, "The Split Brain in Man," *Scientific American* (1967): 24–29.

7. The dichotomy had already announced itself at the end of the nineteenth century. Conservatives in education believed in teaching reading, writing, and arithmetic and an intellectual curriculum. "Progressive education," taking its inspiration from the work of William James and John Dewey, believed there are many kinds of intelligence that complement each other, and that curricula should include music, the arts, and physical education.

8. Hoffer, *The True Believer* (see chap. 1, n. 7).

9. Nobel laureate Roger Sperry did a lot of his most important work on the bilateral functioning of the hemispheres and the slender and vulnerable *commisure*—or neu-

ral connector—called the *corpus callosum* that lies between them. See R. W. Sperry, "The Great Cerebral Commisure," *Scientific American* (1964): 45–52.

10. There are a handful of other neural connections, but, along with the *optic chiasm* and subcortical *limbic* or *thalamic* nonconscious connections, they are extremely small and probably negligible in hemispheric intercommunication. For the sake of metaphor, we can liken them to the other tunnels and bridges that cross the Hudson: the Lincoln and Holland tunnels and the far-away Verrazano Narrows Bridge.

11. Jim Robbins, *A Symphony in the Brain: The Evolution of the New Brain Wave Biofeedback* (New York: Atlantic Monthly Press, 2000).

12. R. J. Davidson, "Cerebral Asymmetry, Emotion, and Affective Style," in R. J. Davidson and Hugdahl, eds., *Brain Asymmetry* (Cambridge: MIT Press, 1995); R. J. Davidson, "Anterior Electrophysiological Asymmetries, Emotion and Depression: Conceptual and Methodological Conundrums," *Psychophysiology*, 35 (1998): 607–614.

13. Again, the situation is more complex than this simple elucidation. Alpha can also be a sign of ADD, anxiety, or brain injury, depending on the amplitude and location. This is a complex field. See Stephen Larsen, *The Healing Power of Neurofeedback: The Revolutionary LENS Technique for Restoring Optimal Brain Function* (Rochester, VT., Healing Arts Press, 2006).

14. Association for Applied Psychophysiology and Biofeedback, national meeting, Las Vegas, 2002. Panel chaired by psychologist Nancy White, participants included Mary Lee Esty and Carol Schneider.

15. Lester G. Fehmi and J. T. McKnight, "Attention and Neurofeedback Synchrony Training: Clinical Results and Their Significance," *Journal of Neurotherapy* 5(1/2) (2001): 45–61. See also George Fritz and Lester G. Fehmi, *The Open Focus Handbook: The Self-Regulation of Attention in Biofeedback Training and Everyday Activities* (Princeton, NJ: Biofeedback Computers, 1982).

CHAPTER THREE: AUTHORITY, RITUAL, AND DISSOCIATION

1. Paul Shepard, *The Others: How Animals Made Us Human* (Washington DC: Island Press / Shearwater Books, 1996), 17; my emphasis.

2. Giacomo Rizzolatti et al., "Premotor Cortex and the Recognition of Motor Actions," *Cognitive Brain Research* 3 (1996): 131–141. See also V. S. Ramachandran, "Mirror Neurons and Imitation Learning as the Driving Force behind 'the Great Leap Forward' in Human Evolution," Edge Foundation; Wikipedia, "Mirror Neuron," http://en.wikipedia.org/wiki/Mirror_cells (retrieved on 1 Nov. 2006).

3. Dwight Pentecost, quoted in Randall Balmer, *Mine Eyes Have Seen the Glory: A Journey Into the Evangelical Subculture in America* (New York: Oxford University Press, 1993), 81.

4. Ibid.

5. Wikipedia, "Kohlberg's Stages of Moral Development," http://en.wikipedia.org/wiki/Kohlberg%27s_stages_of_moral_development.

6. Thom Hartmann, *Beyond ADD: Hunting for Reasons in the Past and Present* (Grass Valley, CA.: Underwood Books, 1996).

7. Daniel G. Amen, *Change Your Brain, Change Your Life* (New York: Random House / Three Rivers Press, 1998), 152.

8. Ibid., 153.

9. Larsen, *The Healing Power of Neurofeedback* (see chap. 2, n. 13).

10. Ibid.

11. Ernest Kurtz and Katherine Ketcham, *The Spirituality of Imperfection: Storytelling and the Journey to Wholeness* (New York: Bantam Books, 1992), 2.

12. "The Wisdom of Ann Coulter," *The Washington Monthly*, October, 2001, washingtonmonthly.com/features/2001/0111.coulterwisdom.

13. Charles Kimball, *When Religion Becomes Evil: Five Warning Signs* (San Francisco: HarperCollins, 2002).

14. "God Tells Pat Robertson: Expect a Good Year for President Bush," *Church & State*, 40 (February 2005): 16, 17.

15. Hoffer, *The True Believer* (see chap. 1, n. 7).

16. The following account of the Branch Davidian tragedy at Waco, Texas is based on James Tabor and Eugene Gallagher, *Why Waco? Cults and the Battle for Religious Freedom in America* (Berkeley and Los Angeles: University of California Press, 1995).

17. Ibid., 32.

18. Ibid., 66.

19. Ibid., 86.

20. Ibid., 208.

21. Ibid., 231 n 22.

22. John Dart, "Buddhist Sect Alarmed by Reports that Leader Kept His AIDS a Secret." *Los Angeles Times*, Home Edition Section, 3 March 1989. "Ösel Tendzin, 45, American-born regent of the international Vajradhatu Buddhist organization . . . whose homosexual activity was known to the movement's insiders, has been infected with the AIDS virus since 1985 but did not acknowledge the problem until last December when a companion was also found to be infected. " www.aegis.com/news/lt/1989/LT890302.html.

23. This was at the Harmonia Mundi conference in 1990 in Newport Beach, California. In addition to the more than one thousand attendees, there were physicians, psy-

chiatrists, social workers, nuns, and monks all working on the rampant problems surfacing in their parishes and consulting rooms.

24. One woman at the conference who had a long relationship with a lama told me that she was touched by his need for her, but that it was difficult and strange, in no way a normal relationship. It fueled her fantasies about having special qualities, but he debunked them. She felt empowered by him, but though he treated her with respect, she was always aware he had other lovers.

CHAPTER FOUR: FRAGMENTS OF THE GODS

1. I think of the phenomenal energies released in the attempted genocide of Tibetan Buddhism, as many accomplished and advanced lamas found themselves without a traditional culture in which to minister. The world was the beneficiary, as Vajrayana monasteries and learning centers were founded around the globe.

2. Larsen, *The Mythic Imagination* (see chap. 1, n. 9).

3. David Miller, *The New Polytheism: Rebirth of the Gods and Goddesses* (New York: Harper & Row, 1974); *Gods and Games* (New York: World Publications, 1970).

4. James Hillman, *Re-Visioning Psychology* (New York: Harper & Row, 1975).

5. See http://www.theonion.com/content/node/28626.

6. Bernard McGinn, *The Antichrist: Two Thousand Years of the Human Fascination with Evil* (San Francisco: Harper San Francisco, 1994), 40, 41.

7. *Encyclopedia Brittanica*, Irenaeus, Saint, *Macropedia*, 1979, vol. 9, 889. The article mentions a biography by F. R. M. Hitchcock, *Irenaeus of Lugdunum*.

8. Hippolytus, *Antichrist* 6. Quoted in McGinn, *The Antichrist*, 61.

9. McGinn, *The Antichrist*.

10. Ibid., 4.

11. Barbara R. Rossing, *The Rapture Exposed: The Message of Hope in the Book of Revelation* (Boulder, CO: Perseus/Westview, 2004); Robert Jewett, *Jesus against the Rapture: Seven Unexpected Prophecies* (Philadelphia: Westminster Press, 1979).

12. McGinn, *The Antichrist*, 5.

CHAPTER FIVE: DUALISM AND MILLENNIALISM IN CHRISTIANITY

1. Charles H. Kahn, *The Art and Thought of Heraclitus: An Edition of the Fragments with Translation and Commentary* (Cambridge: Cambridge University Press, 1981), 183.

2. The name *Persia* comes from one of the Aryan tribes that swept down into it from the north, as did the Medes, who founded the great Iranian empire, roughly around 1000 BCE. The name *Iran*, which means "the land of Aryans," is preferred by the

modern country, which changed the name officially in 1934. Tony Allan, Charles Philips, and Michael Kerrigan, *Wise Lord of the Sky: Persian Myth; Myth and Mankind* (Amsterdam: Time-Life Books, 1999), 7.

3. "Mithraism had much in common with Christian beliefs, symbols and practices, such as baptism for the remission of sins, a symbolic meal of communion including consecrated wine, the sign on the brow, redemption, salvation, sacramentary grace, rebirth in the spirit, confirmation, and the promise of eternal life. The celebration of the birth of Mithra was on the 25th of December, and that of his rebirth at the spring equinox. Indeed, the shocked Christian apologists were driven to denounce the Mithraic beliefs and customs as diabolical and blasphemous caricatures of Christianity." Under "Mithra," in Maria Leach, ed., *Standard Dictionary of Folklore, Mythology, and Legend* (New York: Harper and Row, 1972).

4. Johannes Quasten, *Patrology*, vol 2: *The Ante-Nicene Literature after Irenaeus* (Antwerp: Spectrum, 1953).

5. Elaine Pagels, The Gnostic Gospels (New York: Random House, 1979).

6. Ernest Sandeen, *The Roots of Fundamentalism: British and American Millenarianism 1800–1930* (Chicago and London: University of Chicago Press, 1970).

7. Ibid., 11.

8. Irving's dates, according to Sandeen, are 1792–1834.

9. Sandeen, *Roots of Fundamentalism*, 31.

10. Ibid., 32.

11. Ibid., 38.

12. Thomas Croskery, "The Plymouth Brethren," Princeton Review, i (1872): 48. Quoted in Sandeen, *Roots of Fundamentalism*, 74.

13. T. Robbins and S. Palmer, eds., *Millennium, Messiahs, and Mayhem* (New York and London: Routledge, 1997), 47.

14. Evangelical Alliance, Report of the Proceedings of the Conference Held in London, 1846. Cited in Sandeen, *Roots of Fundamentalism*, 44.

15. Sandeen, *Roots of Fundamentalism*, 43.

16. Noyes, the author of *Strange Cults and Utopias in Nineteenth Century America*, promulgated ideas akin to socialism and practiced "group marriage" in the community he founded.

17. Boyer describes Miller's method: "Making the usual day = 1 year transposition, and starting from 458 B.C. when Artaxerxes of Persia authorized the exiled Jewish priest Ezra to rebuild the Temple in Jerusalem, Miller arrived at 1843." Paul Boyer, *When Time Shall Be No More: Prophecy Belief in Modern American Culture* (Cambridge, MA: Harvard University Press / Belknap, 1992), 81.

18. The source for the recollection of Hiram Edson is Ronald L. Numbers and Jonathan M. Butler, *The Disappointed: Millerism and Millenarianism in the Nineteenth Century* (Knoxville: University of Tennessee Press, 1993); quoted in Boyer, *When Time Shall Be no More*, 81.

19. Boyer, *When Time Shall Be no More*, 54.

20. Doug Hackleman, "The Significance of Ellen White's Head Injury," *Adventist Currents*, 1985. See "Ellen White Research Project," www.ellenwhite.org.

21. John Harvey Kellogg, for example, was a millennialist. See the movie *The Road to Wellville* for a fascinating peek into this world.

22. Robbins and Palmer, *Millennium, Messiahs, and Mayhem*, 212.

23. Boyer, *When Time Shall be no More*, 92.

24. Sandeen, *Roots of Fundamentalism*, 99.

25. Luther also weighed in heavily in this controversy, on the side of "faith alone," whereas many of his contemporaries urged that a life of charity, or "works," was truly necessary for the Christian. But the extreme forms of premillenialism place faith or the big psychological capitulation of "being saved" above any Christlike act of public service. This is why I refer to them as crypto-Gnostics, who think the world is hopelessly in the hands of a twisted archon.

26. It is interesting to note that the year of Scofield's birth (1843) was the same as the first Miller prophecy, and the year of Joseph Smith's death (1844) the same as the second prophecy.

27. Boyer, *When Time Shall be no More*, 96.

28. Sandeen, *Roots of Fundamentalism*, 185.

29. Brookes was also the author of *Maranatha: Or the Lord Cometh* (1870), and the plainspoken *The Truth*. A movement called "the Maranatha" was influential in evangelical Christianity.

30. Boyer, *When Time Shall be no More*, 246.

31. Ibid., 93.

32. Henry Louis Mencken (1880-1956), "Homo Neanderthalensis," *The Baltimore Evening Sun*, 29 June 1925; "The Scopes Trial: Mencken Finds Daytonians Full of Sickening Doubts About Value of Publicity," *The Baltimore Evening Sun*, 9 July 1925; "The Scopes Trial: Impossibility of Obtaining Fair Jury Insures Scopes' Conviction," *The Baltimore Evening Sun*, 10 July 1925. See also Boyer, *When Time Shall be no More*; Grace Halsell, *Prophecy and Politics: Militant Evangelists on the Road to Nuclear War* (Westport CT: Lawrence Hill, 1986); George Marsden, *Evangelicalism and Modern America* (Grand Rapids, MI: William B. Eerdmans, 1984); Mark Noll, *The Scandal of the Evangelical Mind* (Grand Rapids, MI: William B. Eerdmans, 1994).

33. Peter J. Boyer, "The Big Tent: Billy Graham, Franklin Graham, and the Transformation of American Evangelism," *The New Yorker* 22 (August 2005): 42–54.

34. Ibid., 47.

35. Ibid., 51.

36. James Price and William Goodman, *Jerry Falwell: An Unauthorized Profile* (Lynchburg, VA: Paris & Associates, 1981), 130; and Susan Friend Harding, *The Book of Jerry Falwell: Fundamentalist Language and Politics* (Princeton: Princeton University Press, 2000), 69.

CHAPTER SIX: THE ROOTS OF ISLAMIC FUNDAMENTALISM

1. Karen Armstrong, *A History of God: The 4000-Year-Old Quest of Judaism Christianity and Islam* (New York: Random House/Ballantine, 1993).

2. Ibid., 133.

3. Muhammad's dates are conventionally 570–632.

4. Armstrong, *History of God*, 135.

5. Clearly this is a shamanic request. A *kahin* is a medium who channels spirits (*djinn*). Of course, in the high traditions, the inhabiting spirit is not just a local but the cosmic Lord of the known universe—in this case, as known in the seventh century.

6. Ibn Ishaq, *Sira*, 153, in A. Guillame, *The Life of Muhammad*, 106. Quoted in Armstrong, *History of God*, 138.

7. Armstrong, *History of God*, 139.

8. Ibid., 135.

9. Ibid., 144.

10. Ibid., 149.

11. Ibid., 150.

12. Ibid., 154.

13. Martin Riesèbrodt, *Pious Passion: The Emergence of Modern Fundamentalism in the United States and Iran*, trans. by Don Reneau, (1990; repr., Berkeley and Los Angeles: University of California Press, 1993), 141.

14. Jessica Stern, *Terror in the Name of God: Why Religous Militants Kill* (New York: HarperCollins, 2003), 68.

15. In the modern political scheme, it is interesting to note how many of the terrorists who engineered 9/11 were Wahhabists and/or from Saudi Arabia. For all its outspoken criticism of the United States, Shi'a has been less involved in actual violence—an exception being the Iran hostage situation.

16. Stern, *Terror in the Name of God*, 46.

17. Fareed Zakaria, "Islam and Power," *Newsweek*, 13 February 2006, 35–37.

18. Salman Rushdie, *The Satanic Verses* (London: Viking, 1988).

19. Sadik J. Al-Azm, "The Satanic Verses Post Festum: The Global, the Local, the Literary," *Comparative Studies of South Asia, Africa and the Middle East* 20:1–2 (2000): 59.

20. Medhi Mozaffari, *Fatwa: Violence and Discourtesy* (Aarhus, Denmark: Aarhus University Press, 1998), 46.

21. The death sentence was technically not a *fatwa* when it was first issued, according to Al-Azm. A *fatwa* is a specific kind of contract, signed onto by a sheikh or ayatollah who then takes spiritual responsibility for it. The name *fatwa* was applied to the Khomeini Rushdie affair by the European press. Al-Azm, "The Satanic Verses Post Festum," 57.

22. Ibid., 54.

23. Ibid, 60.

24. Isma'il (d.760), son of and designated successor to the 6th imam, Ja'far ibn Muhammad, who outlived him. The Isma'iliyah sect of Shi'ah was founded by his followers. From them descended other influential sects, among them the Fatimids, Qarmatians, and Assassins.

25 Jalalludin Rumi (c. 1273), a Persian poet of mystical love, acknowledged as the greatest of Sufi poets. His creative life was galvanized by his relationship with the martyred Shams ad-Din of Tabriz, to whom much of his verse is addressed. The Mawlawiyah or Whirling Dervishes, founded after his death, continue his ecstatic practice of singing and dancing in meditation. The *Divan-e Shams* and the *Masnawi-ye Ma'navi* are considered his principal works, which are widely translated in the West. See the many beautiful translations of Coleman Barks, among them *The Essential Rumi*, with John Moyne (San Francisco: HarperSanFrancisco, a Division of HarperCollins Publishers, 1995).

26. Huston Smith and Phil Cousineau, *The Way Things Are: Conversations with Huston Smith on the Spiritual Life* (Berkeley and Los Angeles: University of California Press, 2003), 259.

CHAPTER SEVEN: SECULAR FUNDAMENTALISM

1. George M. Marsden, *Fundamentalism and American Culture: The Shaping of Twentieth-Century Evangelicalism: 1870–1925* (Oxford: Oxford University Press, 1980).

2. Feinstein and Krippner, *Personal Mythology* (see chap. 1, n. 9).

3. David Van Biema, "God vs. Science," *Time Magazine*, 13 Nov. 2006, 48.

4. Smith and Cousineau, *The Way Things Are* (see chap. 6, n. 24).

5. Richard Milton, *Alternative Science: Challenging the Myths of the Scientific Establishment* (Rochester, VT.: Park St. Press, 1994), 3.

6. Ibid., 5.

7. Ibid., 179.

8. Encyclopedia Britannica, 15th edition, Macropedia, vol. 11, 827.

9. James S. Gordon, *Manifesto for a New Medicine: Your Guide to Healing Partnerships and the Wise Use of Alternative Therapies* (Reading, MA: Addison-Wesley, 1996), 23; my emphasis.

10. History of Medicine, *Encyclopedia Britanica*, 15th edition, Macropedia, vol. 11, 830, 831.

11. *Encyclopedia Britannica*, vol. 16 (New York, 1979), 529.

12. Ibid.

13. Ibid., 530.

14. Ibid.

15. Allen Kraut, http:history.nih.gov/exhibits/goldberger/docs/pellagre_5htm.

16. William McGuire, ed., *The Freud/Jung Letters: The Correspondence Between Sigmund Freud and C. G. Jung*, trans. by Ralph Manheim and R. F. C. Hull, Bollingen Series 94 (Princeton: Princeton University Press, 1974).

17. Hillman, *Re-Visioning Psychology* (see chap. 4, n. 4).

18. Sharon Begley, "Get Shrunk at your Own Risk," *Newsweek*, 18 June 2007, 49.

19. All quotations are from the website http://skepdic.com/news/newsletter66.html or http://skepdic.com/homeo.html.

CHAPTER EIGHT: THE FIVE-MINUTE FUNDAMENTALIST

1. Though modern technological and literate societies do not really employ shamans in their traditional roles, and I have some problems with psychologists or other healers who hang out a shingle as a "shaman," I consider Brad the real thing. He had his first experience of trance as a young man, falling down outside the collection of Native American artifacts that contained Black Elk's pipe and medicine bundle. Trained as a university professor, he has nonetheless pursued shamanic wisdom all over the world, and has been recognized by elders in a significant number of traditions. See Bradford Keeney, Ph.D., *Shaking out the Spirits: A Psychotherapist's Entry into the Healing Mysteries of Global Shamanism* (Barrytown, N.Y.: Barrytown / Station Hill Press, 1994), for which I wrote the foreword. See also the books on shamanic lore from all over the world that Brad edited published by the Ringing Rocks Foundation: *Profiles of Healing* series (Philadelphia: Ringing Rocks Press).

2. George Lakoff, *Don't Think of an Elephant: Know Your Values and Frame the Debate; A Progressive Guide to Action*, foreword by Howard Dean, introd. by Don Hazen (White River Jct., VT: Chelsea Green, 2004).

3. During the Harmonia Mundi conference, 1990, in San Diego, Dan Goleman, along with other psychologists, was examining the idea of abuse of spiritual privilege. Dan is also author of the influential book, *Emotional Intelligence: Why It Can Matter More Than IQ* (New York: Bantam, 1995).

4. Larsen, *The Mythic Imagination* (see chap. 1, n. 9). Also Larsen, *The Shaman's Doorway* (see chap. 1, n. 2).

5. See any of Jeremy Taylor's excellent books or the classic by Edward Whitmont, *Dreams: A Portal to the Source;* see also Whitmont's *The Alchemy of Healing: Psyche and Soma; The Symbolic Quest: Basic Concepts of Analytical Psychology;* and other titles cited in the bibliography.

6. Tony Schwartz, *What Really Matters: Searching for Wisdom in America* (New York and London: Bantam, 1995).

7. Larsen, *The Healing Power of Neurofeedback* (see chap. 2, n. 13).

8. "The LENS and Self-Actualization and Optimal Performance," paper presented at *The LENS 2007 Conference*, May 3-7, 2007; scheduled for ISNR (International Society for Neurofeedback and Research) Conference, San Diego, Sept. 6-9, 2007.

9. See Doc Lew Childre, Howard Martin and Donna Beech, *The HeartMath® solution: The Institute of HeartMath®'s Revolutionary Program for Engaging the Power of the Heart's Intelligence* (San Francisco, Harper, 1999). See also HeartMath.com and heartmath.org.

10. The reader is also directed to an on-line service, *The Authoritarians*, provided by a psychologist colleague Dr. Bob Altemeyer for analysis and delineation of the connection between fundamentalism and right-wing authoritarian attitudes, which includes numerous questionnaires that have been somewhat standardized through large numbers of experimental participants. See also Altemeyer's *Right Wing Authoritarianism* (Winnipeg: University of Manitoba Press, 1981).

CHAPTER NINE: NATURAL RELIGION

1. Ralph Waldo Emerson, "Essays: History," *The Works of Ralph Waldo Emerson in One Volume: Including the Poems, Philosophic and Inspirational Essays, and Biographical Studies. The Giant International Series* (New York: Walter J. Black, 1925), 83.

2. Robin Larsen, editor, *Emanuel Swedenborg: A Continuing Vision* (New York: The Swedenborg Foundation, 1988).

3. Coincidentally, 1757 also happens to be the year of William Blake's birth. Blake, who later developed a love/hate relationship with Swedenborg's theology, did think this significant.

4. *Arcana Coelestia* 6895[2], quoted in Michael Stanley, "The Relevance of Emanuel Swedenborg's Theological Concepts for the New Age as It Is Envisioned Today." In Robin Larsen, ed., *Emanuel Swedenborg: A Continuing Vision* (New York: The Swedenborg Foundation, 1988), 358.

5. George F. Dole, *A Thoughtful Soul* (West Chester. PA: Chrysalis, 1995).

6. I include a brief study of the Iroquois dream lore in the second chapter of Larsen, *The Shaman's Doorway* (see chap. 1, n. 2).

7. John Neihardt ed., *Black Elk Speaks* (Lincoln, NE: University of Nebraska Press, 1961), 198; see also Joseph Epes Brown, ed., *The Sacred Pipe: Black Elk's Account of the Seven Rites of the Oglala Sioux* (New York: Penguin, 1971).

8. Sharon Begley, "The Man Who Read God's Mind," (*Newsweek*, 16 April 2007), review of the new biography by Walter Isaacson, *Einstein: His Life and Universe* (www.msnbc.msn.com/id/17995521/site/newsweek/page/2/).

9. One of Joseph Campbell's favorite quotes, referenced in *The Inner Reaches of Outer Space: Metaphor as Myth and as Religion* (New York: Harper & Row, 1986): *The Gospel According to Thomas,* Coptic text, tr. by A. Guillaumont, H.-C. Puech, G. Quispel, W. Till., and Yassah 'Abd al Masih (Leiden: E. J. Brill; New York: Harper, 1950), 43, 57.

10. Gérard de Nerval (1854), "Golden Lines," trans. by Robert Bly in Robert Bly, *News of the Universe: Poems of Twofold Consciousness* (San Francisco: Sierra Club Books, 1980), 38.

11. Vusamazulu Credo Mutwa, *Song of the Stars: The Lore of a Zulu Shaman*, ed. by Stephen Larsen (Barrytown, NY: Barrytown / Station Hill Openings, 1996), 201.

12. Ibid., 204.

13. Teilhard de Chardin, *Hymn of the Universe* (New York: Harper Torchbooks, 1961), 20.

14. Tony Schwartz, *What Really Matters: Searching for Wisdom in America* (New York and London: Bantam, 1995), 431.

15. Bruce Lipton, *The Biology of Belief* (Santa Rosa, CA: Mountain of Love / Elite Books, 2005), 183.

16. Ibid., 189.

BIBLIOGRAPHY

Al-Azm, Sadik J. "The Satanic Verses Post Festum: The Global, the Local, the Literary." *Comparative Studies of South Asia, Africa and the Middle East* XX, nos. 1 and 2 (2000).

Allan, Tony, Charles Phillips, Michael Kerrigan, and Vesta Sarkhosh Curtis. *Wise Lord of the Sky: Persian Myth; Myth and Mankind.* Amsterdam: Time-Life Books, 1999.

Almond, Gabriel A., R. Scott Appleby, and Emmanuel Sivan. *Strong Religion: The Rise of Fundamentalisms around the World.* Chicago and London: University of Chicago Press, 2003.

Altemeyer, Robert, Ph.D. *Right Wing Authoritarianism.* Winnipeg: University of Manitoba Press, 1981.

Amen, Daniel G. *Change Your Brain, Change Your Life.* New York: Random House / Three Rivers Press, 1998.

Arendt, Hannah. *The Portable Hannah Arendt.* New York: Viking, 2000.

Armstrong, Karen. *A History of God: The 4000-Year-Old Quest of Judaism, Christianity, and Islam.* New York: Random House / Ballantine, 1993.

_____. *Islam: A Short History.* New York: The Modern Library, 2000.

_____. *A Short History of Myth.* London: Cannongate, 2005.

Austin, James. *Zen and the Brain: Toward an Understanding of Meditation and Consciousness.* Cambridge, MA: MIT Press, 1998.

Balmer, Randall. *Mine Eyes Have Seen the Glory: A Journey Into the Evangelical Subculture in America.* New York: Oxford University Press, 1993.

Barker, John. *Christianity in Oceania.* Lanham, New York, London: University Press of America, 1990.

Bastian, Adolf. *Das Beständige in den Menschenrassen und die Spielweite ihrer Veränderlichkeit.* Berlin: Dietrich Reimer, 1868.

_____. *Ethnische Elementargedanken in der Lehre vom Menschen.* Berlin: Weidmann, 1895.

Begley, Sharon. "The Man Who Read God's Mind." *Newsweek,* 16 April 2007. www.msnbc.msn.com/id/17995521/site/newsweek/page/2.

Benjamin, Daniel, and Steven Simon. *The Age of Sacred Terror.* New York: Random House, 2002.

Black Elk, recorded and edited by Joseph Epes Brown. *The Sacred Pipe: Black Elk's Account of the Seven Rites of the Oglala Sioux.* New York: Penguin Books, 1981. First published by University of Oklahoma Press, 1953.

Bly, Robert, ed. and trans. *News of the Universe: Poems of Twofold Consciousness.* San Francisco: Sierra Club Books, 1980.

Borowsky, Irvin J., ed. *Defining New Christian/Jewish Dialogue.* New York: Crossroad Publishing, 2004.

Boyer, Paul. *When Time Shall Be No More: Prophecy Belief in Modern American Culture.* Cambridge, MA: Harvard University Press / Belknap, 1992.

Boyer, Peter J. "The Big Tent: Billy Graham, Franklin Graham, and the Transformation of American Evangelism." *The New Yorker,* 22 August 2005, 42–54.

Bruner, Jerome S. *Actual Minds, Possible Worlds: The Jerusalem-Harvard Lectures.* Cambridge, MA: Harvard University Press, 1986.

Campbell, Joseph. *The Inner Reaches of Outer Space: Metaphor as Myth and as Religion.* New York: Harper and Row, 1986.

———. *The Masks of God: Primitive Mythology.* New York: Viking, 1959.

Campbell, Joseph, with Bill Moyers. *The Power of Myth.* New York: Doubleday Anchor, 1988.

Childre, Doc Lew, Howard Martin, and Donna Beech. *The HeartMath® Solution.* San Francisco: HarperSanFrancisco, 1999.

Collins, John J. *The Apocalyptic Imagination: An Introduction to the Jewish Matrix of Christianity.* New York: Crossroad, 1984.

Damasio, Antonio. *Descartes' Error: Emotion, Reason and the Human Brain.* New York: G. P. Putnam's Sons, 1994.

———. *The Feeling of What Happens: The Body and Emotion in the Making of Consciousness.* New York: Harcourt Brace, 1999.

Dart, John. "Buddhist Sect Alarmed by Reports that Leader Kept His AIDS a Secret." *Los Angeles Times,* 3 March 1989. www.aegis.com/news/lt/1989/LT890302.html.

Davidson, R. J. "Cerebral Asymmetry, Emotion, and Affective Style." In *Brain Asymmetry,* edited by R. J. Davidson and K. H. Hugdahl. Cambridge, MA: MIT Press / Bradford, 1995.

Dennett, Daniel C. *Kinds of Minds: Toward an Understanding of Consciousness.* New York: Perseus / Basic Books, 1996.

Diamond, Jared. *Guns, Germs, and Steel: The Fates of Human Societies.* New York and London: W. W. Norton, 1997.

Diamond, Sara. *Spiritual Warfare: The Politics of the Christian Right.* Boston: South End Press, 1989.

Edwards, David L. *The Honest to God Debate.* Philadelphia: The Westminster Press, 1963.

Ehrenreich, Barbara. *Dancing in the Streets: A History of Collective Joy*. New York: Metropolitan Books / Henry Holt, 2006.

Ehrman, Bart D. *Jesus: Apocalyptic Prophet of the New Millennium*. Oxford and New York: Oxford University Press, 1999.

Emerson, Ralph Waldo. *The Works of Ralph Waldo Emerson in One Volume: Including the Poems, Philosophic and Inspirational Essays, and Biographical Studies*. The Giant International Series. New York: Walter J. Black, 1925.

Fasching, Darrell J. *The Coming of the Millennium: Good News for the Whole Human Race*. Valley Forge, PA: Trinity Press International, 1996.

Fehmi, Lester G., Ph.D., and George Fritz, Ed.D. "The Attentional Foundation of Health and Well-Being." *Science*, Spring 1980.

_____, and J. T. McKnight, Ph.D. "Attention and Neurofeedback Synchrony Training: Clinical Results and Their Significance." *Journal of Neurotherapy* 5, issue 1/2 (2001): 45-61.

Festinger, Leon, Henry Riecken, and Stanley Schachter. *When Prophecy Fails: A Social and Psychological Study of a Modern Group that Predicted the Destruction of the World*. Minneapolis: University of Minnesota Press / Lund, 1956.

Freud, Anna. *Psychoanalysis: For Teachers and Parents*. Translated by Barbara Low. Boston: Beacon Press, 1960.

Freud, Sigmund. *Beyond the Pleasure Principle*. Edited and translated by James Strachey; introduction by Gregory Zilborg. New York: W. W. Norton, 1961.

_____. *Early Psychoanalytic Writings: Freud's First Studies of Obsessions, Phobias, Anxieties, Hysterias, and Other Symptoms of Neuroses* (part of *The Collected Papers of Sigmund Freud*). Edited and with an introduction by Philip Rieff. New York: Collier, 1963.

Friedman, Thomas L. *From Beirut to Jerusalem*. New York: Farrar, Strauss Giroux, 1989.

Fritz, George, Ed.D., and Lester G. Fehmi, Ph.D. *The Open Focus Handbook: The Self-Regulation of Attention in Biofeedback Training and Everyday Activities*. Princeton: Biofeedback Computers, 1982.

Fromm, Erich. *Escape from Freedom,* in *The Holt Collected Works of Erich Fromm*. New York: Holt, Rinehart, and Winston, 1976.

Galanter, Marc. *Cults: Faith, Healing, and Coercion*. Oxford and New York: Oxford University Press, 1989.

Gazzaniga, Michael. "The Split Brain in Man." *Scientific American,* 1967, 24-29.

Gerson, Michael. "A New Social Gospel." *Newsweek,* 13 November 2006.

"God Tells Pat Robertson: Expect a Good Year for President Bush." *Church and State* 40 (February 2005): 16, 17.

Goleman, Daniel. *Emotional Intelligence: Why It Can Matter More Than IQ*. New York: Bantam, 1995.

Gordon, James S., M.D. *Manifesto for a New Medicine: Your Guide to Healing Partnerships and the Wise Use of Alternative Therapies*. Reading, MA: Addison-Wesley, 1996.

Gore, Al. *The Assault on Reason*. New York: Penguin, 2007.

Gorenberg, Gershom. *The End of Days: Fundamentalism and the Struggle for the Temple Mount*. Oxford: Oxford University Press, 2002.

Guillaumont, Antoine., H. C. Puech, G. Quispel, W. Till, and Yassah 'Abd al Masih, trans. *The Gospel According to Thomas*. New York: Harper, 1959.

Hackleman, Doug. "The Significance of Ellen White's Head Injury." *Adventist Currents* l, no. 6 (June 1985). www.ellenwhite.org.

Halsell, Grace. *Prophecy and Politics: Militant Evangelists on the Road to Nuclear War*. Westport, CT: Lawrence Hill, 1986.

Harding, Susan Friend. *The Book of Jerry Falwell: Fundamentalist Language and Politics*. Princeton: Princeton University Press, 2000.

Hawkin, David J., ed. *The Twenty-First Century Confronts Its Gods: Globalization, Technology, and War*. Albany, NY: State University of New York Press, 2004.

Heard, Alex. *Apocalypse Pretty Soon: Travels in End-Time America*. New York: W.W. Norton, 1999.

Hertzberg, Arthur. *The Fate of Zionism: A Secular Future for Israel and Palestine*. New York: HarperCollins, 2003.

Heschel, Abraham J. "No Religion Is an Island." In *No Religion Is an Island*, edited by Harold Kasimow and Bryan Sherwin. Maryknoll, NY: Orbis Books, 1991.

Hexham, Irving, and Karla Poewe. *Understanding Cults and New Religions*. Grand Rapids, MI: William B. Eerdmans, 1986.

Hillman, James. *Re-visioning Psychology*. New York: Harper and Row, 1975.

Hoffer, Eric. *The True Believer: Thoughts on the Nature of Mass Movements*. New York: Harper Torchbooks, 1951.

Houston, Jean. *A Mythic Life: Learning to Live Our Greater Story*. San Francisco: HarperSanFrancisco, 1996.

Huxley, Aldous. *The Doors of Perception: Heaven and Hell*. New York: Harper and Row, 1954.

James, William. *The Varieties of Religious Experience*. 1902. New York: Longmans, 1980.

Jewett, Robert. *Jesus Against the Rapture: Seven Unexpected Prophecies*. Philadelphia: Westminster Press, 1979.

Juergensmeyer, Mark. *Terror in the Mind of God: The Global Rise of Religious Violence.* Berkeley: University of California Press, 2000.

Jung, C. G. *Symbols of Transformation: An Analysis of the Prelude to a Case of Schizophrenia,* 5th ed. Translated by R. F. C. Hull. 1956. Bollingen Series 20: Vol. 5, *The Collected Works of C. G. Jung.* Princeton: Princeton University Press, 1967.

————. *Memories, Dreams, Reflections.* Recorded and edited by Aniela Jaffé, translated by Richard Winston and Clara Winston. 1961. New York: Random House / Vintage, 1963.

Juster, Susan. *Doomsayers: Anglo-American Prophecy in the Age of Revolution.* Philadelphia: University of Pennsylvania Press, 2003.

Kahn, Charles H. *The Art and Thought of Heraclitus: An Edition of the Fragments with Translation and Commentary.* Cambridge: Cambridge University Press, 1981.

Keay, John. *Sowing the Wind: The Seeds of Conflict in the Middle East.* New York: W. W. Norton, 2003.

Keen, Sam, and Anne Page, photo ed. *Faces of the Enemy: Reflections of the Hostile Imagination; the Psychology of Enmity.* San Francisco: Harper and Row / Perennial Library, 1986.

Keen, Sam, and Anne Valley-Fox. *Your Mythic Journey: Finding Meaning in Your Life through Writing and Storytelling.* 1973. Los Angeles: Tarcher, 1989.

Kersten, Holgar. *Jesus Lived in India: His Unknown Life Before and After the Crucifixion.* New Delhi, India, and New York: Penguin, 1981.

Key, Howard Clark. *Miracle in the Early Christian World: A Study in Sociohistorical Method.* New Haven: Yale University Press, 1983.

Kimball, Charles. *When Religion Becomes Evil: Five Warning Signs.* San Francisco: HarperCollins, 2002.

Klein, Melanie. *Love, Guilt and Reparation and Other Works 1921-1945.* In *The Complete Works of Melanie Klein.* Introduction by R. E. Money-Kyrle. New York: Dell, Delta, 1975.

Klein, Naomi. "Terror's Greatest Recruitment Tool." *The Nation,* 29 September 2005, 14.

Krakauer, Jon. *Under the Banner of Heaven: A Story of Violent Faith.* New York: Random House, 2003.

Kurtz, Ernest, and Katherine Ketcham. *The Spirituality of Imperfection: Storytelling and the Journey to Wholeness.* New York: Bantam Books, 1992.

Lakoff, George. *Don't Think of an Elephant: Know Your Values and Frame the Debate; A Progressive Guide to Action.* Foreword by Howard Dean; introduction by Don Hazen. White River Junction, VT: Chelsea Green, 2004.

Lamy, Philip. *Millennium Rage*. New York and London: Plenum Press, 1996.

Landes, Richard, Andrew Gow, and David C. Van Meter, eds. *The Apocalyptic Year 1000: Religious Expectations and Social Change 950-1050*. New York: Oxford University Press, 2003.

Larsen, Robin, ed. *Emanuel Swedenborg: A Continuing Vision*. New York: The Swedenborg Foundation, 1988.

Larsen, Stephen. *The Healing Power of Neurofeedback: The Revolutionary LENS Technique for Restoring Optimal Brain Function*. Rochester VT: Healing Arts Press, 2006.

———. *The Mythic Imagination: Your Quest for Meaning through Personal Mythology*. New York: Bantam Books, 1990.

———. *The Shaman's Doorway*. 1976. Rochester, VT.: Inner Traditions, 1998.

———. "The Soul and the Abyss of Nature." In *Emanuel Swedenborg: A Continuing Vision*, edited by Robin Larsen. New York: The Swedenborg Foundation, 1988.

———, and Robin Larsen. *Joseph Campbell: A Fire in the Mind; The Authorized Biography*. New York: Doubleday, 1991.

Leach, Maria, ed. *Standard Dictionary of Folklore, Mythology, and Legend*. New York: Harper and Row, 1972.

Leder, Drew. *The Absent Body*. New York and London: University of Chicago Press, 1990.

Lewis, Bernard. *From Babel to Dragomans*. Oxford and New York: Oxford University Press, 2005.

———. *The Multiple Identities of the Middle East*. New York: Schocken Books, 1998.

———. *What Went Wrong: Western Impact and Middle-Eastern Response*. New York: Oxford University Press, 2002.

Lewis, I. M. *Religion in Context: Cults and Charisma*. Cambridge, England: Cambridge University Press, 1996.

Lindorff, David. *Pauli and Jung: The Meeting of Two Great Minds*. Wheaton, IL: Quest Books, 2004.

Lindsey, Hal. *The Late Great Planet Earth*. Grand Rapids, MI: Zondervan, 1970.

Mamdani, Mahmood. *Good Muslim, Bad Muslim: America, the Cold War, and the Roots of Terror*. New York: Pantheon, 2004.

Marsden, George. *Evangelicalism and Modern America*. Grand Rapids, MI: William B. Eerdmans, 1984.

———. *Fundamentalism and American Culture: The Shaping of Twentieth-Century Evangelicalism, 1870-1925*. Oxford: Oxford University Press, 1980.

Maslow, Abraham H. *Religions, Values, and Peak Experiences.* New York: Viking, 1970.

May, Rollo. *The Cry for Myth.* New York and London: W. W.Norton, 1991.

McGinn, Bernard. *The Antichrist: Two Thousand Years of the Human Fascination with Evil.* San Francisco: Harper San Francisco, 1994.

McGuire, William, ed. *The Freud/Jung Letters: The Correspondence between Sigmund Freud and C. G. Jung.* Translated by Ralph Manheim and R. F. C. Hull. Bollingen Series 94. Princeton: Princeton University Press, 1974.

Mencken, Henry Louis. "Homo Neaderthalensis." *The Baltimore Evening Sun,* 29 June 1929.

_____. "The Scopes Trial: Impossibility of Obtaining Fair Jury Insures Scopes' Conviction." *The Baltimore Evening Sun,* 10 July 1929.

_____. "The Scopes Trial: Mencken Finds Daytonians Full of Sickening Doubts about Value of Publicity." *The Baltimore Evening Sun,* 9 July 1925.

_____. "Homo Neanderthalensis." *The Baltimore Evening Sun,* 29 June 1925.

Milgram, S. *Obedience to Authority.* New York: Harper, 1974.

Miller, David Leroy. *Gods and Games: Toward a Theology of Play.* New York: World Publications, 1970.

_____. *The New Polytheism: Rebirth of the Gods and Goddessses.* Harper and Row, 1974.

Milton, Richard. *Alternative Science: Challenging the Myths of the Scientific Establishment.* Rochester, VT: Park St. Press, 1994

Mutwa, Vusamazulu Credo. Edited by Stephen Larsen. *Song of the Stars: The Lore of a Zulu Shaman.* Barrytown, NY: Barrytown / Station Hill Openings, 1996.

Mozaffari, Medhi. *Fatwa: Violence and Discourtesy.* Aarhus, Denmark: Aarhus University Press, 1998.

Naisbitt, John, and Patricia Aburdene. *Megatrends 2000: Ten New Directions for the 1990s.* New York: William Morrow, 1990.

Neihardt, John G. *Black Elk Speaks.* Lincoln, NE: University of Nebraska Press, 1961.

Neuhaus, Richard John, and Michael Cromartie. *Piety and Politics: Evangelicals and Fundamentalists Confront the World.* Washington, D.C.: Ethics and Public Policy Center, 1987.

Newburg, Andrew, Eugene d'Aquili, and Vince Rause. *Why God Won't Go Away: Brain Science and the Biology of Belief.* New York: Ballantine, 2001.

Noll, Mark A. *The Scandal of the Evangelical Mind.* Grand Rapids, MI: William B. Eerdmans, 1994.

Ornstein, Robert. *The Psychology of Consciousness.* New York: Harcourt Brace, 1977.

Pagels, Elaine. *The Gnostic Gospels.* 1979. New York, Vintage, 1981.

Perlman, Fredy. *Against His-Story, Against Leviathan: An Essay.* Detroit: Black and Red, 1983.

Popper, Karl R., and John C. Eccles. *The Self and Its Brain: An Argument for Interactionism.* New York and London: Routledge, 1990.

Pribram, Karl H. *Brain and Perception: Holonomy and Structure in Figural Processing.* Appendices in collaboration with Kunio Yasue and Mari Jibu. Hillsdale, NJ: Stanford University and Radford University / Lawrence Erlbaum, 1991.

_____. "The Cognitive Revolution and Mind/Brain Issues." *American Psychologist* 5, no. 41 (March 1986): 507-19.

_____. "Interview." *Psychology Today,* February 1979, 71ff.

_____. *Languages of the Brain.* Monterrey, CA: Wadsworth, 1977.

_____. "The Neurophysiology of Remembering." *Scientific American* 220 (January 1969): 75–78.

Price, James, and William Goodman. *Jerry Falwell: An Unauthorized Profile.* Lynchburg, VA: Paris and Associates, 1981.

Quasten, Johannes. *The Ante-Nicene Literature After Irenaeus.* Vol. 2, *Patrology.* Antwerp: Spectrum, 1953.

Rank, Otto. *The Myth of the Birth of the Hero and Other Writings.* Edited by Philip Freund. New York: Vintage, 1959.

Ravindra, Ravi. *Science and the Sacred.* Wheaton, IL: Quest Books, 2000.

Reich, Wilhelm. *Character Analysis,* 3d ed. Translated by Vincent R. Carfagno. New York: Pocket, 1976.

Riesèbrodt, Martin. *Pious Passion: The Emergence of Modern Fundamentalism in the United States and Iran.* Translated by Don Reneau. 1990. Berkeley and Los Angeles: University of California Press, 1993.

Robbins, T. and S. Palmer, eds. *Millennium, Messiahs, and Mayhem.* New York and London: Routledge, 1997.

Robertson, Pat. *The Collected Works of Pat Robertson (1990–92).* New York: Inspirational Press / Budget Book Services, 1994.

Robinson, John A. T. *Honest to God.* Philadelphia: Westminster, 1963.

Rose, Jacqueline. *The Question of ZION.* Princeton and Oxford: Princeton University Press, 2005.

Rossing, Barbara R. *The Rapture Exposed: The Message of Hope in the Book of Revelation.* Boulder CO: Perseus / Westview, 2004.

Rushdie, Salman. *The Satanic Verses.* London: Viking, 1988.

Russell, Jeffrey Burton. *The Devil: Perceptions of Evil from Antiquity to Primitive Christianity.* Ithaca and London: Cornell University Press, 1977.

Saliba, John A. *Understanding New Religious Movements.* Grand Rapids, MI: William B. Eerdmans, 1995.

Sandeen, Ernest R. *The Roots of Fundamentalism: British and American Millenarianism 1800–1930.* Chicago and London: University of Chicago Press, 1970.

Sansonese, J. Nigro. *The Body of Myth: Mythology, Shamanic Trance, and the Sacred Geography of the Body.* Rochester, VT: Inner Traditions, 1993.

Saranam, Sankara. *God without Religion: Questioning Centuries of Accepted Truths.* Kerala, India: Stone Hill Foundation, 2005.

Shanks, Niall. *God, the Devil and Darwin: A Critique of Intelligent Design Theory.* Oxford: Oxford University Press, 2004.

Shepard, Paul. *The Others: How Animals Made Us Human.* Washington, D.C.: Island Press /Shearwater Books, 1996.

Simons, Thomas W., Jr. *Islam in a Globalizing World.* Stanford, CA: Stanford University Press / Stanford Law and Politics, 2003.

Smith, Huston and Phil Cousineau. *The Way Things Are: Conversations with Huston Smith on the Spiritual Life.* Berkeley and Los Angeles: University of California Press, 2003.

Smoley, Richard. *The Essential Nostradamus.* New York: Jeremy Tarcher / Penguin, 2006.

Sperry, Robert W. "The Great Cerebral Commisure." *Scientific American,* 1964, 45–52.

_____. *Science and Moral Priority: Merging Mind, Brain, and Human Values.* New York: Columbia University Press, 1983.

Stark, Rodney, and William Sims Bainbridge. *The Future of Religion: Secularization, Revival, and Cult Formation.* Berkeley and Los Angeles: University of California Press, 1985.

Stern, Jessica. *Terror in the Name of God: Why Religous Militants Kill.* New York: HarperCollins, 2003.

Sternhell, Zeev. *The Founding Myths of Israel: Nationalism, Socialism, and the Making of the Jewish State.* Princeton: Princeton University Press, 1998.

Tabor, James, and Eugene Gallagher. *Why Waco? Cults and the Battle for Religious Freedom in America.* Berkeley and Los Angeles: University of California Press, 1995.

Taylor, Jeremy. *Dream Work: Techniques for Discovering the Creative Power in Dreams.*

Foreword by Ann Faraday. New York: Paulist Press, 1983.

Teilhard de Chardin, *Hymn of the Universe.* New York: Harper Torchbooks, 1961.

Trevarthen, Colwyn, ed. *Brain Circuits and Functions of the Mind: Essays in Honor of Roger W. Sperry.* Cambridge, England: Cambridge University Press, 1990.

Van Biema, David. "God vs. Science." *Time Magazine,* 13 November 2006.

Watson, Donald. *A Dictionary of Mind and Spirit.* London: Little Brown / Optima, 1991.

Whitmont, Edward C., M.D. *The Alchemy of Healing: Psyche and Soma.* Berkeley, CA: Homeopathic Educational Services and North Atlantic Books, 1993.

_____. "Changing Ethical and Religious Values in This Epoch of Transition." Series of Six Lectures, March 2–April 13. C. G. Jung Foundation, New York, 1967.

_____. *Return of the Goddess.* New York: Crossroad, 1982.

_____. *The Symbolic Quest: Basic Concepts of Analytical Psychology.* New York: G. P. Putnam's Sons, 1996.

_____, and Sylvia Brinton Perera, Ph.D. *Dreams: A Portal to the Source.* 1989. London and New York: Routledge, 1990.

Wigan, A. L. "The Duality of the Mind: Proved by the Structure, Functions, and Diseases of the Brain." *The Duality of the Mind.* Edited by Joseph Bogen. United States: Joseph Simon, 1844.

Wilson, Bryan. *Magic and the Millennium: A Sociological Study of Religious Movements of Protest among Tribal and Third-World Peoples.* New York: Harper and Row, 1973.

Wojcik, Daniel. *The End of the World as We Know It: Faith, Fatalism, and Apocalypse in America.* New York and London: New York University Press, 1997.

Wolfe, Alan. *The Transformation of American Religion: How We Actually Live Our Faith.* New York and London: Free Press, 2003.

Zaidel, Eran, and D. Frank Benson, eds. *The Dual Brain: Hemispheric Specialization in Humans.* UCLA Forum in Medical Sciences. New York and London: Guilford, 1985.

Zakaria, Fareed. "Islam and Power." *Newsweek,* 13 February 2006, 35–37.

INDEX

abortion, 121
Abraham, 104
Abu Bakr, 131
Achilles, 91
acupuncture, 153, 154, 159
Adler, Alfred, 7
Adorno, T. W., 8
Aesclepius, 148
Against Heresies (Irenaeus), 93
Agnivesh, 201, 202–3
agnosticism, 121
Ahura Mazda, 99
Albert, Geoffrey, 87
Albury Conferences, 111
Alchemy of Healing and Dreams: A Portal to the Source (Whitmont), 207
Alcoholics Anonymous, 44
Ali ibn Abi Talib, 131
al-Lah, 128, 130, 136
allegory, 14
Allen, Woody, 97
alpha male, 51, 53
al-Qaeda, 18, 134
al-Tabari, 136
Altemeyer, Bob, 223n10
Alternate Science (Milton), 145–46
alternative medicine, 153–54
Amen, Daniel, 61
American Medical Association, 153
amygdala, 23, 24, 28, 40, 41, 45, 61
aneurysm, 26
Angra Mainyu, 99, 100
animism, 78–79
Antichrist, 17, 92–95, 113
Antichrist: Two Thousand Years of Human Fascination with Evil (McGinn), 94
Antimessiah, 3, 92
anti-Semitism, 6, 8

Apocalypse, 94, 116
apperception, 28
archetypes, 3
Arendt, Hannah, 8
Aristotle, 5
Ark of the Covenant, 80
Armageddon, 1, 11, 16, 18, 41, 47, 100. *See also* end times
Armstrong, Karen, 127, 129
art, 53
Art of Living (AOL), 201–2
Arya Samaj, 203
Asclepiades, 148
asha, 99
Asherahs, 11
Assagioli, Roberto, 177
Assault on Reason, The (Gore), 28
Assemblies of God Church, 118
astrology, 159
atheism, 121, 144
attitudes, generic, 141–42
Augustine, Saint, 100, 106
Austin, James, 22
Authoritarians, The, (Altemeyer), 223n10
authority
    art and, 53
    behavior and, 50
    cruelty experiment on, 55–56
    and developmental stages, 54–55, 58
    hierarchies and, 51–52, 56
    personality, 8
    spiritual, 52–53, 56–57
    structures, 53–54, 58
ayatollah(s), 132–33, 137, 138
Azm, Sadik al-, 136, 138

Bailey, Catherine, 87–88
Barks, Coleman, 221n25

Bastian, Adolf, 3, 213n1
behavior(ism), 49, 50, 59, 147
beliefs, 69–75, 164–65, 173, 189
Besant, Annie, 190
Beyond the Pleasure Principle (Freud), 7
Bible
    Daniel, Book of, 103, 105
    Deuteronomy, 11, 214n12
    Ezekiel, 102, 103, 104, 105
    Genesis, 198
    Isaiah, 74
    Mark, 93
    Matthew, 101–2, 104
    New Testament, 11, 16
    Old Testament, 11, 16–17, 80, 92, 102
    Revelation, Book of, 17, 93
    Thessalonians, 92–93
    Thomas, 200
Bible Institute of Los Angeles (BIOLA), 121, 122
bicameral mind, 34–36
biofeedback, 179–83
Biology of Belief, The (Lipton), 209
Black Elk, 191, 198
Blake, William, 223n3
Bob Jones College, 124–25
Book of Mormon, The, 118–19
Book of Revelation of St. John, 103–4
Brahma, 13–14
brain
    amygdala, 23, 24, 28, 40, 41, 45, 61
    behavior and, 49
    bicameral mind, 34–36

Quest Books
encourages open-minded inquiry into
world religions, philosophy, science, and the arts
in order to understand the wisdom of the ages,
respect the unity of all life, and help people explore
individual spiritual self-transformation.

Its publications are generously supported by
The Kern Foundation,
a trust committed to Theosophical education.

Quest Books is the imprint of
the Theosophical Publishing House,
a division of the Theosophical Society in America.
For information about programs, literature,
on-line study, membership benefits, and international centers,
see www.theosophical.org
or call 800-669-1571 or (outside the U.S.) 630-668-1571.

To order books or a complete Quest catalog,
call 800-669-9425 or (outside the U.S.) 630-665-0130.

Praise for
Stephen Larsen's
THE FUNDAMENTALIST MIND

"Stephen Larsen has, in great width, approached fundamentalist thinking at its roots. This is an inspired work. Anyone who reads it will benefit from its wealth of knowledge."

—David Lindorff, author, *Pauli and Jung:*
The Meeting of Two Great Minds

"Stephen Larsen has previously opened new doorways for exploring and healing the inner world through shamanism, archetypal studies, and neurofeedback. Now, in his exciting and important new work, *The Fundamentalist Mind,* he combines his expertise with history, politics, and religion to grapple with crises threatening our very survival.

"He exposes how fundamentalism can occur in all intellectual, religious, or political systems. He shows fundamentalism's universal substratum, our vulnerability to it as human beings, and its occurrences throughout history and around the globe. In *The Fundamentalist Mind,* Dr. Larsen teaches mature awareness, compassion, inclusion, world community, and cooperation that together can transcend all forms of fundamentalism. He directs us toward a future that can bring hope, growth, and healing to the entire planet."

—Edward Tick, Ph.D., author, *War and the Soul*
and *The Practice of Dream Healing*

"Stephen Larsen's *The Fundamentalist Mind* stimulates us to look deeper into the spiritual and psychological wellsprings of fundamentalism, whether religious or secular, in all its forms. The journey on which he takes us is not merely political or sociological, but one that leads to the roots of our most cherished beliefs. This is a must-read for understanding our own role in the headlines of fear we face each day."

—Neil Douglas-Klotz, author, *The Sufi Book of*
Life; coauthor, *The Tent of Abraham*